Beggarsbush Barracks
Church
Hospital
Northumberland Road
Officers Quarters
Huts
Lansdowne Terrace
Pembroke Cott
Pembroke Park
Lansdowne Lodge
Beggarsbush
Trinity College Botanic Gardens
Dawson Grove
Mary Villa
Brook Lawn
Hammersmith Ho
Hammersmith Works
Gate Lodges
Turner's Cottages
Pembroke Road
Nursery
Otterdam
Ballsbridge
Elgin Road
Church
Elleville
Lisburne Cottage

Lansdowne FC

Lansdowne FC

A HISTORY

Charles Ivar McGrath

OPEN AIR

canterbury
HUNTERS

Contents

Acknowledgments

For carrying out essential research for the book I would like to thank the ever dependable and excellent Frances Nolan. My thanks to the 2021–2 Club President Colin Goode and Lansdowne FC for facilitating Frances' research and for providing me with access to all of the extant official records and other materials utilized in the writing of the book. We are all also very grateful for the generous financial contribution from David and Cathy Shubotham without whose support this book could not have been written.

My colleague in the UCD School of History, Paul Rouse, led me to this project and I am grateful that he did. My thanks also to my other UCD colleagues who put up with me while I worked on the book.

For management of the project I would like to thank both Michael and Mark Dawson, the latter of whom was my primary Lansdowne point of contact throughout the research and writing process. For agreeing to be interviewed and for providing further follow-up information I am indebted to Stephen Rooney and Paul Van Cauwelaert. For key information on a range of matters I would like to express my appreciation to James Ryan, David Doolin, Eoin Kinsella, David Reynolds, Ian Minch, Peter Minch, Andrew Burke, Rory MacMahon, Caleb Powell, Tom McCabe, Joe Leddin, Ciaran O'Reilly, Frank Forrest, Aidan Delany, Michael Cassidy, Michael Daly, Derry Shaw, Frank Kenny, Dermot McCarron, Patrick Halpenny and Luke Healy. For providing all of the necessary administrative support my thanks go to Michael Diskin and Elayne Power. Both Ciaran O'Mara and Michael Daly provided me with invaluable information regarding the Lansdowne FC members who fought and died in the First World War, and I am very grateful to them both for so doing. And of course a huge debt of thanks to all the Lansdowne rugby players, officials, administrators, supporters, families and friends – past and present – who keep the true spirit and ethos of the Club alive on the pitch, in the pavilion, and in the wider community.

For assistance with map images and copyright I would like to thank Jane

Nolan of UCD library, Daniel O'Connell from the OS*i*, and Angela Cope from University of Wisconsin Milwaukee Libraries. For help with other images I owe thanks to Mark MacWhite, Gavin Johnston of IPAG (Ireland) Ltd, and Berni Metcalfe and Chris Swift from the National Library of Ireland. I also wish to thank Michael O'Brien for providing a range of Club photos and assisting more generally in that regard. Likewise, I am very grateful to Patrick Flood and family for providing access to the image archives of the work of Patrick's father, the late Vincent Flood, who was a long-time photographer of all things to do with Lansdowne FC. All images in the book are courtesy of Lansdowne FC unless noted otherwise.

My thanks also to Michael Kearney and Mark Dawson for reading through the final manuscript and for their very helpful insights, comments and suggestions. Any errors that may remain are wholly my responsibility. My thanks also to Martin Fanning and all the team at Four Courts Press for their support, input and management of the whole publication process.

I am particularly indebted to Marnie Hay for reading, commenting on, editing and discussing the whole book in manuscript and to Ivar Will Hay-McGrath for keeping me company at Lansdowne matches and patiently listening to my ramblings about rugby more generally. To the two of them, I owe the greatest debt of thanks and gratitude.

Introduction

1872

Lansdowne Football Club (FC) was established in 1872. This book provides a social and cultural history of the Club from its foundation up to 2022. It is a study that contextualizes the sporting club and its people within the wider fabric of society, economy and culture in Ireland and beyond over the period of 150 years.

Lansdowne FC not only has the most iconic and distinctive rugby club name in Ireland, but it is also one of the earliest such clubs established in the country. This history of Lansdowne offers a unique insight into the development of Irish rugby from the early days of codification of sports more generally in the British Isles. As a central player in the establishment of local, provincial, national and international governance and organization structures for rugby, the Lansdowne name came from the Club's home ground on Lansdowne Road. It was a ground that soon became headquarters for the Irish

Lansdowne FC circa 1895.

rugby team as well and grew into one of the most well-known, as well being the oldest, international rugby grounds. For more than 125 years the name 'Lansdowne Road' was emblematic of Irish rugby. Despite the renaming of the Stadium after its redevelopment in 2007–10, the international association with Lansdowne Road is sustained to this day by the Club.

Described interchangeably as 'Headquarters', 'HQ' and simply 'the Road', Lansdowne FC has always been synonymous with the Lansdowne Road Stadium. In 1958, when Lansdowne became the first Irish rugby club to play at Twickenham, the team was described as 'the famous headquarters side' in a match in which they defeated the much-distinguished London Harlequins at the home of English rugby. And as T.D. Burke wrote in the *Evening Herald* a year later, 'The story of Lansdowne Football Club is to a very considerable extent interwoven with the story of Irish Rugby, for before the Irish Rugby Union was founded and before Ireland had played an international game the famous Headquarters Club was in existence'.[1]

It is also the case that at the heart of every sporting activity is sociability – the desire and need of people to associate and interact. Sporting clubs are central to fulfilling such desire and need, and it is the people who make up the clubs – the players, administrators, supporters, members, families and visitors – that are the life-blood of all such organizations. This book therefore also looks at the social and cultural world of club-life and the people who make it happen. From fund-raising to tea-making and from pitch to pavilion, the driving forces behind the success and survival of a sporting club over 150 years, through wars and revolution and global economic depressions and health pandemics, are the people themselves. The history of Lansdowne FC epitomizes the ability of people to associate and come together in order to overcome calumny, penury, death and disease in a journey that is universal in nature: to strive to do better, and to be better.

Chapter 1

Finding a Name, Establishing the Game

1872–1899

As with all good stories, this one starts with a mystery. Cloaked with uncertainty, obscured by time, muddled by memory: that is the very nature of history, and Lansdowne FC is no exception. During the 1920s H.W.D. Dunlop, the Club's founder, recounted that in 1871 he set up the Irish Champion Athletic Club (ICAC), the umbrella sporting body that incubated Lansdowne FC. However, Dunlop also acknowledged he had 'a shocking memory for names and dates'. It is not surprising therefore that 1872 is more commonly agreed upon as the founding date for the ICAC, though at what point in the year remains uncertain, though very pertinent.[1]

The modernization of society within the British Isles during the nineteenth century led to increased spending power and more leisure time among the

H.W.D. Dunlop, founder of Lansdowne FC and first Club President in 1903–4.

wider populace. Combined with the commercialization of sport and a greater emphasis upon physical fitness at the time, all of these factors led to a growing need for greater organization of sporting activities in order to accommodate the ever-increasing numbers of people taking part. These early days of greater codification, regulation and bureaucratization of sporting activity at a local and national level were accompanied by the inevitable quarrels and schisms over access, governance and control. The establishment of the ICAC hints at such early discord. As reported in the English paper, *The Sportsman*, on 5 October 1872, the Dublin Amateur Athletic Club (DAAC) had recently been established in compliance and accordance with the rules and regulations of England's Amateur Athletic Club 'as are in vogue in our universities and elsewhere'. According to *The Sportsman*, the DAAC 'was established under the most encouraging circumstances, and under patronage and management that are respectively gratifying'. Yet the paper had 'now learnt of the proposed starting of another club, under the title of the "Irish Amateur Champion Athletic Club," with some surprise'. The problem for *The Sportsman* was that the ICAC's stated purpose was to facilitate the winners of 'leading Irish athletic sports, and others who may wish to run to contend against each other for the title of champions, provided they be "Irish gentlemen amateurs."' With Imperialistic condescension, *The Sportsman* trumpeted that the 'chief races at nearly all the leading Irish clubs, including the open races at the Civil Service and Trinity College Sports, have invariably been won by [English] gentlemen', and this was 'almost certain' to continue, 'notwithstanding the great advancement of the Irishmen within the last few years in athletic excellence'. Assuming that it was the aim of the ICAC to bar English competitors, *The Sportsman* arrogantly contended 'we can hardly see where the fields of winners are to come from to contest at the sports of this club'.[2]

The Sportsman presumed – or wanted people to believe – that the ICAC was to be exclusive, like the two leaders in Irish athletic organization in the 1860s, Dublin University Athletic Club and the Irish Civil Service Athletic Club. However, according to the English newspaper at least, the DAAC was intended to be inclusive, 'with the object of giving races open to gentlemen amateurs throughout the universe'. Such a club was greatly needed in Ireland, 'where athletics have hitherto been under the sway of some few individuals'. Yet in reality the DAAC wanted to be the governing body for Irish athletics. It was also the case that the Dunbar family, owners of *The Irish Sportsman* newspaper, were centrally involved in the Club, a fact that may have caused their newspaper's English namesake to take up the cause of the DAAC in 1872.[3]

The issues at stake were in part about access to sporting clubs for the wider population, and the freedom to compete. There was also clearly a national context, arising out of the suggestion that Dublin University, the Civil Service and the DAAC were closely aligned with the English athletic governing body. The matter was clarified on 11 December 1872, in the *Dublin Daily Express*.

Under a heading 'Irish Champion Athletic Club', an appeal was made to the

> athletic strength of the whole of Ireland .... to lend itself to the establishment and furtherance of a national club. Heretofore it has been College men against collegiate: the Civil Servicemen against Government officials. But now the sphere of action is to be enlarged, and any amateur who hails from the Green Isle, and is approved of by a committee, will be eligible. Much has been done by the leading athletic clubs in Ireland to promote the interests of manly pastimes, but more remains to be done, and will we trust, be effected by the Irish Champion Athletic Club.

The exclusiveness of Dublin University and the Civil Service was being challenged, and on a national platform at a time of increasing national awareness in Ireland.[4]

The *Dublin Daily Express* report had followed hot on the heels of the release of the ICAC's printed *Explanatory Circular* on 9 December 1872. The pamphlet clearly stated the new organization's rationale: 'It has been long felt that Amateur Athletes have not in Ireland sufficient opportunity for competing with each other, owing to the fact of there not being any liberal and comprehensive club to which they can all belong'. The ICAC was to be that club, with its meetings 'open to all approved Irish Amateur Athletes'. The circular provided a list of the ICAC's patrons (including ten peers of the realm), the plans for an annual event bringing together all the winners of competitions around the country, and information on membership, subscriptions, and trophies designed by 'two of the best students at the Royal Dublin Society's School of Art'.[5]

The decision to print the *Explanatory Circular* had been taken on 22 November, at one of the earliest recorded meetings of the ICAC executive committee. Those in attendance were Herbert Wilson, E. Dillon, J.D. Ogilby, Reginald Miller and of course H.W.D. Dunlop, who along with Miller held the position of honorary secretary. In early 1873 the rules of the ICAC were agreed and printed, and plans commenced for the first national event that summer. In March, at the first Annual General Meeting (AGM), the first resolution of members was that the ICAC, 'being a National Club and not the result of mere rivalry, is worthy of the support and co-operation of all Athletes and Athletic Bodies and of the Public throughout Ireland'. It was also noted that the brothers and co-managers of their family brewing business, Sir Arthur and Edward Guinness, had been unavoidably detained from attendance, though their original intention of so doing implied support for the endeavour, which would have resonated with the family's philanthropic activities more generally.[6] Rivalry or not, the ICAC clearly meant business.

The uncertainty over the actual foundation date of the ICAC was added to in May 1873. Despite their claim otherwise, the evident ongoing rivalry with the DAAC caused Dunlop to write to the *Dublin Daily Express* to disabuse readers of the belief that he represented that organization:

> I beg you will help me to dispel any such idea. I am not, have not been asked to become, and do not intend to be, in any way connected with that body, as I have had the honour of representing since its formation in May, 1872 – before the Dublin Amateur Athletic Club was started – the interest of the now flourishing 'Irish Champion Athletic Club.' This body, having now 250 members, requires no other legs than its own 500 to stand upon and by them is likely to be well supported.

Clearly Dunlop's desire was to establish seniority and precedence for the ICAC over the DAAC.[7]

Precedence also required action. To that end, the ICAC's first Irish Championship meeting took place in July 1873. As the Club did not yet have their own grounds, the meeting was hosted by Dublin University. By all accounts, the meeting was a success, despite a postponement because of the weather. The ICAC later claimed via the press that an Irish athlete had set a new United Kingdom record for the high jump (5ft 10¼ inches), an achievement acknowledged 'even by our English rivals'.[8]

In the interim, discussions had commenced about getting a plot of ground of their own on the vast South Dublin estate of one of the ICAC's first

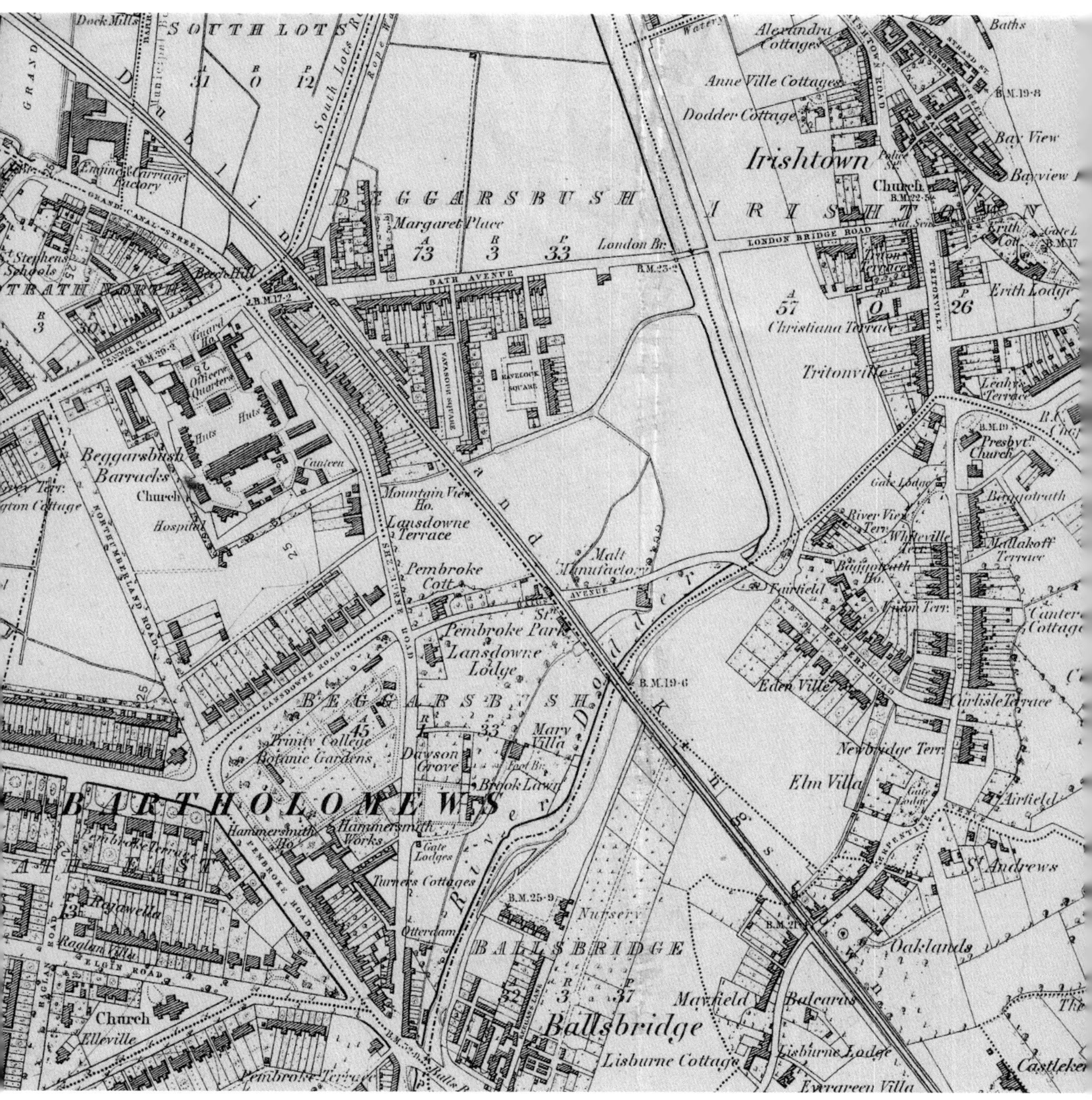

Lansdowne Road, 1874. Source: 'Map of the city of Dublin and its environs, constructed for Thom's Almanac and Official Directory', held by UCD School of Geography, Planning & Environmental Policy. © Public domain. Digital content: © University College Dublin, published by UCD Library, University College Dublin http://digital.ucd.ie/view/ucdlib:33001.

patrons, the earl of Pembroke. In later years, Dunlop suggested that the need to find alternative grounds transpired because the ICAC had been banned from Trinity College because the Provost had given permission for the 1873 event without consulting the Board of Dublin University. If so, then Dublin University's loss was Irish rugby's gain.[9]

In reality, the search for a more permanent home had already commenced before the ICAC's first Athletics meeting. In May 1873, a newspaper report stated that the honorary secretary of the ICAC had entered into discussions for grounds near Sydney Parade train station. By late October–early November the ICAC had agreed to lease this seven-acre site and to raise £1,000 for enclosing, levelling and further developing the ground with pitches for cricket, football and hurling, as well as a cinder running track, and to make it all available to other sporting clubs. It was also noted at that time that there was 'no reasonable probability' of getting access to Dublin University in the future. However, by late November a new plot of ground had become available, also on the Pembroke estate, beside Lansdowne Road train station. It was quickly decided to drop the Sydney Parade plan and instead to lease this new plot and develop it as previously proposed. The desire to include other sporting groups was also acted upon immediately following a request from Wanderers FC. Access to the grounds was granted at a cost of '£10 per season, they playing as often as they wished until another Club should join, but to have two days a week in any case and a third on two days' notice.'[10]

As a result of the change of ground, Sydney Parade FC never came to be – but Lansdowne FC certainly did. The ICAC's desire for a permanent ground was, according to the *Irish Times*, so as to 'provide for the young men of the south side of Dublin what those of the north side already possess in the Phoenix Park – the great boon of a large piece of ground on which they can indulge in the healthy sports of cricket, football, [and] athletics.'[11]

With a unique clarity of vision regarding the emerging understanding about the great benefit organized sporting activity could have for a modern society, Dunlop instigated a process that would result in the emergence of one of Ireland's leading rugby clubs. Lansdowne rugby was born out of a desire to widen access to sporting activities in Ireland for a greater percentage of

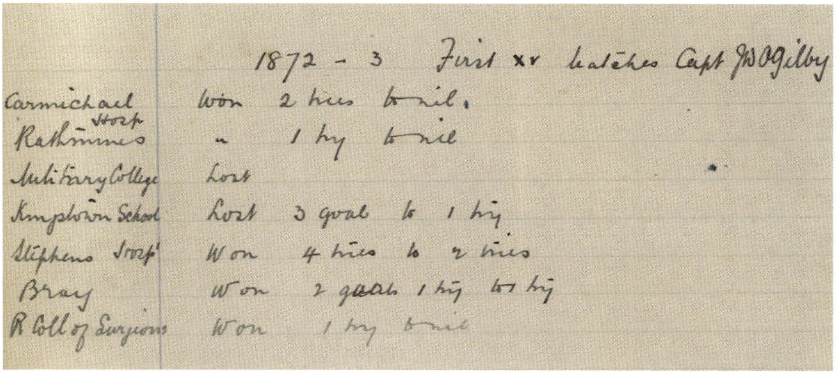
1872 - 3 First XV Matches Capt JWOgilby

Carmichael Hosp	Won	2 tries to nil.
Rathmines	"	1 try to nil
Military College	Lost	
Kingstown School	Lost	3 goals to 1 try
Stephens Hosp'	Won	4 tries to 2 tries
Bray	Won	2 goals 1 try to try
R Coll of Surgeons	Won	1 try to nil

Lansdowne FC's first season of fixtures, 1872–3.

the population, and to create an identifiable brand of Irish sporting activity, played by and run by Irish people. It was a desire to emerge from the sporting shadow of the Imperial, and imperious, 'Mother Country' and to generate a unique sense of Irish sporting identity. This was however by no means separatist nationalism; it was rather about recognizing different cultural identities within the wider framework of the Empire.

* * * * *

There remains one further mystery to be resolved in the foundation story of Lansdowne FC. Dunlop reminisced in the 1920s that Lansdowne's first game was played in the winter of 1872–3 against Wanderers FC, one of only two rugby clubs – the other being Dublin University FC – in existence at that time. It was also the case that the team was heavily dependent upon Dublin University for its players on this first occasion, and also in 1874 when next they played against Wanderers. The first game Dunlop described as 'a fiasco'; the second a Lansdowne victory by a try scored by F.W. Kidd, a future Club President in 1910–11.[12]

However, the first Lansdowne FC Fixture Book records seven games being played by the Club in its inaugural 1872–3 season, although none of them were against Wanderers. Instead, the eclectic mix of opponents included Carmichael Hospital, Rathmines School, Military College, Kingstown School, Steevens

Hospital, Bray FC, and the Royal College of Surgeons. Wanderers did make a winning appearance among the ten teams played against the following season, 1873–4, when other newcomers included Phoenix and Athlone School.[13]

These early games for the Club did not take place at Lansdowne Road. The lease for the plot of land was only signed in January 1874, at which time work also commenced for laying out the pitches and running track. The following month the ICAC agreed the rates of fees to be paid for playing different sports at Lansdowne Road, including 5*s.* per annum for 'Football' subscribers, while the new grounds were officially opened in May by Queen Victoria's viceroy in Ireland, the duke of Abercorn, who also agreed to become a patron of the ICAC. The following month the ICAC convened their second annual Championship Athletics meeting – and their first at Lansdowne Road – while in August there was even an exhibition baseball match held there.[14]

Several months later, however, the focus of the ICAC shifted towards creating a more competitive and successful rugby team from among the *ad hoc* assemblage of players that had been playing under its auspices since 1872 as the nucleus of Lansdowne FC. In late October 1874 it was reported that an 'Irish Champion Football Club' was being organized at Lansdowne Road. It was deemed to be a much-welcomed occurrence, 'since there has been no club sufficiently large or sufficiently representative to enable its members to compete successfully with our English neighbours'. There were to be daily training sessions at Lansdowne Road, with 'two or more matches weekly'. The season was to commence at the beginning of November and would continue till March 1875. All those who were interested in 'this truly excellent game' were exhorted to join the Club by applying for membership to the ICAC organizers, H.W.D. Dunlop and F.J. Jones.[15]

As a result, on 13 November 1874 the 'inauguration match' for the ICAC-backed rugby club, as reported in the *Irish Times*, took place at Lansdowne Road. Thirty men played in the game, in which 'Ogilby, Granby Burke, Spunner and Jones showed to advantage'. A management committee was chosen straight afterwards and twenty of those who had played signed up for the Club. Three of the four named players were current or future Lansdowne members: J.D. Ogilby, who was also an ICAC committee member, captained the team from 1872–3 to 1874–5; H. Spunner was included in the 1875–6 team; and Burke played every season from 1872–3 to 1876–7.[16]

Once again it would appear that Dunlop was keen to move beyond the overly loose structures then in existence and perceived a need to put the rugby team on a more formal footing as a club in its own right, in keeping with the trend at the time for greater codification and organization of sporting activities. It was also to be a team that would have its own subscribing membership rather than being reliant on players from Dublin University. This latter problem, as Dunlop later recalled, had resulted in the team being called 'Second Trinity'.[17]

The prescience of Dunlop and his ICAC colleagues was also evident when, in December 1874, the Irish Football Union (IFU) was founded with a view to promoting the game throughout the country and organizing international matches against England and Scotland. Although Dublin University was the driving force behind the initiative, the formalization by Dunlop and his colleagues two months earlier of the structures of the emergent Lansdowne FC surely facilitated two of its playing members, Ogilby and Burke, being appointed to the first IFU committee.[18]

During 1875 the Club began to emerge more clearly from the shadow of the ICAC. In October a meeting of the Club took place at 39 Grafton Street under the new name of 'Lansdowne Football Club', at which time the Club Captain for 1875–6, D.T. Arnott, was chosen as honorary secretary, with J. Neligan as assistant honorary secretary and D.J. Stokes as honorary treasurer. The out-going captain and representative on the IFU, Ogilby, was one of four committee members, along with fellow Lansdowne players W.J. Hamilton, T.W. Harpur and J.W. Richards. The meeting also 'provisionally adopted' the bye laws of Wanderers FC. An inaugural game to publicize the Club's new name was also planned.[19]

The first game of the 1875–6 season played using the new Club name of Lansdowne FC was against Bray FC on 24 November 1875. This was also the first match to be reported in the newspapers, when the *Irish Times* noted that the game, played at 'the LFC ground', resulted in a 'no side', even though 'it was manifestly a "draw" in favour of the home club'. The latter outcome was also recorded for posterity in the Club fixture list, though only after the initial record of 'no result' had been crossed out.[20]

There were still some minor teething problems with the new name, however. When D.T. Arnott played rugby for Ireland at the Leinster Cricket Ground in December 1875 in the first ever home game against England (the first encounter between the two countries having taken place in London at the Oval Cricket Ground in February 1875), he was recorded as representing 'Lansdowne Road' rather than Lansdowne FC. Even still, a corner had clearly been turned, and the Club was firmly on the map of Irish rugby history.[21]

These early years were not without their challenges. At the end of 1875 at the ICAC AGM, where it was noted that there were now clubs for cricket, archery, croquet and tennis under their auspices, it was pointed out that 'the Lansdowne Football Club has, through great difficulties and discouragements, fought its way to the front'. Money was always of course a problem for young clubs – the ICAC raised funds in numerous ways, including allowing sheep graze on the Lansdowne ground 'on payment of 1*d.* per night per head.' But the single-greatest hurdle remained the reliance upon Dublin University for players, which was reflected in a resolution at a General Meeting on 13 October 1876, when it was agreed that 'any man joining Lansdowne FC should pledge himself to play primarily for that Club against any other Dublin club, except Dublin University FC'. Two weeks later it was reported in the press that a visit to Lansdowne Road on a Saturday had found the place vacant. Where the Lansdowne team was 'no one could tell; but then they were more of a "fifteen" than a distinctive club, and consequently so much importance does not attach to the absence of their members, who were certain to be well engaged elsewhere.'[22]

It was under the guidance of F.W. Kidd, who was elected Club Captain for the 1876–7 season, that Lansdowne began to become more self-reliant. Prior to that time, the team colours had been the ICAC's blue and yellow, which was also used for the first four honour caps awarded 'for superior play on behalf of the Club'. But in November 1876 at a special general meeting, it was agreed to adopt new colours of black, red and yellow, similar to those of an amateur

English touring cricket team called I Zingari, which played each summer in Ireland during the 1870s. In February 1877 Kidd was selected to play for Ireland in the third international against England, once again at the Oval in London, and by the end of the season Lansdowne had truly consolidated its position, having finally managed to avoid defeat to Wanderers 'in a dead "draw"', which was reported in great detail in the *Irish Times*, and having defeated 'the, until then, invincible First and Second Fifteens of Kingstown School'. A first victory over Wanderers would come the following season, when the Club Captain was J.W. Richards.[23]

A newspaper review of the 1877–8 season highlighted the challenges the new game faced. Some clubs, like Bray FC, had not managed to field a team at all, while others such as Kingsbridge FC had permanently folded. Kingstown School was described as a combination of past and present students, though there was no clarity as to how far back the captain could go in selecting past players, which led to occasional surprises for opponents when the 'boys' turned out to be fully grown men. As for Lansdowne, the hopes for the future were high when 'a good number of men … joined for the coming season'.[24]

The review of the 1878–9 season expressed similar hopes for Lansdowne, possessed as it was 'of about the best ground of any club in Dublin'. It was mused that it would do exceedingly well 'if the members will only work together and attend punctually and regularly when required'. More generally, the game in Ireland seemed to be growing more popular, with more new clubs being established and increasing attendances at matches. At a national level, developments were afoot also. In October 1879 the IFU and the Northern Football Union amalgamated to form the IRFU. The process had been preceded in January of that year by a series of interprovincial games between Ulster, Munster and Leinster in Dublin (the first ever interprovincial game had occurred in November 1875 in Belfast between Ulster and Leinster, with the second between the same teams in December 1876 at Lansdowne Road). It was therefore apt that, with the amalgamation of the two Unions, three Provincial Branches were also formally established in Leinster, Ulster and Munster, each with representatives on the IRFU committee. The Lansdowne captain for the 1878–9 season, George Scriven, had been instrumental in the process and so was elected a member of the IRFU, while another Lansdowne member, C.B. Croker, was appointed as honorary treasurer of the Leinster Branch.[25]

Such developments demonstrated that Lansdowne was now clearly established as a leading rugby club in Ireland. The first volume of *The Irish Football Review*, published in 1880, declared that Lansdowne 'now holds a foremost position among the clubs in Dublin'. With fifty members, twenty-four of whom had joined in the 1879–80 season, it was predicted that the Club would soon be 'top of the tree'. Part of the success was put down to the fact that Lansdowne Road was 'the best ground' with the 'most complete dressing arrangements … in the vicinity of Dublin'. The fact that members were entitled to free admission to all sporting events at the ground during the rugby season was also deemed to offer 'great pecuniary advantages'. These included free entrance to all interprovincial games and, since the Ireland-England game played there in March 1878, all home international matches.[26]

There had also been some important re-structuring in the background in the late 1870s, primarily relating to Dunlop and the ICAC. Mounting debts and a conflict over sporting ethos among ICAC members led to Dunlop resigning as honorary secretary of that organization in late 1877. The following year he took on the role of managing the Lansdowne FC Second XV and also became honorary secretary for the Club. The ICAC eventually dissolved itself for financial reasons at the end of 1880, at which time the tenancy of the ground was transferred to Lansdowne FC before being taken over in 1886 by Harry Sheppard. It was also in 1880 that Wanderers moved permanently to Lansdowne Road.[27]

A significant occurrence for restricting players to one club only and, as a result, a boon for Lansdowne, was the establishment of the Leinster Senior Challenge Cup in 1882. With only five teams in the first competition in February of that year, Lansdowne got a bye into the semi-final but lost the match to the ultimate winners, Dublin University. The following season Lansdowne beat Kingstown in a replay in their semi-final but lost the final, after another replay, to Dublin University once again.[28]

Despite the establishment of the Leinster Senior Cup, the small number of matches played by Lansdowne in these early years, and the variety of teams played against, was synonymous with a game at an embryonic stage of formation. Matches per year ranged from seven to eleven in total, with teams such as the Nomads, Survey FC, Southern Counties FC, 93rd Highlanders, Dundalk, Armagh Royal School, Egremont, Kildare FC, The Garrison, Hibernians, Wakefield Trinity and Halifax turning up in the fixtures for the Lansdowne First XV during the first decade of seasons, alongside the likes of Wanderers, Dublin University, Clontarf and Wesley College. Once the Second XV came into being in 1876–7, games were also played against teams such as Morehampton, Portarlington School, Military Academy, Merrion Rovers, St Columba's College, North Wexford, Dundrum, and Adelaide Hospital, as well as the likes of Monkstown, Bective Rangers and Second XVs from Wanderers and Clontarf. The Third XV first appeared in 1881–2 with fixtures against Dublin University and Kingstown School.[29]

The eclectic mix of teams played against in these early years, including a number of secondary schools, demonstrated both the small number of clubs in existence at that time and the fact that the development of rugby in Ireland, as in England, was predicated upon the enthusiasm for the game first and foremost in middle- and upper-class private, fee-paying schools such as Kingstown, Rathmines and St Columba's College. It was also the case that although initially most rugby players came from Protestant backgrounds, the rapid embracing of the game in private middle- and upper-class Catholic schools such as Clongowes Wood College, Castleknock College, Blackrock College and St Mary's College, and in the latter two instances the ensuing establishment of associated senior clubs, ensured that a more ecumenical mix on playing fields and in clubhouses quickly developed as well. A prime example was Thomas Shanahan, who after finishing at Castleknock College in 1880 played on the Lansdowne First XV from 1883–4 to 1887–8. He was also capped for Ireland five times during that same period and is accredited with being the first Castleknock graduate to play for the national team.[30]

The important role from early on of touring teams coming from England and Scotland for the growth of the game in Ireland was also evident from the Lansdowne fixtures against Egremont from Liverpool in November 1880 and Wakefield Trinity and Halifax, both from Yorkshire, in early 1882.

In all instances, the post-match sociability loomed large, with toasting of all and sundry from 'the Queen' and 'the umpires' to 'the Press' and 'the ladies' more generally. The first reciprocal Lansdowne tour was to Yorkshire in late November 1882, when they played return matches against both Halifax and Wakefield Trinity. The English press similarly reported much convivial post-match dining, drinking and general entertainment. The importance of sociability in amateur associational club culture was not unique to rugby clubs and remains to this day a hugely important aspect of sustaining amateur club activity across a wide range of sports.[31]

Wakefield were back in Dublin in November 1883, with Lansdowne returning to Yorkshire in November 1884 when they also played against Huddersfield. The next biennial trip to Yorkshire in November 1886 included a game against Hull FC, though the return fixture at Lansdowne Road in November 1887 became a source of controversy, testing the limits of sociability in the emerging class-war centred around amateur versus professional status. The Irish sports journalist, J.J. McCarthy, reflecting the snobbish and elitist mentality of many of the middle and upper classes at the time regarding the involvement of the working classes in the higher levels of organized sporting activities, reported after the game that the Hull captain was a mill-owner and that the team was made up from his paid employees. This accusation of professionalism in an amateur game was coupled with blatant prejudice: McCarthy claimed the Hull players 'look like artisans or mechanics of some sort' and wondered who had paid all the costs of 'those anything-but-aristocratic-looking Yorkshiremen'. McCarthy also expressed his disdain for the Hull committee men, who apparently joined the two teams at the Lansdowne-hosted dinner after the game. His prejudice appeared again as he recounted that forty-five Hull 'camp-followers' turned up for the dinner, 'dirty, with their mouths open'. He concluded by arguing that Hull should not be invited again: 'we can get lots of teams of gentlemen – every club in Scotland is such; every one in Ireland … also … and [plenty] in England' as well. The flagrant classism and prejudice aside, this event also highlighted the early stages of a wider issue in England relating to the different financial perspectives and challenges of the working-class teams of the north and the rest of the country's middle- and upper-class clubs, differences that would ultimately result in a split in the 1890s and the emergence of professional Rugby League. Amateurism was the luxury, and bias, of the economically better-off.[32]

More immediately, Lansdowne, the Leinster Branch and the IRFU understandably took umbrage at McCarthy's very considerable insult to Hull. Letters to that effect were sent to Hull FC, with permission for their publication. The Lansdowne letter wholly rejected McCarthy's 'disgraceful statements' and put them down to the fact that he had been 'black-balled' from the Club a few years before and seemed to have retained a major grudge as a result. Despite the controversy, Lansdowne returned to Yorkshire the following season to play Hull, Bradford and Huddersfield. In the ensuing seasons such tours continued while new itineraries were added, such as to Cardiff and Newport in 1894 and Northampton in 1898 and 1899, ensuring that the importance of hosting touring sides and going on tour continued to loom large as part of the ethos of the Club thereafter.[33]

Internal tours were also growing in importance during the 1880s and 1890s. Along with trips to and from Ulster for games against North of Ireland FC (NIFC), Methodist Collegians and Malone, Lansdowne also toured to and hosted teams from Munster, including Queen's College Cork, Garryowen, Limerick County, Tralee and Rockwell College, while also playing closer to home against sides such as Carlow College, Clongowes Wood College, and Kilkenny County and City.[34]

Off the pitch, however, the process of improving facilities at Lansdowne Road was slow. In October 1884 the small wooden grandstand was burnt to the ground in what was believed to be a malicious attack, though some considered it a blessing in disguise given the poor condition of the structure. By 1892 a new stand had been erected which seated 800 people. Early the following year a new pavilion built by Harry Sheppard was provided for the use of Wanderers. Lansdowne, 'not to be outdone', also began building a new pavilion, having shifted their old wooden one over to the side of the new grandstand for use as a changing room for visiting teams. The maintenance of the grounds also had some unexpected side effects. In 1897 the new black pony employed to pull the pitch roller proved to be an avid rugby fan and ‘frisks and frolics about like mad’ whenever there was a score, after which he would turn on the water-tap with his teeth for a cooling drink. The Club also initiated an annual place- and drop-kicking competition at Lansdowne Road at the end of each season in March–April, which continued for many years. In time it became the day on which team photos were taken and the annual dinner took place.[35]

Such activities were all part of the evidence for the growing popularity of rugby in Ireland, which was also seen in the increasing number of fixtures played, with the Lansdowne First XV undertaking on average twelve games per season in the 1880s and fifteen per season in the 1890s. Of course, during those two decades the most important fixtures each season were in the Leinster Senior Cup. In the 1883–4 season, under the captaincy of J.B. ‘Buffer’ Moore, Lansdowne beat Wanderers but then lost the final on a replay to Dublin University by a disputed goal. Moore, who had been Club Captain since 1881, was wholly committed to the game. In 1886 he was one of Ireland’s three representatives when the International Rugby Football Board (IRB) first met in Dublin and was a member of that body from 1906 to 1927, while also having served as President of the IRFU in 1898–9.[36]

A first-round exit to Wanderers awaited in the 1884–5 season, which was the first of six years that Lansdowne was captained by R.G. ‘Bob’ Warren. A Dublin University graduate, Warren had previously attended the prestigious Rathmines School, one of the early seed-beds for rugby in Ireland, which had also provided viable playing opposition for the first clubs in those formative years. The loss to Wanderers was avenged in the 1885–6 season though once again Dublin University triumphed over Lansdowne in a replayed final. In February 1887 the Club lost to Wanderers in the first-round match by two tries to two goals. However, the result was deemed to be ‘one of the greatest surprises’ not least because the referee had prevented Lansdowne charging down the free kick that resulted in one of Wanderers’ goals. The reporter believed that ultimately ‘the team that worked harder won’, but also that there was ‘no doubt’ that Lansdowne were the better side. In both March 1888 and February 1889 Lansdowne lost to Dublin University again in first-round ties. Growing frustration within Lansdowne over the lack of success in the

Leinster Senior Cup, 1890–1. Standing: T. Edwards, E.S. Jacob (Hon. Sec.), E.J. Walsh, H. Le Fanu, J. Sibthorpe (Hon. Treas.), R.E. Smith, H. Jameson, J.B. Moore, A.J. Robinson. Seated: M.J. Bulger, R. Hogarth, V.C. Le Fanu (Capt.), J.S. Jameson. On Ground: F.E. Davies, E. Doran, S.C. Smith, R.G. Warren, A.W. Rutherford.

Leinster Senior Cup resulted in Dunlop writing to the Press to desire that the rules of the competition be more strictly enforced.[37]

With the number of clubs in the Senior Cup increasing, in the 1889–90 season Lansdowne beat Bective in the first round but again lost to Dublin University in the final in March 1890. It was Warren's last season as Club

Captain, and surely a frustrating one, but during his time in charge at Lansdowne he had also had the distinction of captaining Ireland in 1887, when England were beaten for the first time, as well as in 1889 and 1890, and went on to serve as President of the IRFU in 1895–6, President of Lansdowne in 1909–10, and honorary secretary of the IRB for an incredible thirty-seven years from 1898 to 1934.[38]

Although no longer Club Captain, Warren continued to play on the Lansdowne First XV under the leadership of V.C. Le Fanu, a fellow Ireland international, during the 1890–1 season. It was fitting after all his endeavours for the Club, that Warren should still be playing the season that Lansdowne finally got their hands on the Holy Grail of Leinster rugby. In the first months of 1891 an initial victory over Monkstown in the first round of the Senior Cup was followed by the defeat of Bective after a replay in the semi-final. As usual, Dublin University awaited in the final in late March. On this occasion, however, the result went emphatically Lansdowne's way, by two goals and one dropped goal to nil, or 11–Nil in old scoring values. The long-awaited first Leinster Senior Cup Champions title had arrived. As noted in the *Irish Times* on 30 March, 'The victory of Lansdowne was very popular', despite the attempted belittling of the Club's achievement by the clearly still disgruntled McCarthy.[39]

It had taken twenty years from the date of foundation, and ten years from the start of the Leinster Senior Cup itself, for Lansdowne to win their first title. Yet in so doing the Club had truly come of age. Patience and persistence had won out over adversity and calumny. Those former traits would still be needed however in the coming years, as the remainder of the 1890s turned into another decade of near misses before the status of Champions would be conferred once again, with further losses in the final to Dublin University in 1893 and 1898, and to Monkstown in 1899. However, behind the scenes individuals such as R.W. Jeffares, Club Captain from 1896 to 1898 and a future Lansdowne President in 1911–12 and long-serving member of the IRFU, were instilling greater organization and consistency of play which in time would lead to a second Senior Cup success. The building blocks were being put in place, and time would tell.[40]

First XV, 1892–3. Standing: J.B. Moore, J. Sibthorpe, H.W. Pennington, W.L. Norwood, R.W. Brew, E.J. Walsh, R.E. Smith, R.G. Warren. Seated: V.C. Le Fanu, J.S. Jameson, E.G. Brunker, F.E. Davies (Capt.), A.A. Brunker, S.C. Smith, A.C. Smith. On Ground: R.S. Dyas, T. Edwards, G. Martin, J.J. Leahy.

Nor did the Leinster Senior Cup defeats of the later 1890s detract from the huge progress that had been made overall, highlighted by the fact that during these early years of the Club's existence a total of twenty-six Lansdowne players had played for Ireland. With a variety of caps from one to nineteen, the players were: D.T. Arnott; J.C. Bagot; A.A. Brunker; L.Q. Bulger; M.J. Bulger; J.J. Coffey; H.G. Cook; A.P. Cronyn; F.E. Davies; B.R.W. Doran; E.F. Doran; G.P. Doran; T. Edwards; A.J. Hamilton; J.S. Jameson; T.R. Johnson-Smyth; F.W. Kidd; V.C. Le Fanu; P.J. O'Connor; J.P. Ross; W.G. Rutherford; T. Shanahan; R.E. Smith; E.J. Walsh; R.G. Warren; and W.J. Willis. As F.E. Davies recalled in February 1951 shortly before he died, this very significant international representation for the fledgling Club included the selection of five players in the Irish XV who defeated Wales in 1892 by one goal and two tries to nil. All of the points in the game were scored by Lansdowne players: E.J. Walsh got two tries; Davies got the third; and Edwards kicked the goal. The other two Lansdowne players on the Irish team that day were J.S. Jameson and V.C. Le Fanu. All five players had also been part of the first Lansdowne Leinster Senior Cup winning side in March 1891.[41]

Of the other Lansdowne internationals of that era, G.P. Doran had played against both England and Wales during Ireland's second Triple Crown and third Championship success in 1899, while L.Q. 'Larry' Bulger had the distinction of having been invited to play for the British Isles touring side in South Africa in 1896. A winger who played for Lansdowne in 1896–8, Bulger managed to score nineteen tries in twenty-one games on the tour. Speed ran in the family, as his older brother, Daniel, was a very successful field and track athlete in sprint, hurdles and long-jump, and had played for Lansdowne during the 1880s. A third brother, Michael J. Bulger, was also an Irish international and had been on the Lansdowne Cup winning side in 1891, having first appeared for the First XV in 1885–6. Hailing from a Catholic, middle-class background in Kilrush, County Clare, all three boys had attended Blackrock College and Dublin University, with both Larry and Michael acquiring medical degrees. All three emigrated to London in the later 1890s, where Michael chaired the inaugural meeting of London Irish Rugby Club.[42]

The first three decades of Lansdowne's existence had seen the Club established as a crucial part of the embryonic development of rugby in Ireland. Envisioned as part of a wider expression of a separate Irish national sporting identity within the British Empire, the Club was a key player in the codification and organization of the game in Ireland. Lansdowne members

Gasometer
Gas Works
Pembroke Township
Main Sewerage Works
BEGGARSBUSH
Margaret Place
London Br.
Dodder Cottages
Irishtown
Pumping Station
Church
LONDON BRIDGE ROAD
BATH AVENUE
Tritonville
TRITONVILLE ROAD
Guard Ho.
Officers Quarters
Beggarsbush Huts
Barracks
Canteen
Lansdowne Lawn Tennis Ground
LANSDOWNE ROAD
Ivanhoe
River Dodder
Fairfield
HERBERT ROAD
Eden Ville
Elm Villa
Gate Lodge
Trinity College Botanic Gardens
Hammersmith Works
Brook Lawn
Gate Lodges
PEMBROKE ROAD
Nursery
BALLSBRIDGE
Dublin Society's Branch
Ballsbridge
Station
Mayfield
Oaklands
Lisburne Lodge

Lansdowne Road, 1898. Source: 'Map of the city of Dublin and its environs, constructed for Thom's Almanac and Official Directory', held by UCD School of Geography, Planning & Environmental Policy. © Public domain. Digital content: © University College Dublin, published by UCD Library, University College Dublin http://digital.ucd.ie/view/ucdlib:33009.

were instrumental in the formation of both the IRFU and the Leinster Branch, while the foresight of Dunlop had ensured that the Club's home ground was also Ireland's premier rugby facility, and the one which hosted the national team. Situated in an increasingly urbanizing South Dublin, the Club was perfectly placed – geographically, socially and culturally – for further growth, expansion and success. Only war or revolution could really threaten the future of Lansdowne FC.

Chapter 2

In War and Revolution 1899–1924

Sports clubs reflect wider society in many ways and in turn are impacted by wider non-sporting events. Lansdowne FC was no exception. In the first two decades of the twentieth century the British Isles and the wider world experienced a series of seismic events that impacted upon and helped define Lansdowne. The South African or Boer War of October 1899 to May 1902 was the first such occurrence. As a war of the British Empire, it directly impacted Ireland in numerous ways. The first months of conflict saw very significant British casualties, and with Irish regiments involved in the fighting, many families in Ireland were directly affected. In the continuing absence of proper British governmental provision for the families of soldiers killed in action, a special fund for that purpose was set up by Sir John Arnott and his wife, Caroline Sydney. Arnott was not only a member of the famous Irish department store family but was also centrally involved in running the *Irish*

Times, becoming the managing director and chairman in 1900. It was no surprise then that this new Irish Soldiers or Regimental Widows and Orphans Fund was promoted through the newspaper via the organization of a Charity Rugby Match in November 1899 between Lansdowne and Dublin University at Lansdowne Road.

The event itself included a military band that played for an hour before the game and at the interval as well. The ball was provided for free by Lawrence & Sons of Grafton Street, with Lynch & Sons of Westmoreland Street providing the stewards' badges for free. Both Lansdowne's and Wanderers' season ticket holders forewent their right of free entry to the ground for the occasion. The event and the fund were also supported by the Commander-in-Chief of the army in Ireland, the Anglo-Irishman Frederick, Lord Roberts, who within two months would take over command of the British army in South Africa.[1]

Roberts' appointment to South Africa was as a result of a series of military setbacks experienced by his predecessor, Lieutenant General Sir Redvers Buller, the last of which had been the British defeat at Vaal Krantz in Northern Natal in early February 1900. Part of that battle had taken place at Potgieter's Drift, where T.R. Johnson-Smyth, a forward in the Lansdowne team of 1882–3, was killed serving with the Durham Light Infantry. He was remembered 'as a footballer of some note', who had been capped for Ireland against England in 1882.[2]

Such charitable matches were not unusual. Lansdowne players also took part in the annual Hospitals Charity Match, togging out for the County Dublin team against the United Hospitals. Lawrences and Lynches always provided the ball and badges for free, while on occasion a band was provided by either the Dublin Garrison or the Dublin Metropolitan Police. The games were played at Lansdowne Road, with the ground also being provided without charge.[3]

Charity matches aside, in terms of the real rugby business of the Leinster Senior Cup, having lost in the first round in the 1899–1900 season to Dublin University, a second title was finally secured by Lansdowne under the captaincy of B.R. 'Bertie' Doran in the 1900–1 season, ten years on from when the Club had first been crowned Leinster Champions. Having warmed up

Leinster Senior Cup, 1900–1. Standing: R.W. Jeffares (Hon. Sec.), H.W.D. Dunlop, J.J. Coffey, A.E. Freear, J. Gargan, H.J. Knox, J.J. Warren, T.R. Malcolmson, J. Anderson (Hon. Treas.). Seated: R. Simmonds, A.C. Rowan, B.R. Doran (Capt.), G.P. Doran, R.R. Boyd. On Ground: R.S. Swan, J.R. Magee, C.J. Law, W.B.A. Moore.

by going on tour to Scotland in February 1901, Lansdowne beat Wanderers 6–Nil in the first round and then went on to defeat Old Wesley in the semi-final 15–6. Dublin University awaited once again in the final, a game that went Lansdowne's way 8–3, with both tries for the winning side scored by the captain's brother, G.P. 'Blucher' Doran. The nickname was ostensibly because, like the duke of Wellington's Prussian ally Marshall Blücher at Waterloo in 1815, Doran had a tendency to arrive late though always in sufficient time to save the day.[4] The Club's erstwhile press critic, McCarthy, begrudgingly

Leinster Senior Cup, 1902–3. Standing: H.W.D. Dunlop, C.M. Burton, R.S. Swan, J.J. Stokes, T.R. Malcolmson, W.J. Law, J.J. Warren, L.M. Bayley, J. Johnston, F. Studdert (Hon. Sec.). Seated: B.R. Doran, G.P. Doran, J.J. Coffey (Capt.), A.W. Waters, W.P. Bridge. On Ground: W.B.A. Moore. M.J. D'Alton.

acknowledged the victory as 'meritorious' and liable to provide further stimulus to the development of the game in Dublin: 'It was not out of their turn that Lansdowne won the Cup for the second time, and that this trophy should go around is for the good of the game. Lansdowne deserved the win and Trinity for once in a way deserved to lose'.[5]

In what was an excellent season for Lansdowne, the Second XV also won their first Junior League title, with a highly impressive 241 points for, including fifty-eight tries, and only fourteen points against in twenty games. Those paying close attention to the Second XV's recent seasons would not have been surprised by their success, given their previous season's 270 points, including sixty-six tries, and only thirty-nine points against, all of which hinted at a free-flowing, heads-up style of play.[6]

The demands of maintaining a livelihood saw Lansdowne lose one of their Cup-winning players, A.E. Freear, at the start of the 1901–2 season when he departed for Swansea, having taken up a post there for the Harbour Commissioners. He had been capped for Ireland for all three games in the previous season's Four Nations competition. The Winter of 1901 also saw the first visit to Ireland by the recently established London Irish RFC, captained by Louis Magee, who had led Ireland to Triple Crown victory in 1899. The touring side got the better of Lansdowne 3–Nil on 23 December.[7]

In competition matters, the Leinster Senior Cup was not retained in the 1901–2 season. Having defeated Wanderers and Blackrock, Lansdowne were beaten by Monkstown in the final. However, at the beginning of the 1902–3 season hopes were high for renewed success, reflected in the Club embarking upon building a new and better pavilion. It was also the case that the Lansdowne three-quarter line was considered to be potentially the best in Leinster. The captain for the season was one of the Club's great stalwarts, J.J. Coffey, an Ireland international since 1900 who had been a regular on the Lansdowne First XV since 1897–8, having previously learnt his rugby at one of Ireland's leading Catholic private schools, Blackrock College. Accordingly, in a season when it was proudly noted that Blucher Doran scored nine tries, converted thirteen and kicked a further three penalties and two dropped goals, Lansdowne secured a third Cup title. In the first round, revenge was gained over Monkstown in a 6–Nil victory, which was followed by a 16–3 defeat of Old Wesley. In the final, the old foe Dublin University were overcome 5–3 in a closely contested game in April 1903. Once again, the winning try was scored in style by Blucher Doran, who latched on to a loose ball, chipped the fullback and won the footrace to the line.[8]

A fourth Leinster Senior Cup title – and the first back-to-back – was achieved the following season and once again under the captaincy of Coffey, with victories over Blackrock, Old Wesley and, in the final, Clontarf. The winning score of 5–3, while evidently close, belied the fact that Lansdowne had been all but defeated 3–Nil with five minutes left on the clock, before R. Swan scored what was reported to be a 'sensational try', converted by Blucher Doran. Lansdowne were deemed very lucky, having been beaten 'almost hollow' for most of the game. It was notable that the attendance at the game was estimated at over 4,000, demonstrating the growing popularity of club rugby at the time.[9]

The 'treble event' as it was termed in the newspapers – three Leinster Senior Cup titles in a row – was not to be, however, in the 1904–5 season. Although Lansdowne made it to the final, beating Bective Rangers and Monkstown on the way, once again Dublin University, who had dominated the Cup since its inception with twelve titles, secured their thirteenth by a score of 22–11 in April 1905. Public interest was also continuing to increase, with a full house of 5,000 people at the match.[10]

Large attendances were a clear sign of the increasing popularity of the game in Dublin in particular. This was once again evident when the 'Originals' New Zealand touring side played Ireland at Lansdowne Road. The demand for tickets outstripped capacity, with one irate member of the public complaining of the 'very inadequate accommodation' for spectators. With 5,000 one-shilling tickets all sold out, 'not to speak of schoolboys', the existing infrastructure at the ground was deemed wholly insufficient for the expected crowd. As for the match itself, two Lansdowne players, Coffey and H.J. Knox, were included in the Ireland team which lost 15–Nil.[11]

Such increasing popularity clearly required improved facilities, but it also impacted upon Club structures. The most notable change in the latter regard was the decision to institute the office of Club President in 1903. It was a decision that was not taken lightly nor without debate, a 'heated discussion' of the matter occurring at the Club AGM on 17 April. However, once resolved upon, it was unanimously agreed to elect Dunlop as the inaugural holder of that office. Indeed, Dunlop had been so central to the founding of the Club and its survival during the first three decades of its existence, being later described as the 'driving force and guiding genius' of those early days, that he has come to be remembered and honoured as the President for all those preceding years.[12]

Another important change to Club structures addressed the previously ad hoc, and opaque, manner of team selection. In October 1906 it was agreed to introduce a more formal process with two sub-committees to be appointed each year for selection of the Second and Third XV. It was also agreed that each week a number of committee members be sent to attend Second and Third XV fixtures and report back on player performance. However, the desire of some members to have a similar sub-committee for selection of the First XV continued to be rebuffed. Other aspects of the Club's formalization of structures were more readily agreed, most notably in October 1910 when a wide range of Club administrative activities were amended and formalized, including the holding of two General Meetings per year in April and October and the printing and circulation of the annual accounts.[13]

With regard to the facilities at Lansdowne Road, a new wooden Club pavilion had been completed at the end of 1902, while additional work was carried out to further improve the pavilion and bar in 1907–8. Prior to 1903 the facilities for washing had been described as 'the most primitive', with 'just a few tin basins and watering cans' of which there were never enough for both teams, with the quickest players being the cleanest. As for refreshments, there was usually 'a crate of stout for those who imbibed, and a crate of minerals for the teetotallers'. By the early 1900s tea was served under the uncovered stand, where there was also an 'outside bar'. The indoor members' bar was located between the teahouse and the uncovered stand.[14]

With the passing of Harry Sheppard in December 1906, the IRFU took over the lease for Lansdowne Road and commenced significant work on remodelling the grounds by realigning the pitches and building new stands. At times the differing priorities of Lansdowne FC and the IRFU in terms of developments at the ground could lead to tension, be it with regard to the use of each other's facilities on match days or either organization's plans to improve or expand such facilities. In 1907, for example, there was disagreement for a time over the use of the promenade by Club members on IRFU match days. But such issues tended to get resolved in time, as ultimately the various developments of the ground aimed to improve the experience for all involved, be they players or spectators. In that regard, in 1911 the IRFU undertook to

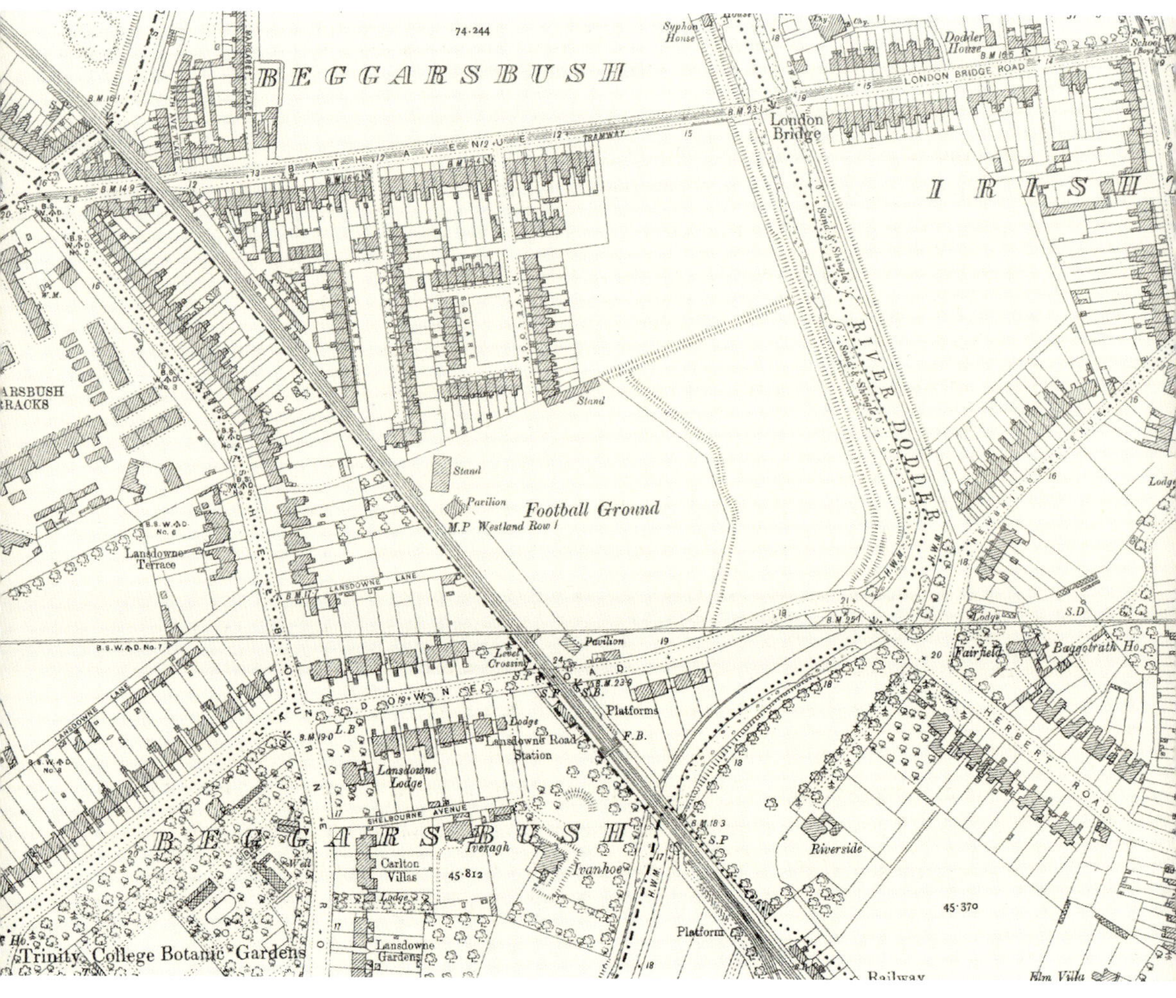

Lansdowne Road, 1907. Source: OSi 25inch Dublin 18–12 / 18–16, 1907 edition. © Ordnance Survey Ireland/Government of Ireland Copyright Permit No. MP 000122. All rights reserved. Courtesy of UCD Library.

further improve the spectator experience, with a plan 'to erect in the ground dividing the Lansdowne and Wanderers' grounds banking accommodation for 10,000 people.'[15]

Basic as the Club facilities may have been, they were central to the associational nature of the organization. Although membership fees were the main source of income for the Club, the social side of the game and increasing public interest helped to improve the financial picture as well. In the 1905–6 season income from the teahouse was £6 10*s.* 2*d.* while £35 13*s.* 8*d.* was brought in at the bar, which was more than the gate receipts of £28 6*s.* 3*d.* The following season income from tea sales increased to £20 9*d.* with the bar bringing in £47 12*s.* 11*d.*, again more than the gate receipts of £42 5*s.* 3*d.* However, the 1908–9 season was a bumper year in terms of gate receipts thanks to two matches in particular, the first against a touring South African student team, which brought in £28 16*s.* 6*d.*, and the second, which brought in £25 9*s.*, against Stade Français, whom Lansdowne had previously played during a brief tour to France in November 1906. These amounts compared to averages of about £3 per game otherwise. However, the touring sides cost money in guarantees and entertainment – the South Africans totalling £29 18*s.* and Stade costing £40 17*s.* But these types of games improved receipts elsewhere, as was evident from tea sales of £29 16*s.* 2*d.* and bar receipts of £59 14*s.* for that season.[16]

Unfortunately, the improving finances were not matched in those years by results on the pitch. Between 1906 and 1914 Lansdowne exited the Leinster Senior Cup in either the first or second rounds. Results from regular season matches were not auspicious either. A significant turnover in players, including some moving overseas, was a major contributing factor. At a time when there continued to be significant migration from Ireland for economic and other reasons, most notably within Protestant communities but applicable across all religious denominations, it was noted at the Lansdowne General Meeting in October 1910 that the Club Captain D.H. Weldon had departed for Persia, while 'two other promising players', W. D'Alton and M.U. Manly, had also emigrated. A year later it was recorded that two more First XV players, G.J. Henebry and W.B. Burke, had left Ireland as well. Even still, Club membership continued to grow which ensured a healthy and vibrant community continued to exist despite on-field results. In the 1909–10 season, for example, turnover in players meant that forty-six men played over the season on the First XV, when only three matches were won. The Second XV won thirteen of twenty-five matches, while using seventy-six players, and the Third XV won fourteen out of thirty-six matches and used over ninety players. So, despite poor results and even with players playing on more than one team at times, the overall picture was one of a vibrant Club having a poor run of games. This healthy state of affairs was particularly evident in the numbers playing at Thirds level, where since 1906–7 the Club had started to field a Third A XV as well, and from 1910–11 a Third B XV also. And results-wise it was not all doom and gloom: in the 1911–12 season, the Second XV finished top of their league, with eighteen wins from twenty-one matches.[17]

Neither were poor on-field results allowed to get in the way of continued planning for further improving Club facilities. In 1910 plans were put in place for hot baths in the pavilion as well as a shower in the visitors' changing room. Eventually in October 1913 it was concluded that a wholly 'new pavilion or tearoom' was needed, with permission to build one being granted by the IRFU in December. On 31 March 1914 it was agreed to proceed with the building of 'additional pavilion accommodation' at a cost of £500, a decision endorsed at the General Meeting the following month.[18] However, such plans were to come unstuck as once again international affairs looked to impact Lansdowne FC and the game of rugby more generally.

The escalating international crisis during the summer of 1914 culminated in various declarations of war mounting up during the early days of August. As the world began to face into the reality of the first global war, so too did the rugby fraternity in Ireland and elsewhere. On 10 August the IRFU organized a meeting at Lansdowne Road with two representatives from each club with a view to discussing the formation of a 'Rugby Football Volunteer Corps'. Such a move was in keeping with similar activities across the whole range of sporting organizations in England, Scotland and Wales. In Ireland, while many other such sporting groups saw large numbers of their members volunteering for service, had their sporting activities either greatly restricted or wholly suspended during the following four years, and saw many members killed or permanently disabled, rugby was from the outset seen to be to the forefront of Ireland's sporting commitment to the war effort.[19]

During the First World War the volunteer soldier took on an added dimension in Ireland as politically the imposition of conscription remained too contentious. Volunteers were therefore all the more important, but also were seen to be making a political statement, be it as outright supporters of the Union and the British Empire or as constitutional nationalist supporters of Home Rule, which was placed on the Statute Books in the autumn of 1914 but was immediately suspended until after the war. When the Irish Parliamentary Party Leader, John Redmond, called for voluntary enlistment in September 1914 from the 170,000 Irish Volunteers, a body formed originally in 1913 as a nationalist counterblast to Ulster Unionist threats of violent opposition to the implementation of Home Rule, it proved to be a political disaster as the body split with a small core of hard-line nationalists, controlled by the militant Irish Republican Brotherhood, breaking away and, in time, instigating the 1916 Easter Rising. Yet of the 150,000 who remained in the re-named National Volunteers, many, like their rugby counterparts, would go on to voluntarily sign up to serve in the war.

As a result of the meeting on 10 August 1914, about 250 men had joined the IRFU Volunteer Corps by the end of the month, with Lansdowne Road being used as their drill training ground. The Corps was inspected at the grounds on 1 September by General Sir Bryan Mahon, who was responsible for raising the 10th (Irish) Division. The Royal Dublin Fusiliers (RDF) were part of that division, and the 7th Battalion thereof was under the command of Lieutenant-Colonel Geoffrey Downing, an ex-Monkstown FC First XV player from the 1880s. Downing had agreed to reserve D Company in the 7th Battalion RDF for the IRFU volunteers. As a result, on 17 September, with a

The 'Pals' at Lansdowne Road, September 1914.

Royal Irish Constabulary (RIC) band in attendance, the first detachment of the Corps to enlist in the army, numbering 120 men, marched from Trinity College to Kingsbridge (Heuston) Station to travel to the Curragh to join the 7th Battalion RDF. The RDF were known colloquially as the 'Old Toughs', so not surprisingly their new middle-class, professional Dublin recruits became known as the 'Young Toffs', and D Company became known as the 'Pals'.[20]

The departure of the 'Pals' to the Curragh had been preceded four days earlier by an IRFU announcement, following the lead from the English RFU, that all fixtures other than schoolboy or charity games were to be suspended for the 1914–15 season. In reality, there would be no senior club rugby played thereafter until the war ended. However, with a significant number of volunteers remaining in Dublin, in early October 1914 a trial match took place at Lansdowne Road with a view to playing a charity match against the newly formed D Company of the 7th RDF. The trial included six Lansdowne players: J. Burke-Gaffney, R. Donnelly, T.A. Whitty, R.N. Mitchell, W. Doolin, and C. Hadden. Of these, Burke-Gaffney and Donnelly were selected for the Volunteer Corps team that played the rugby recruits of D Company on 17 October. To great fanfare and before a large crowd at Lansdowne Road, with the RIC band once again performing for everyone's entertainment, the guiding light behind the Volunteer Corps, the IRFU President, F.H. Browning, was presented with a gold watch before the match for his efforts. The proceeds from the game, which had resulted in an honourable draw, were donated for the purpose of the purchasing of a field kitchen for the RDF regiment.[21]

By that time, as reported to the Lansdowne FC General Meeting on 14 October, at least fifty Club members had already 'engaged in service of their Country'. Despite the very significant depletion of funds resulting from such a large military enlistment of members, the Club had also agreed to contribute £10 10*s.* to the National Relief Fund. Not surprisingly, at the same time it was agreed to put the new pavilion accommodation project on hold till the war ended, though thoughts also turned to further charitable activities in support of the war effort, which resulted in Lansdowne's only fixture for that season, a match against Wanderers on 14 November in aid of the Red Cross Society.[22] The dramatic impact of the war was also seen in the annual Hospitals Charity

Match, which was now played between Dublin County and 'the Military of Ireland'.[23]

Following the first flurry of recruitment into the regular army from the IRFU VC, attention turned to the usefulness of the Corps at home. While rugby players continued to enlist, there were many Club members too old or otherwise incapacitated for military service. Browning therefore pushed for formal government recognition of the Corps as a volunteer body alongside the regular army, and in May 1915 the IRFU VC formally affiliated with the Irish Association of Volunteer Training Corps. The IAVTC served on a part-time basis in a formal uniformed capacity in support of the military in Ireland and were nick-named the 'Gorgeous Wrecks' by Dubliners because of the initials G.R. ('Georgius Rex') on their uniform armbands. Although thereafter part of this wider IAVTC, the IRFU VC continued to operate out of Lansdowne Road.[24]

Despite the inactivity on the pitch, Lansdowne's Club committee continued to meet to manage administrative matters. In a show of solidarity with their military colleagues, on 12 April 1915 the committee resolved unanimously 'that all members of the Club engaged in His Majesty's Forces shall be and are hereby elected Honorary Members of the Club during the duration of the War'. The harsh reality for such members was evident at the General Meeting in November 1915, when the printed report noted that over 100 members were now in military service, while the names of thirteen members and nine past members were recorded as killed in action or died of wounds received. The differentiation between current and past members was primarily on the basis of those whose fees had either been fully paid or not in 1914. However, in recognition of the impact of the war, the General Meeting resolved unanimously to suspend the annual practice of reading out the names of those who had defaulted on their fees.[25]

Behind the stark statistics of Lansdowne members killed in action lay the reality of war: the 'Pals' of D Company had shipped out for Gallipoli in August 1915 as part of General Mahon's 10th (Irish) Division and suffered the same fate of all those sent there. Reports of the fighting at Suvla Bay highlighted the heroic actions of the 'Pals', including one account of D Company soldiers entering into the trenches 'with a dash for all the world like a wild forward rush at Lansdowne Road'. Particular notice was taken of the actions of Lansdowne's Richard P. 'Paddy' Tobin, who was posthumously awarded the Military Cross, a distinction given to officers for gallantry in the field. Other Lansdowne members killed during August–September in Gallipoli, serving both with the 'Pals' and the other Irish regiments of the 10th Division, included Edward Theaker Weatherill, William Purefoy Bridge, Arnold Wilson Moss, William Stewart Collen, Harold (J.A.H.) Taylor, John Errol Burke, Fredrick 'Fred' Gibson Heuston, John Henry Frederick Leland and Thomas Anthony Whitty, the last of whom had played in the Volunteers trial match back in October 1914. Another, Thomas Samuel Cuthbert Black, had been injured at Suvla Bay in August and died from his wounds in September in a hospital in Egypt. By the end of September, only seventy-nine of the original 239 'Pals' who had landed at Suvla Bay had survived. What was left of D Company shipped out to Solonika on 30 September, and thereafter members were dispersed to other theatres of war in Europe and beyond.[26]

At the beginning of 1916 the *Sport* newspaper highlighted the fact that the rugby fraternity across Britain and Ireland continued to be to the fore in supporting the war effort. Such commitment continued to prevent any regular senior rugby in Ireland, but one-off games and charity matches continued alongside Schools rugby. The players serving overseas even found time for a game behind the frontline in February when the RDF beat the Munster Fusiliers 12–Nil. One of the RDF forwards, W.J. 'Billy' Young, was a Lansdowne player who had also been involved in an earlier failed attempt in Solonika to play a match against the Welch Regiment, then considered to be the rugby 'Champions of the Balkans'. It appears that having marched thirty miles for the purpose, the men were initially too tired to play a game and then the realities of war intervened again before the match could take place. Young was also apparently renowned among his fellow soldiers for standing stark naked and having himself doused in ice-cold water first thing in the morning in the snow-strewn Macedonian mountains.[27]

Back in Ireland, four retired Lansdowne players took part in a big charity match at Lansdowne Road on 22 April 1916 between the old 'Crocks' of

Leinster and Ulster. With all four playing on the Leinster team, they were J.J. 'Johnny' Warren, J.J. Coffey, and both Blucher and Bertie Doran. All four were previous Lansdowne Club Captains, while the latter three were also Irish internationals. Also, Bertie Doran, Coffey and Warren would all go on to serve as presidents of the Club in succession to each other from 1922 to 1925, while Coffey also served as Club Secretary from 1924 to 1945. The proceeds from the 'Crocks' charity match went to the Dublin Central Soldiers Club and other Irish war charities.[28]

The 'Crocks' charity match had taken place two days before the outbreak of the 1916 Easter Rising. The playing of the match – with the bands of the RDF and IATVC entertaining the large crowd – was, like so many other public and private events that Easter weekend, evidence of the complete absence of knowledge among most of the Irish population of what was about to unfold on the streets of Dublin. However, just as international war was impacting upon Lansdowne and the wider Irish rugby public, so the Easter Rising did as well. As noted at the General Meeting in October 1916, 'one of our oldest members', William John Rice, was killed 'during the performance of his duties during the Rebellion', as was a past member, Holden Stoddart, who was 'killed by rebels while attending to the wounded as a Red Cross Worker'. Stoddart, who had grown up close to Lansdowne on Northumberland Road and had attended The High School, was an employee of Guinness Brewery. As Corps Superintendent of the St John Ambulance Brigade in Dublin, he had organized medical centres throughout the city during the Rising and on the afternoon of 26 April had left the Royal City of Dublin Hospital on Baggot Street with a stretcher party when he was killed by rebel gunfire on Northumberland Road while trying to attend to a wounded man. Like Stoddart, Rice was also an employee of Guinness Brewery. He lived at Sandford Terrace in Ranelagh and had won a Lansdowne Second XV Honours Cap in 1903–4, a memento which left Ireland with his widow and was still treasured by his descendants in Durban, South Africa, in 1987. Rice had been working as a night clerk in the Guinness Malthouse on 28 April 1916 when he was killed alongside a fellow employee and two soldiers from King Edward's Horse Regiment by members of the 5th Battalion RDF who were patrolling in the Brewery. Ostensibly mistaken for rebels, the four men may have been the victims of a callous murderer, even though the NCO commanding the RDF patrol was acquitted at a court martial hearing. Also killed in the Rising was the IRFU President, Browning, and three other men of the IAVTC. Although unarmed, they were shot by rebels on Northumberland Road late on the afternoon of 24 April, the first day of the Rising, as they marched back to Beggars Bush Barracks following a routine training exercise in the Dublin Mountains.[29]

The Club General Meeting in October 1916 also recorded that the number of war casualties had increased further to twenty-one members and fifteen past members. It was noted though with pride that in total 120 of the members were now on active service, which accounted for three-quarters of all those eligible to enlist. It was also recorded that five Military Crosses and a Distinguished Service Order (DSO) had been awarded to members.[30]

During 1917 Lansdowne Road remained the focus for war-related charity activities. In April the IRFU were involved in arranging a rugby match between Irish and Scottish Regiments, which attracted a crowd of 7,000 spectators. In September, two Lansdowne past captains and past and future presidents, Rupert Jeffares and J.J. Warren, were IRFU representatives on the organizing committee of a Military Tournament at the ground. Reported as a 'Brilliant Gathering', with the Viceroy and his wife among those in attendance, the event was intended to raise money for the support of RDF soldiers who were prisoners of war in Germany. The Central Advisory Committee of the RDF estimated that it cost them about £1,000 per month to provide the necessary assistance to these prisoners.[31]

The increasing heavy toll of the war ensured that at the Club General Meeting in November 1917 the casualties were up to thirty members as well as twenty past members. By then, a further seven members had received Military Crosses, while a further two had been mentioned in dispatches. Billy Young, a serving member of the 'Pals' who had played in February 1916 in the Frontline game against the Munster Fusiliers, was elected Club Vice-Captain in place of T.C. Jones Nowlan, one of the nine members killed in action that year. Young served as vice-captain for the 1918–19 season as well and continued to play on the Lansdowne First XV into the 1922–3 season. He also served as Club

President in 1943–4.[32] One of the game's characters, a newspaper report in 1938 described how Young had retired from rugby because of disquiet every Monday at his place of employment about his bruised appearance, which he ascribed to the fact that the Lansdowne team he played on 'had a huge forward called Sammy Campbell and my face seemed to have a fatal attraction for his boots'. His love of the game however ensured he could not stay retired, so on being asked to tog out for a match he told the team captain to list him with some sort of pseudonym, though he had not expected it to be 'Ludendorff', after the German First World War general.[33]

With the final Armistice of the war declared on 11 November 1918, a sign of the changing times was evident just two weeks later at Lansdowne's bi-annual General Meeting. With no new members having been proposed since October 1914, two new names were put forward at the meeting – F. Milligan and E. McCrea – while it was also resolved to start playing again as soon as possible. The four years of war had also left the Club's finances in a precarious position, though there was a small balance of £29 in the bank thanks to some arrears of membership fees being paid and £2 sent from Palestine by Lieutenant C.A. Murray, a member of the First XV in 1911–13 who was still on active service with the army. Particular notice was taken at that time of the death of Lieutenant-Colonel Henry Moore, who had been a member of the Club for thirty years and had been President in 1906–7.[34] A medical doctor, Moore's obituary recorded how he had served throughout the war in the Army Medical Corps, had been mentioned in dispatches in 1916 and 1917 and had received both the DSO and Military Cross. It was said that no one better understood how to run a field ambulance and advanced dressing station, or 'rendered greater service to suffering humanity'. He had been mortally wounded at Ypres while working at an advanced post. In December 1920 the Colonel Moore Memorial was erected at the Royal City of Dublin Hospital.[35]

As reported at the end of December 1918, no sport in Ireland had been 'hit heavier than the rugby game' by the war. For Lansdowne, from a position of having over 300 members before the war, by the beginning of 1919 their ranks had been reduced to one tenth of that figure, with more than 145 having served in the armed forces alongside more than 120 past members. In total,

Henry Moore, MC, a medical doctor, was a long-time member of Lansdowne FC and Club President in 1906–7. He died from wounds received at Ypres in May 1918 while serving at an advanced station as part of the Army Medical Corps. Courtesy of the Royal College of Surgeons, Ireland.

seventy-three of those men had died – thirty-eight members and thirty-five past members. Most of them had been killed on the Western Front, while two more, Rice and Stoddart, had been killed in Dublin during the 1916 Rising. By war's end, a further twelve Military Crosses had been awarded, bringing to twenty-four the total number of Lansdowne members so honoured, alongside three DSOs and two mentions in dispatches.[36]

It was notable that many among Lansdowne's war dead were not originally from Dublin. These included the likes of Harold Taylor, a Limerick teacher previously employed in St Columba's College; Thomas Samuel Cuthbert

Black of South Africa and County Monaghan; Thomas Henry Clesham of County Mayo who died at the Somme in July 1916; Robert Lepper Valentine of Enniskillen who was killed in France in April 1916; and Marshall Alfred Hill from County Kerry who died of wounds in May 1918. All of them had found a welcome at Lansdowne, a fact that was reflective of one of the Club's greatest strengths throughout its history of offering a friendly and supportive home to players from all parts of the island of Ireland as well as those from overseas.[37]

That Lansdowne tradition was seen once again as the Club looked to get back on its feet in January 1919 when eight new members were proposed and elected. These eight included the twenty-seven-year-old W.E. 'Ernie' Crawford, a former pupil of Methodist College, Belfast, who had been a very promising young player with Malone before enlisting at the outset of the war with the Royal Inniskilling Dragoons. Badly wounded at Arras in 1917, he thereafter served with the Ministry of Munitions. His appointment as accountant and chief financial officer of the Rathmines and Rathgar Urban District Council in early 1919 was to prove to Lansdowne's benefit in acquiring the services of one of the finest fullbacks – and greatest characters – of Irish rugby.[38]

January 1919 had also seen the outbreak of the Irish War of Independence, following the landslide victory for Sinn Féin in the December 1918 General Election, as Irish political life concluded its journey from the constitutional nationalism of the Irish Parliamentary Party and Home Rule to majority support for Republican separatism 'by any and every means'.[39] Yet even as guerrilla warfare began to take hold in Ireland, people still looked to re-establish their lives in the aftermath of the First World War.

With the 1918–19 playing season already half over before rugby matches recommenced, there was no official record kept of games played, but a start was made. Lansdowne's first match was on 18 January 1919 against the North Lancashire Regiment. The difficulty of getting fifteen players together was noted in the match report, which also pointed out that ten of Lansdowne's First XV from 1914 had died in the war. As a result, many of those involved in the match had never played the game before. Having run out 17–Nil victors, the following Saturday the Club was brought back to earth with a Nil-Nil result against the South Lancashire Regiment, though the match was graced

Lansdowne versus NIFC, *Irish Life*, 3 December 1920. The use of cartoons to present amusing reports on matches was common in the first decades of the twentieth century. In this instance, the rain- and mud-affected match between Lansdowne and NIFC was used to make fun of the fact that Ernie Crawford also played soccer for Dublin's Bohemians. Courtesy of the National Library of Ireland.

by a fine performance at fullback from Crawford. Further matches were played in the following months against the likes of Monkstown, Wanderers, Bective, Clontarf, Dublin University and NIFC, though at times games were cancelled as clubs struggled to field sides. Such challenges also meant that other clubs, including St Mary's College RFC, did not get re-established until much later. Not surprisingly, Lansdowne only managed to put out one team during the Winter and Spring of 1919, though the Club did participate in a respectable eighteen games during that time. With rapidly increasing membership at the same time, the Club and the game of rugby more generally were bouncing back from one of the most testing times yet to have been experienced by both.[40]

The 1919–20 season was the first full season played since 1914. The new Club Captain was Noel M. Purcell, who had first played for Lansdowne back in 1910 and had served throughout the war in the Leinster Regiment. Described as a 'burly' forward from Belvedere College, Purcell was a multi-talented athlete, having won an Olympic Gold Medal in 1920 for Britain in water-polo, a sport in which he also captained the Dublin University team and in which he went on to represent the newly independent Ireland at the 1924 Paris Olympics, thereby becoming the first man to compete in the Games for two different countries. In later years he went on to referee, including an England–Scotland game for which he wore his Lansdowne jersey, much to the consternation of the English media. He also served as Club President in 1937–8.[41]

The Leinster Senior Cup also got underway once again during the 1919–20 season, though Lansdowne went out in a first-round replay to Blackrock Nil–3. However, overall, the First XV had won ten of their eighteen games, drawing five and losing only three. Even more importantly for the successful future of the Club, the Second and Third XVs had also completed their first season in six years, with the Seconds winning eleven and losing five of their seventeen games and the Thirds winning five out of eight played.[42]

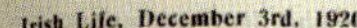
Irish Life, December 3rd, 1920.

273

North of Ireland v. Lansdowne.

WANDERERS WENT UNDER TO QUEEN'S OF BELFAST — BUT LANSDOWNE REVERSED THINGS BY BEATING "NORTH" ("NORTH" IS NOT THE PROVINCE OF ULSTER ———— BUT WE WONT SPOIL LANSDOWNES LITTLE JOKE).

"COCKY" ROWLAND FINDS A SIMILARITY IN TOGS ——— ADDED TO BY THE MUD.

A LITTLE WELL DIRECTED WILL-POWER MIGHT, INDEED, HAVE BEEN EFFECTIVE.

THANKS TO WHICH THE SLIGHTEST SUGGESTION OF A TACKLE WAS SUFFICE.

CRAWFORD'S ATTEMPT TO DEMONSTRATE THAT SOCCER IS A CLEANER GAME THAN RUGBY WAS A FAILURE.

THIS IS CUNNINGHAM, WHOM I RECOGNISED AFTER SOME TIME.

AND THESE ARE A FEW OF THE OTHER OUTSTANDING MEN.

With International Rugby back on the fixture list at the beginning of 1920, Crawford won the first of his thirty caps for Ireland. The Club's committee minutes of 16 February recorded a vote of congratulations to him on his selection and 'his magnificent play in the match against England' at Lansdowne Road. At the Club General Meeting later that year it was recorded that Crawford's 'play was the feature of the Irish XV' that season. It is only to be surmised how many more caps he would have won had the First World War not postponed the inevitable until he was twenty-eight years old. The Lansdowne scrumhalf, Willy J. Cunningham, was also capped that season against Wales and went on to play a further seven times for Ireland before he emigrated to South Africa in late 1923. A dentist by profession, in 1924 he was drafted in to replace the injured scrumhalf, A.T. Young, in one of four Tests played against South Africa by the newly named 'British Lions'.[43]

At the beginning of the 1920–1 season, attention turned once again to the need for better facilities for the Club, and as an interim measure it was proposed to erect an army hut as a tea-room, and in keeping with the gender inequalities and assumptions of the time, it was to have a Ladies Committee to manage it. A longer-term solution to the facilities issue would have to wait a while though, as the 1914 plans for the pavilion accommodation extension were postponed once again. An evident desire for further improvement on the field was also seen on 31 January 1921 when the Club decided 'after discussion that a trainer should be engaged' for the First XV for the remainder of the season. Crawford was given responsibility for pursuing the matter. It would seem there had been a degree of tension over the issue, presumably on the grounds that employing a trainer might undermine the amateur ethos of Rugby Union. Despite another exit in the first round of the Leinster Senior Cup, on this occasion to Bective Rangers, overall the First XV won fourteen and lost only five of their twenty games.[44]

The season also saw two more Lansdowne players capped for Ireland. Purcell, in his second season as Club Captain, was selected for all four of Ireland's Five Nations matches in 1921. The other player to be capped was the centre, Harry Jack, who played in the game against Wales. At the time he was actually employed in the British Colonial Service in Malaya but was at home in Cork on extended leave, and so would travel up to Dublin each week for

Lansdowne's matches. Later in life he was a founder of the Malaya Rugby Union in 1936 and served as President of the Fiji Rugby Union during which role he oversaw a tour to New Zealand that resulted in Fiji winning eight out of their nine games to the consternation of their hosts; he also served as President of Lansdowne in 1959–60.[45]

In preparation for the 1921–2 season, in April 1921 Crawford was elected as Club Captain. His appointment heralded the start of a very successful season for the Club, but it was not to be one without tragedy. On 10 February 1922 the Lansdowne three-quarter, John Hubert Wogan Browne, an Irish Catholic serving in the British Royal Field Artillery, was murdered by an armed gang as he returned from a bank to the artillery barracks in Kildare with cash for soldiers' pay. He had been a regular on the Lansdowne First XV that season and had been due to play for the Club the following day. His death was recorded in the Club Minutes on 13 February. With the War of Independence only recently concluded in July 1921, the ensuing Treaty only ratified by the Dáil in January 1922, and British army units still in the country, such an attack on a serving British army officer was potentially explosive, not least because

Lansdowne versus Wanderers, *Irish Life*, 7 October 1921. Action during a 24–Nil victory over Wanderers. Courtesy of the National Library of Ireland.

similar attacks on barracks and post offices by Irish Republican Army (IRA) detachments opposed to the Treaty was part of the process of the quick slide into Civil War in Ireland during 1922. It was therefore not surprising that Michael Collins, Chairman of the Irish Provisional Government, sent a telegram to Winston Churchill informing him of the arrest of the three men believed to be responsible for the 'abominable' attack and promising that if found guilty they would face the full rigours of the law. As a member of a long-established gentry family in the area, Wogan Browne's funeral was considered the most impressive ever seen in Naas. The attendance included representatives of both the British army and the IRA, a body that was in the process of splitting into the Free State army on the one hand and the Irregulars on the other as civil war loomed.[46]

The last recorded action of Wogan Browne on a rugby pitch was scoring a try in Lansdowne's 16–3 victory over Bective Rangers in mid-December 1921. Like so many other Irish rugby players who had similarly served in the British army throughout the First World War, it must have been poignant for Wogan Browne that the substantial gate receipts of £81 that day were donated to the planned IRFU War Memorial. At the same time, Lansdowne had also commenced considerations for a Club Memorial for the war dead, discussing on 19 December whether they could fund one large enough to include both deceased members and past members. Following Wogan Browne's death, as a mark of respect the Club cancelled a Dance planned for 15 February, but as the player himself would surely have wished, the rugby continued.[47]

It therefore seemed fitting that, after a hiatus of eighteen years, Lansdowne concluded the 1921–2 season by winning the Leinster Senior Cup for the fifth time, defeating old rivals Wanderers and Dublin University on the way to a 15–5 victory over Monkstown in the final. The game was probably most notable for the fact that Crawford suggested to the referee that Lansdowne's second of three tries be disallowed because Monkstown had been distracted by a Lansdowne injury. The referee deemed otherwise, and so Crawford duly converted. To add icing to the cake, shortly thereafter the First XV beat Cork Constitution 6–5 in the final of the newly inaugurated Bateman Cup, a charity competition in aid of Lady Dudley's Nurses Fund which was played between the Cup winners from each of the four provinces. The Cup itself was donated by Dr Godfrey Bateman of West Cork, in memory of his sons Reginald and Arthur who had been killed in the First World War. Along with Crawford, Purcell and Cunnigham, the 1921–2 team also included Arthur Aslett, one of the many British soldiers still stationed in Ireland and a future England player from 1926 to 1929 as well as a later Vice-President of the RFU. Apparently, the team for the final also included the pseudonymous Ludendorff – a.k.a. Billy Young – in place of the injured A.D. Brennan in the forwards.[48]

Leinster Senior Cup and Bateman Cup, 1921–2. Standing: J.J. Warren, G.E. Clarke, W.J. Young, A.D.J. Brennan, L. Healy, F. Dearden, F.C. Joynt (Pres.), C. Van Heerden, J.S. Pettigrew, H. Bell, N.M. Falkiner, C.P.S. Randell, J.J. Coffey. Seated: P.J. Whitty, J. Bell, W.A. Cunningham, W.E. Crawford (Capt.), N.M. Purcell, R.E. McGuire, C.E.G. Nunns. On Ground: R.M. Campbell, G.E. Larkin.

April 7th, 1923. Irish Society and Social Review. 19

RUGBY SEMI-FINAL: Lansdowne v. University College

Low visibility, rain and mud gave variety if not interest to the Rugby Semi-Final at Ballsbridge last Saturday. Our artist gives his own ideas why the result might have been different.

Lansdowne versus UCD, Leinster Senior Cup semi-final, *Irish Society and Social Review*, 7 April 1923. Rain-affected matches always offered opportunity for cartoons. Courtesy of the National Library of Ireland.

The summer of 1922 also saw the recommencement of plans for improving the Club's facilities at Lansdowne Road. The proposal now was for a new tea pavilion along with alterations to the old pavilion accommodation, all at an estimated cost of £960. With contracts agreed and a subscription list opened in October, work finally commenced that winter. Considerations for the Club War Memorial also continued, including the reversal of the earlier decision to include all past members' names. Instead, it was only to include ex-members who had played on Cup teams. As a result, the final Memorial included the thirty-eight members killed during the war plus a further four past members, bringing the total names on the Memorial to forty-two. The names of the remaining thirty-one past members killed during the war, as well as those of Rice and Stoddart who had been killed in Dublin during the 1916 Rising, were not included.[49]

On the pitch, Crawford remained Club Captain for the 1922–3 season, while also starring for Bohemians in soccer. The Lansdowne First XV achieved fourteen victories and nine losses in twenty-five games, though having beaten both Wanderers and Monkstown in the Leinster Cup, the Club's interest in the competition that year was ended by a 5–6 loss in a semi-final replay with University College Dublin (UCD). The match seems to have been decided as much by the rain and mud as it was by the players themselves. The Second XV for their part won nineteen and lost only three of their twenty-three games. Unfortunately two of those losses were to Dublin University, in the Metropolitan Cup and the Junior League final. It seems Dublin's rugby-playing students were no friends to Lansdowne that season.[50]

The early months of the 1923–4 season were consumed by final work on the new tea pavilion and the improved dressing room facilities with proper showers and a plunge pool, as well as final alterations to the Club War Memorial. With the latter mounted in the new tea pavilion, it was planned to unveil it at the official opening of the new facilities on 26 October 1923. It was appropriate that H.W.D. Dunlop was invited to perform the official duties on the day. Noted at the time in both the newspapers and the Club's minutes as 'the founder of the Club', Dunlop duly obliged at what was described as 'a simple but remarkably impressive ceremony', with the reading of the names, the playing of the 'Last Post', and the observation of two minutes silence. The Memorial was inscribed with the words 'They Played the Game' above the list of the war dead. The whole event had taken place immediately prior to the commencement of a game against Queen's University Belfast.[51]

With regard to playing matters, in April 1923 Willy Cunningham had been elected Club Captain for 1923–4. However, in what proved a disrupted season on the pitch, in November he stood down as he was about to emigrate to South Africa. The Club Vice-Captain, P.J. 'Paddy' Whitty, took over as captain, while T.V. Harris was elected in turn to Whitty's old post. With only eight victories in their twenty-three games that season, it was not surprising that the Club suffered a first-round exit at the hands of Blackrock in the Leinster Senior Cup.

But short-term results on the pitch in 1923–4 did not tell the bigger and more important story. Much had been achieved by Lansdowne FC in the first two-and-a-half decades of the twentieth century, not least in the growth of Club membership before the war and the re-invigoration of that membership after 1918, especially in the re-establishment of Second and Third XV fixtures from 1919–20 onwards. It was also the case that despite five years without any international rugby, ten Lansdowne players had been capped for Ireland during the years 1899–1924. With a variety of caps from two to thirty, the players were: J.J. Coffey; W.E. Crawford; W.J. Cunningham; B.R.W. Doran; G.P. Doran; A.E. Freear; Harry Jack; H.J. Knox; J.W. McConnell; and N.M. Purcell. Of those players, G.P. Doran and Cunningham had been invited to play with British Isles touring sides respectively in Australia in 1899 and South Africa in 1924. Behind such successes lay the hard work and endeavour of many individuals on the Club committee and as Club Officers, all of which helped to further develop and improve the Club structures and facilities and kept the Club financially viable. Alongside people such as R.G. Warren, J.J. Warren, J.J. Coffey and Rupert Jeffares there were the likes of Frank C. Joynt, who served as Club Secretary from 1906 to 1923 (with a brief respite for serious

A sketch of the Lansdowne tea pavilion which was officially opened by H.W.D. Dunlop in October 1923.

illness in 1912–13) and as President for two years during that time in 1920–2; or Arthur Sibthorpe, Club Treasurer throughout the war years and beyond to 1929; or Fred F. Denning who remained President throughout the war. The opening of the new tea pavilion and the improved changing facilities, as well as the unveiling of the War Memorial, were tangible evidence of all that hard work and endeavour. As recorded in the Lansdowne Centenary publication in 1972, 'At last there was room for a civil cup of tea after a match and space for members to bring wives or female friends'. It was also the case that the new tea-room was from the outset graced by the presence of Mary Kavanagh, who had started serving teas at the Club immediately after the war and would continue to do so through to her retirement in 1974.[52] Associational culture is sustained first and foremost by people and sociability, the life blood of every club. Despite the very dramatic and serious challenges of more than two decades of war and revolution, by 1924 Lansdowne FC, both on and off the pitch, was building towards a better and brighter future.

Chapter 3

Building a Tradition, Establishing a Legacy 1924–1945

The establishment of the new Free State in the twenty-six counties and the creation of the border with Northern Ireland had a significant impact upon Irish society and politics, as well as creating new challenges for everyone living on the island. These changes also took place within a wider context of re-building of societies, governments and nations in Europe and beyond in the aftermath of the First World War. Rugby, like all other sporting organizations and activities, had to learn to adapt, accommodate and evolve in light of these new realities. Lansdowne FC was no exception to that rule. The years 1924–45 were testament to how readily and successfully the Club rose to the challenge.

Despite the new geo-political reality on the island and the emergence of a new national border, rugby continued to function on a thirty-two-county basis both at national and club level. For Lansdowne, this meant that games proceeded uninterrupted against teams based in the new six-county Northern Ireland. The Club continued to play regular fixtures against the likes of NIFC, Queen's University Belfast, Instonians and Malone, alternating every other season as to which team was home or away. However, overseas tours and visits from abroad were slower to build up again after the First World War. Apart from an away trip to Coventry in 1921–2 and a visit from Oxford University in 1924–5, it was not until the second half of the decade that some semblance of normality would resume in that regard.[1]

As was common at the time, in preparation for the 1924–5 season Lansdowne held a trial match in September 1924. Reported in the *Irish Times*, it was noted that Ernie Crawford was as ever looking very fit, 'thanks to, as is his custom, a month's hard Association [Football] with Bohemians'. Despite one of the forwards, L. Healy, having moved to London and the outhalf, G. Roberston, being out with a long-term injury, the reporter's assessment of Lansdowne's First XV was that 'the team is young, but should do quite well this season'. There was also a rumour at the time that the UCD centre, G.P. Sarsfield Hogan, previously of the Catholic University School (CUS) on Leeson Street, was moving to Lansdowne – it would be another season however before that move actually occurred. On the pitch, with P.J. Whitty as Club Captain for a second season, there was some improvement on the previous year with eleven victories, ten losses and five draws, though having beaten Blackrock in the first round of the Leinster Senior Cup on St Patrick's Day, Lansdowne lost a semi-final replay 8–11 to Bective Rangers. It was not a season without success, however, as the Second XV, captained by H.V. Millar, won the Junior League for the second time, beating Dublin University 17–12 in the final. The team apparently included on occasion the pseudonymous Ludendorff. It was proudly noted at the October General Meeting that the Second XV had not 'lost a match in the Competition'. The Club also continued to increase its membership, with about 200 players taking part at the various junior levels. This was possible not least because the Third As ostensibly played sixty-five matches that season, though presumably this in reality involved several levels of Third XV teams.[2]

The 1924–5 season also included New Zealand's second tour to the British Isles. 'The Invincibles', as they became known, won all thirty-two of their matches, including beating Ireland 6–Nil at Lansdowne Road on 1 November. Ernie Crawford was the only Lansdowne player on the defeated side.[3]

However, with the First World War still fresh in people's minds, a more significant and particularly poignant event for Irish rugby that season was the unveiling in February 1925 of the IRFU War Memorial at Lansdowne Road. The occasion was presided over by Lansdowne's J.J. Coffey, then President of the IRFU, and took place the day before the international match between Ireland and Scotland on 28 February. In his speech, Coffey spoke of

> his proud honour to preside over this gathering of sportsmen, and yet his thoughts were tinged with sorrow when he looked back over his long career – twenty-five years – and recollected what grievous havoc the four years of war had wrought among the ranks of Rugby footballers … His own thoughts, he was sure, were the thoughts also of most Rugby men present – the sense of personal loss that they felt at the passing, in the prime of life, of men whom they had played with or against or whom they had watched playing. There was no greater brotherhood than that of Rugby football. Only those who played it could realize all that it stood for. To the lover of the game it would always be the training ground for the development of those manly qualities – pluck, courage, chivalry, good fellowship, and *esprit de corps* – which made decent fellows and good soldiers.

Coffey went on to remind the crowd of several hundred people that 'When the call to arms came … no class of sportsmen answered more unanimously than Rugby footballers'.

Other Lansdowne members representing the IRFU that day were R.G. Warren, Rupert Jeffares and J.B. Moore, while the President of the Leinster Branch was J.J. Warren. Former Lansdowne players among the ex-Irish Internationals in attendance included Noel Purcell and B.R. Doran, while the Club was represented by Ernie Crawford, Arthur Sibthorpe, J. Gargan, R.

Simmons and R. Donnelly, who had also designed the Memorial. The very significant contribution of the Club to the event was evident and had of course included the substantial financial donation of the gate receipts from a match against Bective Rangers in December 1921. The inscription on the Memorial reads: 'To the memory of Irish Rugby Football players who made the supreme sacrifice in the Great War[.] Greater love hath no man than this[:] That a man lay down his life for his friends'. The Memorial remains today at the re-developed Lansdowne Road.[4]

Lansdowne could also take some consolation from the 1924–5 playing season in that their semi-final opponents Bective Rangers had gone on to win the 1925 Leinster Senior Cup when they defeated UCD in the final. Of even more relevance in that regard for Lansdowne was the fact that some of UCD's 'sparkling back play' in their 1925 Cup run, and which had also helped the students win the Cup for the first time in 1924, was making its way to Lansdowne Road for the 1925–6 season in the form of Sarsfield Hogan and T.V. Davy. Another new recruit to the First XV was T.A. 'Tommy' O'Reilly at scrumhalf, who had learnt his rugby at Castleknock College and was to be a regular on the team through to the 1935–6 season, including being Club Captain in 1933–4. He would go on to serve as Club President in 1953–4, while also serving as honorary secretary of the Leinster Branch between 1949 and 1961 and ultimately as President of the IRFU in 1963–4. He was clearly a sporting all-rounder also, as in August 1926 he won the Liffey Swim. The 1925–6 season, however, also saw the loss to the Club of the services of Whitty, the outgoing captain, who had moved overseas. But with a new captain in T.V. Harris, the Club record was deemed to have been 'well maintained' with ten wins and eleven losses for the First XV. However, despite the recruitment of Sarsfield Hogan and Davy from UCD back in September, the students still got the better of Lansdowne 12–8 in the first round of the Leinster Senior Cup.[5]

While travel and mini-tours were always considered a crucial part of club life in every season, it was of particular note that in 1925–6 various Lansdowne teams had undertaken 'a considerable amount of travelling' within Ireland. This included visits to Belfast on three occasions, as well as matches in Cork, Galway, Kildare, Kilkenny, Longford, Waterford, Wexford and Wicklow. The

Eugene Davy, one of the greats of Irish rugby, was capped thirty-four times for Ireland. He played nine consecutive seasons for the Lansdowne First XV, captaining the Club to back-to-back Leinster Senior Cup and Bateman Cup 'doubles' in 1928–9 and 1929–30.

'Touring account' for the year totalled £187 1*s.* 2*d.*, in comparison to £98 3*s.* 6*d.* the previous season. It was notable however that, as had been the case since 1921–2, there had not been any trips overseas, nor had any overseas sides visited. This hiatus in international club tours would finally come to an end the following season.[6]

Contributing to a growing tradition of UCD students making a new home for themselves at Lansdowne FC after their College days, one of the greats of Irish rugby, Eugene Davy, came in as outhalf for the Club for the 1926–7 season, which was to be the first of nine consecutive seasons he would play for the First XV as both an outhalf and, on occasion, as a centre. Davy had already been capped five times for Ireland while playing for UCD and would go on to win a further twenty-nine international caps during the remainder of his playing career at Lansdowne up to and including the 1934–5 season. The re-uniting of Davy with his old College clubmate Sarsfield Hogan augured well for the Club.[7]

Early in the season the first overseas mini-tour since before the war took place, with games against Waterloo FC, which was won 9–8 and included a try by Davy, and Manchester FC, which was lost 3–5. It was to be one of only five losses out of twenty-seven games that season for the First XV – the remaining twenty-two all resulted in victories, with 332 points for and only 85 against over the whole season. The Second XV were similarly impressive, with nineteen victories out of twenty-two games, with 366 points for and only 79 against. Such statistics signalled a Club playing try-scoring rugby, as was evidenced on 13 January 1927 when it was reported that Lansdowne's three teams had scored a combined total of eighty-seven points the previous Saturday, which was considered an Irish record at that time for one club on any given match day. However, neither the First nor Second XV's seasonal record included the visit to Enniscorthy in early January 1927 by a Lansdowne selection boasting five of the First XV. While the match itself resulted in a draw, the media attention was directed primarily toward the side-line, where Ernie Crawford, in the guise of an 'interested spectator', was congratulated by Enniscorthy's rugby fans for captaining Ireland to victory in Paris on New Year's Day. After the match, all headed to Rosslare for the Enniscorthy RC's annual dance.[8]

Such occasions were part of the evidence that the game was growing in popularity across the country, a fact noted in the newspapers when the Leinster Senior Cup draw was made at the beginning of February. Lansdowne were pitted against Bective Rangers in the first round, both teams being considered to be among the top four in the Province that year. The other two top clubs, Dublin University and Monkstown, had also been drawn together. Lansdowne defeated Bective 9–Nil before dispatching Old Wesley 20–Nil in the semi-final. Once again, they faced Dublin University in the final. In a rain-affected match, Lansdowne ran out 8–Nil winners with a dominant display up front and with the only try of the match scored in the second half

Leinster Senior Cup, 1926–7. Standing: J.J. Coffey (Hon. Sec.), W.G. Browne, J.J. Winters, M.J. Dunne, J.F. Cullen, T.V. Harris, J.A. Gargan (Pres.). Seated: W.E. Crawford, W.W. Rossiter, G.P.S. Hogan, T.O. Pike (Capt.), J.E. Arigho, E.J. Lightfoot, J.E. McEnery. On Ground: E.O'D. Davy, T.A. O'Reilly.

by O'Reilly, the scrumhalf, whose all-round play, along with that of Davy, was singled out for praise in the Press. The Club Captain, T.O. 'Ted' Pike, had kicked a penalty goal in the first half as well as the second-half conversion. It was of note that Lansdowne had not conceded a single point in their Cup run.[9]

Although the First XV did not manage to win the Bateman Cup, having beaten Bohemians before losing to Instonians in the final 8–16, it had been a stellar season for the Club. The Second XV, captained by Leslie Heaney, did the 'double' by winning both the Junior League and the Metropolitan Cup, defeating Blackrock 3–Nil in the third replay of their League final in March and Bective Rangers 21–12 in April in the Cup final. The Third XV also had three replays of their Minor League final, but ultimately lost by a penalty goal to Nil. Reported as the Club's best season in its fifty-five years in existence, among other notable occurrences was the fact that the Third As and Bs had played ninety-two matches, utilizing over 100 players.[10]

The increasing numbers playing Junior and Minor rugby in Lansdowne was replicated across Leinster and beyond. In 1922–3 there had been eleven Junior clubs affiliated with the Leinster Branch, while by 1926–7 there were twenty-nine. At the same time, the number of teams playing in the Junior and Minor leagues had increased from fourteen in 1920 to thirty in 1926–7, with sixteen teams taking part in the Metropolitan Cup and eighteen in the Provincial Towns Cup.[11]

Increased numbers of players of course also meant more people availing of club facilities. In that regard, the shadow of the new Irish State was seen most directly for Lansdowne FC in relation to new licensing laws. After several attempts, in September 1927 the Club finally managed to agree new rules to bring the sale of alcohol on the Club premises in line with the Intoxicating Liquor Act of 1924. Apart from outlining the times when alcohol could legally be sold and imbibed at the Club by members, the new rules also deemed all visiting rugby players to Lansdowne Road to be honorary members from 2–7 p.m. on the days on which they were playing against Lansdowne or were otherwise using the grounds with the Club's permission. The new rules thereby demonstrated that the essential conviviality and sociability of club life would not be undermined by conservative officialdom.[12]

As highlighted by a tribute in the English paper, *Sporting Life*, by C.W. Packford, the beginning of the 1927–8 season heralded the end of Ernie Crawford's international career. Packford described Crawford as a 'complete sportsman' who was a 'relentless being' on the pitch when guarding the Irish line: 'A great patriot, a great sportsman and player, a man who fought relentlessly for Ireland, we shall miss him'. Despite the eulogistic nature of the tribute, Crawford was not in fact dead, and continued to play on the Lansdowne First XV for the next two seasons and would go on to serve as Club President for two years in 1939–41, as an Irish selector and as President of the IRFU in 1957–8. He has also been credited with coining the term 'Alickadoo', when on a train to London he took umbrage – apparently exclaiming 'Yew an' yer bloody Ali Khadu!' – when a discussion of a fellow-player's book about an oriental prince held up the poker game.[13]

The Club Captain for 1927–8 was Sarsfield Hogan and early in the season the re-emergence of touring sides from Britain saw Cardiff visit Dublin for the first time. Travelling as Welsh club champions and with a very strong reputation, Cardiff were however defeated 11–6, with a late Lansdowne try sealing the game in contentious circumstances. As Sarsfield Hogan later recounted, Davy had placed the ball for a penalty kick at goal, but when the three Cardiff forwards at the mark turned their backs, Crawford whispered to Davy to take a tap and go, which resulted in the latter scoring the try in the corner. Described in the Press as 'a rugby ruse', Cardiff protested at Davy's actions but to no avail. For his part, Sarsfield Hogan maintained that the episode led to the IRB changing the rules in the first instance so as to require that the placed ball be kicked at least ten yards, and then later on to the requirement that once placed, the ball had to be kicked at goal. Disputed rules aside, as a sure sign that British club sides were travelling once again to Ireland, Heriot's FP also arrived over from Scotland that season to commence a long-running series of reciprocal visits with Lansdowne, with the visiting side winning the first match 8–10, while Manchester and Waterloo both visited as well.[14]

The Leinster Cup was marred that season by the tragic death of a promising young Lansdowne prop-forward, Brian Fitzgerald Hanrahan, as a result of an injury sustained in the first-round victory over Dublin University on 3 March 1928. A native of Clonmel in Tipperary and former student at Castleknock College, Hanrahan was a twenty-two–year-old clerk who lived in South Richmond Street and had played on the victorious Lansdowne Second XV that had done the 'double' in 1926–7 when winning both the Junior League and Metropolitan Cup. He was the younger brother of Charles F. Hanrahan of Dolphin and Ireland, who was also a future President of the IRFU. The injury had occurred at a scrum about fifteen minutes into the match, when what was described at the time as a violent collision between the two front-rows resulted in Hanrahan sustaining a broken neck. A doctor on the side-line came to his aid and was informed by Hanrahan that he was unable to move. Suffering from total paralysis, he was taken to the Royal City of Dublin Hospital on Baggot Street where he later lost consciousness and died the following day. The tragedy was widely reported, as was the inquest, at which Lansdowne were represented

Brian Fitzgerald Hanrahan tragically died the day after he sustained a broken neck playing for Lansdowne FC in the first round of the Leinster Senior Cup in March 1928. His memory lives on with his picture on permanent display in the Zurich Room of the Lansdowne Clubhouse.

by J.J. Coffey. The inquest recorded evidence that the injury had been caused by a collapsed scrum, though another witness stated that Hanrahan himself had said that he had been involved in a head-to-head collision. Hanrahan's older brother, Edgar, identified the body at the inquest, where a verdict of 'accidental death' was returned.[15]

Hanrahan's funeral on 6 March in St Mary's Catholic Church on Haddington Road was a concelebrated Requiem Mass. Large numbers attended, with representatives from rugby clubs throughout Ireland. The IRFU and Leinster Branch were also represented, as were the Association of Referees. A large turn-out from Lansdowne included all Hanrahan's team-mates and other Club members, while many of those he had played against were there from Wanderers, Old Wesley, Bective Rangers, UCD, Dublin University, Palmerstown, Monkstown, Blackrock, CYMS, Civil Service RFC, Bank of Ireland RFC, Cork Constitution, Athlone, Carrick-on-Suir, Dolphin, Bohemians, Garryowen, Young Munster, and Rockwell and Castleknock Colleges. Various other sporting organizations were also represented, while the many wreaths laid on the grave included one from the Ulster Branch of the IRFU. Hanrahan's tragic death had clearly affected many sporting people around the country. Of Hanrahan's teammates who played that fateful day, Sarsfield Hogan recounted how 'none of us … will ever forget the avoidable chain of circumstances which destroyed a young life'. As a result of the accident, the IRB amended the laws of the game to preclude front-rows charging into each other. As for Hanrahan himself, his memory lives on in the twenty-first century as a central, if ghostly, character in the *Rugby Spirit* fiction series by Gerard Siggins.[16]

Despite the tragedy, the Leinster Senior Cup continued with Lansdowne facing Wanderers in the second round. A close 6–4 victory was followed by a cliff-hanger 6–3 semi-final win over Bective Rangers, when both O'Reilly and Davy were absent with winter ailments. With both men back in harness for the final against Blackrock, Lansdowne won 13–Nil, the same score-line with which they had commenced the Cup campaign against Dublin University. In the face of 'stonewall' defence from Blackrock, all Lansdowne's points in the final were scored in the second half. The captain, Sarsfield Hogan, led the way with a try himself and then, 'in true Lansdowne style', threw a pass over the head of his fellow-centre, Morgan Crowe, to the winger, J.E. 'Jack' Arigho, thereby creating the space for the latter to race in for 'a grand try'. A long pass from Davy to Sarsfield Hogan, who drew his man and passed to the other Lansdowne winger, E.J. 'Ned' Lightfoot, created the third and final try of the match. Both Arigho and Lightfoot were in their second season on the First

Leinster Senior Cup, 1927–8. Standing: J.C. McClelland, W.W. Rossiter, N.H. Lambert, W.G. Browne, J.J. Coffey (Hon. Sec.), M.J. Dunne, M.P. Crowe, W.E. Crawford, E.O'D. Davy. Seated: A.C. Sibthorpe (Pres.), J.C. Bermingham, F. Conroy, G.P.S. Hogan (Capt.), J.E. McEnery, T.O. Pike, J.J. Warren. On Ground: T.A. O'Reilly, J.E. Arigho. Inset: E.J. Lightfoot.

XV, while Crowe was in his first. All three would continue to play at senior level well into the 1930s, with Lightfoot serving as Club Captain in 1934–5 and Arigho doing likewise in 1935–6. All three also went on to play for Ireland, with Arigho winning sixteen caps between 1928 and 1932 and scoring a record of five tries in three home nations games in 1928, Crowe getting thirteen caps in 1930–4, and Lightfoot securing eleven caps in 1931–3.[17]

Lansdowne's second Leinster Senior Cup victory in a row – and seventh overall – and 'the play of the side during the whole season', was deemed by the *Irish Times* to be a fitting 'tribute to the fine modern idea of play cultivated by the Lansdowne backs, an idea that might well be set up as a standard for other clubs and schools to follow'. Once again, however, the Bateman Cup escaped Lansdowne's clutches soon after when losing the final to Young Munster 6–3. The victory was much against popular expectation, but was deemed a very merited win by the Young Munster team, competing in their first ever Bateman final after having just secured their first ever Munster Cup.[18]

Overall, however, it had once again been a highly successful season for the Club at all levels in 1927–8. Captained again by Leslie Heaney, who would go on to serve as Club Honorary Treasurer from 1929 to 1951, the Second XV had won the Junior League for a second year in a row (and fourth time overall), beating Old Wesley 16–Nil in the final, and had also reached the final of the Metropolitan Cup. For their part, the Third XV had just missed out on winning their section of the Minor League, while the Third As and Bs had played sixty-one matches between them and utilized over 100 players in so doing. It was also reported at the Club General Meeting in late April 1928 that the First XV had used forty-seven players through the season, which apparently demonstrated that 'the policy of trying out everyone has much to recommend it'. Ultimately it was concluded that the playing resources of the Club were 'very high'. Certainly the fact the First XV had scored 431 points in winning twenty-one of their thirty games, while only conceding 166, suggested that player rotation was not undermining the free-flowing game that was a recognized hallmark of the Club. This ethos of the Club was summed up in the minutes of the General Meeting in April: 'we do not consider that the winning of these trophies make a great season. We consider that our play and

Junior 1 League, 1927–8. Standing: D. Robertson (Manager), W.C. McNeaney, A.G. Anketell, N.H. Lambert, J.T. Moran, M.E. Bardon, T.V. Harris, M. Bell, W.G. Brown, V.J. Fielding, A.C. Sibthorpe (Hon. Treas.). Seated: J. O'Connor, W.M. Keogh, M.P. Ruddle, L.J. Heaney (Capt.), J.G. Roberston, E.A. Heard, J.F. Cullen. On Ground: H. Gibson, P. McPhillips.

the fixtures we fulfilled during the season are more advantageous to rugby'.[19]

Central to that ethos was travelling around the country and abroad to spread the game. In that regard, as the Club headed into the 1928–9 season, Ernie Crawford continued to be a key member of Lansdowne. His enthusiasm to grow the game in Ireland had long since led to him picking scratch sides for Sunday games against provincial clubs in various parts of the country at a time when 'Sabbath-breaking' was still much frowned upon in certain quarters. In keeping with such activities, in October 1928 he selected a Dublin side to play against a visiting Llanelli team, who had had a drawn match the day before against a Dublin County side. Crawford's selection, chosen from Lansdowne, Wanderers, Bective Rangers, Old Welsey, Dublin University and UCD, lost 15–Nil. This was sandwiched in between journeying north with Lansdowne for a 12–6 victory over Malone and then heading off to Scotland for a two-match Club mini-tour to Heriots and Watsonians.[20]

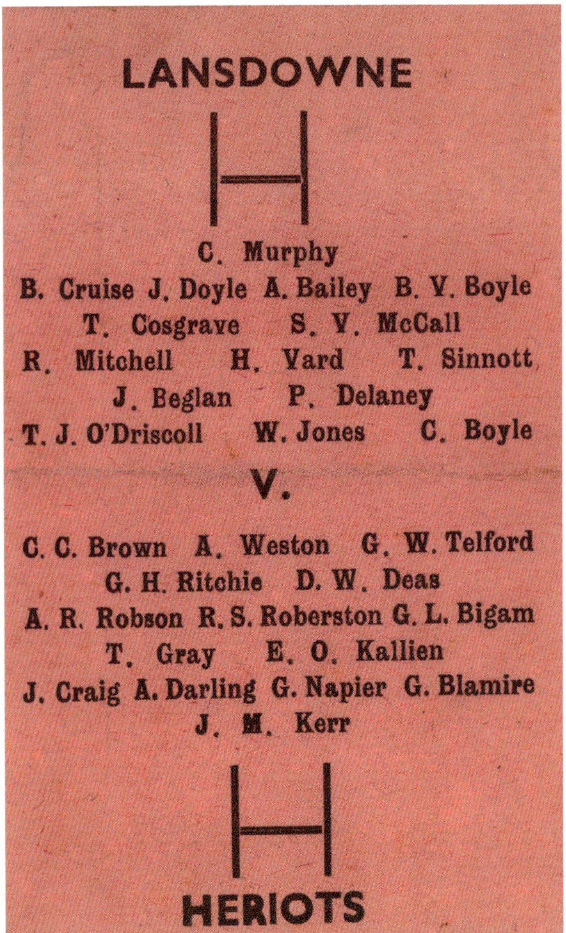
LANSDOWNE

C. Murphy
B. Cruise J. Doyle A. Bailey B. V. Boyle
T. Cosgrave S. V. McCall
R. Mitchell H. Vard T. Sinnott
J. Beglan P. Delaney
T. J. O'Driscoll W. Jones C. Boyle

V.

C. C. Brown A. Weston G. W. Telford
G. H. Ritchie D. W. Deas
A. R. Robson R. S. Roberston G. L. Bigam
T. Gray E. O. Kallien
J. Craig A. Darling G. Napier G. Blamire
J. M. Kerr

HERIOTS

The team sheet for the 1938–9 Lansdowne FC versus Heriots FP match held at Lansdowne Road. This recurring annual fixture on a rotating home or away basis against the Scottish club was first established in the late 1920s and early 1930s.

Although both Scottish matches were lost, the rest of the season panned out extremely well. In the first year of Eugene Davy's Club captaincy, and when Cardiff also came visiting once again, the Leinster Cup was retained for the Club's first three-in-a-row. Having dispatched Palmerston 30–6 in their first Cup game, Lansdowne had a much tighter 3–Nil semi-final victory over Wanderers before going on to win the final 45–Nil against Monkstown. In so doing, Lansdowne made history with the biggest result for a Cup final, scoring nine tries in the process. Davy kicked six conversions, a dropped goal and scored two tries in an all-round captain's performance, Crowe scored a hat-trick, and Arigho, Lightfoot, M.J. 'Mick' Dunne and Frank Conroy all got one a piece. The match was a prime example of Lansdowne's open running rugby that defined this golden era of results at the Club. In heaping praise upon the skills of all the Lansdowne backs 'who have become famous the world over', the *Sport* newspaper opined that in a 'dazzling display', the 'gospel of attack as the best form of defence has been adopted … with … the most satisfactory results'. It was also of note that Arigho, Lightfoot and Dunne had all come from Castleknock College, like O'Reilly before them, thereby establishing another strong Club tradition within a Dublin Catholic secondary school that continued in future years. With a slightly peripatetic schooling, Arigho had actually only spent his final year in 1925 at Castleknock, having attended both Blackrock and Belvedere College beforehand, including helping the latter beat Castleknock in the Schools Senior Cup final in 1924.[21]

The Bateman Cup was also secured later in April 1929 with another stylish display of passing rugby in a 32–11 victory over Galwegians, on an occasion when seven of the Lansdowne team were Irish internationals – Crawford, Davy, Arigho and Crowe, as well as Dunne who won sixteen caps between 1929 and 1934, J.C. Bermingham who had won four caps in 1921, and J.S. Synge who won one cap in 1929. The team also included three future Ireland players in Lightfoot, M.E. Barden, who got one cap in 1934, and N.H. 'Ham' Lambert, who got capped twice the same year. The latter's rugby career was cut short in 1934 at the young age of twenty-three owing to a ruptured cruciate ligament, though he defied the odds to go on to maintain a lengthy playing career in cricket with Leinster, as well as a highly successful international rugby refereeing career in the late 1940s and early 1950s. He also took a leading role in establishing the Irish Wolfhounds club for the promotion of rugby in rural Ireland, served as Lansdowne President in 1961–2, and pursued a lengthy administrative career with the Leinster Rugby Referees Association, which culminated in 2005 in the IRFU awarding him a special cap for his services to Irish refereeing.[22]

Overall during the 1928–9 season the Lansdowne First XV had scored 537 points in thirty-two games, with only 179 conceded. This thrilling playing style may also have accounted in part for the continuing popularity of the

Leinster Senior Cup and Bateman Cup, 1928–9. Standing: M.J. Dawson (Pres.), J.C. Cathcart, A.G. Anketell, M.E. Bardon, J.C. Bermingham, J.J. Warren, M.J. Dunne, W.F. Power, J.C. Powell, J.J. Coffey (Hon. Sec.). Seated: N.H. Lambert, E.J. Lightfoot, W.E. Crawford, E.O'D. Davy (Capt.), J.E. McEnery, M.P. Crowe, F. Conroy. On Ground: T.A. O'Reilly, J.E. Arigho.

game, as seen at a match in Limerick in January 1929 against Bohemians attended by 3,000 spectators who saw Lansdowne win 13–6, and another game at Lansdowne Road in February in front of a 'big gathering' when a visiting Halifax team won 13–8.[23]

The importance of strength-in-depth for any club was seen in the astounding 100 per cent record of the Third XV who won the Minor League for the first time in 1928–9, defeating Blackrock 6–5 in the final. Captained by Bill Demery, the team included T.C. 'Tom' Fox, who served as Club President in 1957–8 while also serving as honorary treasurer from 1951 till his death in 1965, and T.C. 'Tishy' Byrne, who was Club President in 1969–70. The team scored a phenomenal 410 points with only eighteen conceded over nineteen matches, with fourteen games won to Nil. The Third As and Bs also continued their high number of games, with fifty-four played, thirty-three won and 590 points for and 309 against.[24]

The continuing success of the Third XVs and the large number of Club members more generally playing rugby increased the pressure on the Club to find more pitches for training and matches. The ability of a city club to attract lots of players from its surrounding hinterland was a double-edged sword, as increasing urbanization reduced the amount of green space available for sporting purposes. The quest to find a dedicated alternative grounds for the Thirds was challenging. In September 1928 arrangements to use grounds on Sandymount Road and Claremont Road fell through. Then in October 1929 it was agreed to acquire a ground for the junior teams, and Crawford was directed to investigate a potential location at Beech Hill in Donnybrook. Nothing came of this initiative, however, and the issue remained unresolved as the Club prepared to head into the 1930s.[25]

The Club's success on the pitch was also reflected in the Club coffers, to the extent that in April 1928 it was proposed to approach Davy Stockbrokers with a view to investing surplus Club income in what was termed 'trustee stock'. Davy's was a new company just established by Lansdowne's Eugene Davy and his older brother James. In September the process was initiated, when the honorary treasurer was empowered to make arrangements with James Davy for the investment. With a balance of £535 in the bank, it was agreed at the General Meeting on 24 September to invest £400 in a Free State Loan, with the treasurer and secretary, Sibthorpe and Coffey, acting as trustees for the Club. The £400 was invested by Davy's 'at cost' of £391 1*s*. in the Irish Free State 5% National Loan, which saw a dividend payment to the Club of £10 by September 1929, increasing thereafter to an annual return of £20 in the early 1930s.[26] It may not have seemed an auspicious time for the Club to be investing in the stock market, especially after the Wall Street Crash of October 1929 and the ensuing global economic depression. But Ireland was not overly affected by such world events owing primarily to the conservative fiscal policies of the 1920s Free State government. As a result, Ireland managed to avoid the hyper-inflation experienced elsewhere in the 1930s, with governmental fiscal rectitude resulting in the country maintaining an excellent international credit

Eugene Davy, Ernie Crawford and Jack Arigho, Ogden's and Wills's cigarette cards. Sportspeople were depicted on cigarette cards as a form of brand promotion. Source: Courtesy of Frances Nolan.

rating. It was also the case that purchasing government debt secured by the national legislature was one of the safer stock-market investment strategies, but it also suggested that Lansdowne had sufficient confidence in the new twenty-six county Free State to be willing to invest significant income in it.[27]

But not all was rosy in Irish rugby. The 1929–30 season commenced with a looming crisis within the administration of the game. The issue arose as a result of an IRFU ban that year on gate-receipted league or cup rugby being played on a Sunday. Both the Munster and Connacht Branches resisted what has been described as both a classist and religiously motivated ruling. Sport on Sundays was particularly objectionable to Protestant Sabbatarians, but the reality was that working-class players in particular had less free time at weekends with six-day working weeks still being common, and Sunday rugby was often all they could manage. Without it, there was increased danger of fixture congestion, especially in Munster and Connacht. Middle- and upper-class players with greater leisure time and working flexibility were less impacted by the ban. There was also an old-school Victorian classist attitude within the higher echelons of the IRFU, where it was believed that Sunday Junior rugby, especially in Limerick, was excessively violent and was undermining the 'prestige, traditions and discipline of rugby'.[28]

In light of the ban, on 21 October 1929 Lansdowne FC received a letter from the Leinster Branch requesting a reduction in the Club's non-Dublin fixtures. The desire of the Leinster Branch, in keeping with the IRFU ban, was to free up more Saturdays for Dublin club fixtures. The matter continued to be discussed during the following months, though ultimately efforts were made to reduce the number of games played outside of Dublin. For much of the 1930s, Lansdowne's number of matches against non-Dublin clubs dropped from around twelve or thirteen per season to seven or eight.[29]

More immediately, the IRFU ban on Sunday games led to tensions within the club game. On 21 October 1929 Lansdowne received a letter regarding the 'resolution on Sunday football' from UCD FC, who were very supportive of facilitating Sunday rugby and were also lobbying the IRFU on the matter. However, although Ernie Crawford had long been an advocate of Sunday rugby, other members of Lansdowne were more reticent about openly defying the IRFU. This was evident on 25 November when the Club committee considered whether they should fulfil a fixture with Galwegians 'unless prohibited by' the IRFU. When the Connacht Branch then informed Lansdowne that Galwegians had consented to the Branch resolution to continue Sunday matches despite the IRFU ban, the committee decided that 'under the circumstances' they felt reluctantly … compelled' to cancel their annual fixture for that year. However, a quick response from Galwegians stating that 'they did not in any way' intend to 'break the resolution' of the IRFU, coupled with a private communiqué from the Connacht Branch, facilitated Lansdowne re-scheduling the fixture.[30]

The issue of Sunday rugby would rumble on, and ultimately needs to be viewed within the context of the continuing growth in popularity of the game. At the heart of spreading that popularity was Crawford, who finally retired from playing for the Lansdowne First XV during the 1929–30 season, though not before turning out for London Irish against London Welsh in February 1930. He had previously made a couple of guest appearances for Cardiff in the mid-1920s. The connection with London Irish was also strong at that time,

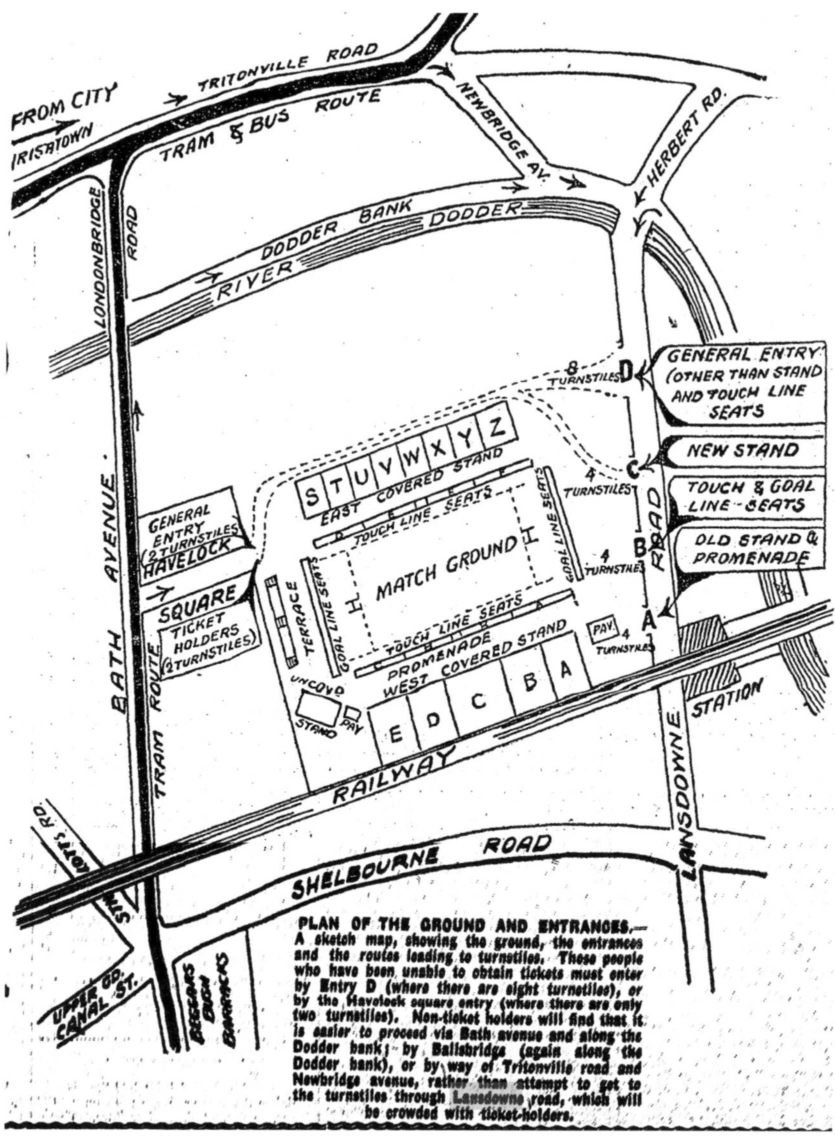

PLAN OF THE GROUND AND ENTRANCES.—A sketch map, showing the ground, the entrances and the routes leading to turnstiles. Those people who have been unable to obtain tickets must enter by Entry D (where there are eight turnstiles), or by the Havelock square entry (where there are only two turnstiles). Non-ticket holders will find that it is easier to proceed via Bath avenue and along the Dodder bank; by Ballsbridge (again along the Dodder bank), or by way of Tritonville road and Newbridge avenue, rather than attempt to get to the turnstiles through Lansdowne road, which will be crowded with ticket-holders.

Lansdowne Road, *Irish Times*, 8 February 1930.

Lansdowne having commenced annual fixtures in 1928–9 with, as they were described in official records, 'Anglo-Irish', which continued through to 1934–5 (excluding 1930–1).[31]

Despite Crawford's retirement, the First XV, with Davy as captain once again, continued to have great success on the field in 1929–30. Having beaten Monkstown 32–3 and Palmerston 33–Nil en route to the final of the Leinster Senior Cup, Lansdowne then defeated Bective Rangers 9–Nil to claim their fourth Leinster Cup title in a row and, in so doing, equalled Dublin University's historic run of four titles in 1895–8. With Davy playing in the centre owing to injuries to both Crowe and Lambert, the match reports highlighted the contribution once again of O'Reilly at scrumhalf, partnered on the occasion by Jim Jones who had been promoted from the Second XV to play at outhalf. The same halfbacks steered Lansdowne to a second Bateman Cup title in a row, with Young Munster beaten 16–Nil in the semi-final and NIFC defeated 19–12 in the final, when Arigho scored a hat-trick of tries, Lightfoot added a brace, and Jones kicked a dropped goal.[32]

In another excellent season for the Club, the Second XV only lost out on winning the Junior league in a replayed final with Bective, while the Third As and Bs continued to rack up phenomenal statistics, with sixty-seven matches played during the season. Not surprisingly, the junior team honorary secretary, Eddie Carthew, was commended at a General Meeting on 28 March 1930 for his efforts in getting so many teams out to play. It was also noted at that time that two Club players, Dunne and Crowe, had been invited to tour New Zealand and Australia with the Lions in the summer of 1930. While Dunne actually went on the ensuing tour, Crowe had to pull out owing to an injury sustained playing in the Hospitals Cup.[33]

Presumably with tongue-in-cheek, though possibly also with some of the more vocal and dissident Lansdowne members in mind, Coffey's honorary secretary's report to the March 1930 General Meeting concluded as follows:

> The committee are rather disappointed with the Junior players as we have only had one player, J. MacNeaney, to come on to the 1st XV. Now we want understudies for all our players and surely we should be able out of all our members to get a second Tommy O'Reilly. Some of you may think we want new blood on our committee, well now is the time, I want a rest and would like a successor. However, if

> you do elect some of the 'Alakdoos' don't grouse afterwards at what we do.[34]

If Coffey's intention had been to silence dissent, he was unsuccessful. When the matter of extending the pavilion at a cost of £425 was thereafter raised at the meeting, Crawford, Heaney and Davy all argued that the money would be better spent on acquiring a junior ground. They were defeated in this regard, and an attempt by Crawford to put forward an amendment to the decision was ruled out of order. But Crawford's persistence on the matter paid off in September 1930, when it was reported at the next General Meeting that the Club were in negotiation for a junior ground and hoped to be in possession of it that season. At the end of the month Crawford was empowered to negotiate the acquisition.[35]

Leinster Senior Cup and Bateman Cup, 1929–30. Standing: W.E. Crawford, M.J. D'Alton (Pres.), F. Conroy, J.C. Powell, J.C. Bermingham, V.V. Drennan, M.E. Bardon, D. Moran, J. MacNeaney, J.J. Warren, J.J. Coffey (Hon. Sec.). Seated: J. Hanlon, W.G. Browne, E.J. Lightfoot, E.O'D. Davy (Capt.), J.E. McEnery, J.T. Moran, J.W. Jones. On Ground: J.E. Arigho, T.A. O'Reilly.

The 1929–30 season had also seen a new initiative in December 1929 when committee member W. MacNeaney was empowered to arrange Christmas vacation fixtures for the Club's schoolboy members. In early January 1930, with both teams unbeaten at that point, Lansdowne schoolboys defeated Bective Rangers schoolboys in the final game. As part of that initiative, in December an advertisement had been run in the *Irish Times* advising any schoolboys wishing to take part in these Christmas vacation rugby matches to send their names to Ernie Crawford at 12 Sandford Terrace.[36]

As was evident throughout the 1929–30 season, Crawford's retirement from playing had not diminished his massive commitment to, and passion for, the game. His drive to acquire a proper ground for the Club's junior teams was testament to his recognition that the game was much more than the First XV. Likewise, his promotion of schoolboy rugby at Lansdowne over the Christmas holidays was just a microcosm of his commitment to the development of rugby in general. He had long-since kept a keen eye on the schools game in order to identify future club players. As a result, it made sense that on his retirement he was appointed as honorary secretary of the Leinster Schools Branch of the IRFU.[37]

The great success of the 1929–30 season was however tempered by a number of significant deaths of Club members during the spring and summer of 1930. On 16 April H.W.D. Dunlop passed away at the age of eighty-six. His death was recorded in the Club minutes on 21 April, when it was noted that, as well as founding Lansdowne FC, he had been a member for fifty-eight years. A wreath was also sent to the funeral in Mount Jerome, which although a private family affair included twelve members of Lansdowne, among whom was Eugene Davy, who later recalled how at home matches in the 1920s Dunlop had been 'a regular fixture on the old, uncovered stand beside the Tea House … consistent in support and encouragement.' He was also credited with inventing a 'curious sort of loose string gloves to make handling easier in bad weather', a pair of which he apparently presented to Davy in the tea pavilion just as the latter prepared to go onto the pitch for an international match. Dunlop also came up with a knitted toe cap intended to make it easier to kick a wet ball – apparently neither invention caught on. Following Dunlop's death, the Club raised a fund for the support of his widow and family, which resulted in £32 8*s*. 8*d*. being passed on for that purpose.[38]

Another death occurred in June, when the Club recorded the tragic passing of Cecil Bulmer, a promising young player with the Third XV who had won an Honours Cap that season. Then, in early August, the death occurred of Claud J. Law, the incoming Club President for the 1930–1 season, who had been elected at the General Meeting on 28 March 1930. He had been a member of Lansdowne for thirty years and had played at number 8 on the Cup-winning side of 1901 as well as captaining the Second XV to their first Junior League title in the same year. He died before formally taking office, though as his wife, Mary, recorded forty-nine years later, the position was left vacant for that season in his memory. She also recalled how during the two years of their engagement and eighteen years of marriage, Lansdowne Road had 'played an important part in our lives. The teas in the pavilion after the matches were so enjoyable'. Even in 1979 after many decades living in London the sense of a wider Lansdowne community was still so strong for Mary Law, not least in the fact that an English interdenominational service organized at that time by her daughter, Diana, was officiated at by an ex-Lansdowne player, Bishop Victor Pike. The Club was officially represented at the service by the bishop's brother, Sir Theodore Pike, while Mary wore her late husband's cup winners medal as a brooch on the occasion.[39]

For their part, the Pikes were long-connected with Lansdowne. Theodore O. 'Ted' Pike first played for the First XV in the 1922–3 season, and was a regular thereafter until the 1930–1 season, as well as being Club Captain in the Cup-winning 1926–7 season. He was capped eight times for Ireland in 1927 and 1928. His younger brother, Victor J. Pike, played for Lansdowne in both the 1930–1 and 1931–2 seasons, and was also capped for Ireland on thirteen occasions between 1931 and 1934. They were however just two of the five Pike brothers who played for the Club in the 1920s and 1930s. A.H. 'Andy' Pike had played on the First XV with Ted in 1922–3, while R.B. 'Bobs' Pike played with Ted in the 1923–4 and 1924–5 teams. A younger brother, St John Pike, played on the First XV from 1933–4 to 1936–7, in which latter season he was also Club Captain. Coming from a large Church of Ireland family in Thurles, Tipperary, with a clergyman father, it was not unusual that some of the Pike sons went on to be clerics themselves, though the fact that Victor, Bobs and St John all rose to the rank of Bishop was exceptional. Ted chose instead the well-worn alternative route of British colonial service, eventually ending up as Governor of British Somaliland in the later 1950s during which time he was knighted as Knight Commander of the Order of St Michael and St George.[40]

With three such significant deaths in the Spring and Summer of 1930, the 1930–1 season commenced in a sombre mood for Lansdowne. Yet at the same time, it was noted that the Club's success was such that it had nearly a thousand members, one-tenth of whom were current players.[41] The season commenced with renewed concerns being expressed by members over the lack of transparency in team selection. As a result, once again, it was agreed that two Club committee members attend junior fixtures for that purpose. At the same time, the increasing focus on weekly training sessions resulted in discussion taking place as to the installation of 'artificial lights' in Lansdowne Road for training in December and January. Although the IRFU refused permission at that time, by 1934–5 such illumination had been agreed to and put in place.[42]

History beckoned for Lansdowne in 1931 as the Club entered into the Leinster Senior Cup as joint recordholders with Dublin University with four wins a piece in a row. With a bye for the first round, in the second Lansdowne defeated Palmerston 43–3, while Monkstown were overcome 8–Nil in the semi-final. It was fitting that the final was against one of the Club's oldest rivals, Wanderers, who had had a harder run of Cup games against UCD, Dublin University and Bective Rangers. Expectations were for a close match, with Wanderers' forward supremacy pitted against Lansdowne's back-play. This latter assumption was well made, given that the whole of the Irish three-quarter line at that time was comprised of Lansdowne players in Davy, Arigho, Crowe and Lightfoot. In a singular distinction for the Club, the four men played together in the Ireland games that year against Wales, Scotland and South Africa.[43]

In the end, history was indeed achieved in the Leinster Cup final. Captained by J.E. 'Jimmy' McEnery, Lansdowne played true to themselves and although

Leinster Senior Cup and Bateman Cup, 1930–1. Standing: J.J. Coffey (Hon. Sec.), J. MacNeaney, J.C. Powell, T.O. Pike, F.E. Davies (Vice-Pres.), D. Moran, M.E. Bardon, J. McGuire, J.J. Warren. Seated: N.H. Lambert, M.P. Crowe, M.J. Dunne, J.E. McEnery (Capt.), J.E. Arigho, V.J. Pike, E.J. Lightfoot. On Ground: T.A. O'Reilly, E.O'D. Davy.

the game remained in the balance for a long time, the constant threat of the Lansdowne backline eventually told in the final quarter. Davy was dominant throughout, ably assisted by O'Reilly. A Davy dropped goal in the first half was followed early in the second by a Lambert try off a Davy break. Wanderers responded with their own converted try, but a scintillating solo-effort from Davy for his own try and a final touch-down for Lightfoot off yet another Davy break sealed the match 17–5, McEnery having kicked two conversions. Shortly after, the Bateman Cup was retained for the third year running with victory over Loughrea 13–3 and then 16–5 against Belfast Collegians in the final.[44]

At the Spring General Meeting Coffey, the honorary secretary, in noting that the Club was then fifty-nine years old, declared that 'never in its existence has it achieved such success. The Club stands as the first in Ireland'. This was in part owing to the fact that 'we have picked our teams paying no attention to the advice of "well-wishers or the Press statistics"'. On that happy note, he listed the season's statistics: the First XV had won twenty of their twenty-three games; the Second XV had won fifteen out of twenty and, having beaten Palmerston, CYMS and Dublin University in the Metropolitan Cup, only lost out in the final 3–6 to Bective Rangers; and the Third XV had won seventeen of their twenty-six games, being pipped for the Minor League title on a third replay by Dublin University. Meanwhile, the Third As, Bs and Cs had played seventy-one matches between them. It was appropriate that the General Meeting concluded with the presentation by F.E. Davies, one of the oldest Club members and the temporary acting chairman in light of the earlier death of Claud Law, of a silver tea service, an illuminated album with a list of subscribers, and a wireless set to Coffey for his service to the Club as both a player and administrator for over thirty-five years.[45]

However, the General Meeting had also been marked by a significant point of conflict within the Club. As the issue of Sunday matches had demonstrated, there was a growing sense of disconnect between the upper echelons of the IRFU and the grass roots of the game in Ireland.[46] That divide was also seen in microcosm within Lansdowne. Older Club members such as Coffey, Rupert Jeffares, and both R.G. and J.J. Warren were of a different generation and mindset, and as leading figures within the IRFU and IRB, were protective of those organizations. Younger members such as Crawford, Davy and Sarsfield Hogan were willing to challenge the status quo and the establishment in order to improve the system for all. In that regard, there was a sense of continuity from H.W.D. Dunlop, who had challenged the Imperial arrogance of the English Athletic governing bodies.

The point of conflict arose over a resolution put forward by Crawford, and seconded by P.W. Byrne, stating that the 'present Constitution and By-laws' of the IRFU were 'inadequate to cope with the growth of the game' and that 'immediate steps' be taken to 'bring about the necessary alterations'. The idea was for this resolution to be sent to all rugby clubs as the expressed view of the members of Lansdowne FC. However, there was clearly bad feeling among the members over the proposed resolution, and a protracted debate ensued.

Crawford's key bone of contention was the presence of all past IRFU presidents on the General Council which meant that the seventeen representatives from the four provincial Branches – five apiece from Ulster, Munster and Leinster, and two from Connacht – could always be outvoted by what was perceived as the older, more conservative and traditional element of the organization. He also took issue with the fact that the Council's select committee of eight could in theory come from one province, city or club, thereby leading to potential regional bias in decision-making. Among those won over by Crawford's argument was Davy, who said that it was all a 'revelation' to him, while Sarsfield Hogan felt that the passing of such a resolution by Lansdowne at a time of pre-eminence in the club game 'would have all the greater effect'.[47]

Coffey however put up a staunch defence of the IRFU, stating that they were just trying 'to keep the game clean and to … uphold all that is good'.[48] B.M. Doran and Michael Dawson, two former Club presidents, also spoke in opposition to the resolution, with the former arguing that Lansdowne should not 'fight the battles of provinces or bodies who might have grievances'. It was also argued that the resolution would do a great deal of damage to the Club, which had always been well treated by the IRFU. Yet all of these arguments could be seen as elitist and exclusionary, especially in light of the Sunday games issue. The debate went on close to midnight, when a compromise was agreed that the Club committee would consider the matter and an EGM would be convened a month later.[49]

The divisiveness of the issue was highlighted by the fact that a newspaper report of the incident pasted into the Club Minute Book, and initialled by F.E. Davies, had the picture of Crawford pencilled out. There was also dismay that the whole affair had been leaked to the Press. When the EGM convened on 15 May, the same sides were evident in the debate, with Sarsfield Hogan arguing that 'direct representative of the provinces should be on the Union, and that the powers of the ex-presidents should become ineffective'. With 116 members recorded as in attendance, the resolution was finally put to a vote and was defeated by what was termed 'a large majority'.[50]

Press and public interest in the matter stemmed from the fact that dissatisfaction with the lack of reform within the IRFU went beyond just members of Lansdowne FC. Crawford's resolution and the debate that had ensued 'created a great sensation in Irish rugby circles', and shortly thereafter Bective Rangers, UCD and Blackrock as well as a large number of junior clubs in Munster adopted similar resolutions. The pressure on the IRFU led to proposals being brought forward from the Leinster Branch for increasing provincial representation on the General Council, but it came to nought as conservative power and resistance to such reform remained too strong at the time. Yet the issue had awoken an impetus for reform within the Leinster Branch, which started to pay dividends in the mid-1930s and in time took effect within the IRFU as well.[51]

Whether or not the arguments in the committee-rooms affected performance on the pitch during the 1931–2 season is unknown. However, in terms of the Leinster Cup, Lansdowne's drive for six in row came to a grinding halt in the first round in a 5–6 loss to Bective Rangers, who went on to win the Cup. The evidence would suggest, however, that the Club ethos of playing attractive rugby first and foremost was continued under the captaincy of Mick Dunne, regardless of the Cup loss. One of the players on the First XV that year was W.G.M. Jones, who had previously attended St Columba's College. He only played one season for Lansdowne before moving to England, but fifty years later on his first return to Ireland – to see the new pavilion of the team whose fortunes he had followed from afar for half a century – he recalled it as the Club at which 'I passed the happiest season of my football career'. The kindness shown him in 1980 on his return made his belated sojourn just as memorable.[52]

Despite the fact the Leinster Cup had not been retained in 1932, the April General meeting noted that Lansdowne continued to play an exciting and positive brand of rugby, which was once again deemed more important than winning trophies. Likewise, despite the Leinster Branch disapproving of 'cross-channel' fixtures, the Club were resolved to continue to arrange two or three such matches per season as 'we have learned a good deal … from our Scottish and English friends'. Other matters that arose at that time included the presence of too many non-members in the members bar, which constituted a breach of the Intoxicating Liquor Act, and concerns over an anti-rugby bias in some sections of the Press.[53]

In the latter regard, the 1920s and early 1930s were challenging times for everyone living in the new Irish Free State. Precarious state finances, post-Civil War politics, and historically divided national and religious allegiances all contributed to areas of conflict and discontent within the Irish sporting world. The confessional overtones of the IRFU's ban on Sunday matches was one example, but other issues bubbled to the surface in the early 1930s as well. One such area of conflict related to the question of taxation on sporting activities. In 1916 the British government had passed the Finance (New Duties) Act, which imposed an excise duty or tax on entrance charges to sporting events, defined as an 'Entertainment Tax'. The GAA had lobbied to be excluded from the tax on the grounds that they were a cultural organization involved in reviving national pastimes. Although unsuccessful in this regard, the GAA thereafter refused to pay the tax anyway. Other sports toed the line, including rugby, as was evident from the tax returns noted in the Lansdowne annual accounts when 2*s*. 6*d*. was paid in 1915–16, 6*s*. in 1916–17, and £1 15*s*. in 1919–20. Thereafter the War of Independence and Civil War greatly disrupted such matters, but in 1925 the Free State government looked to rationalize matters by granting an exemption from the Entertainment Tax for 'any games or sports which are ordinarily played or contested out-of-doors by two or more persons or by two or more groups of persons'.[54]

Matters became complicated again in 1927 when a new Finance Act imposed an income tax upon sporting clubs and organizations, but exempted the GAA. Within the wider context of the GAA's continuing ban on 'foreign sports' such as rugby and soccer, the introduction of what was seen as a purely punitive tax on those same sports smacked of political discrimination and certainly was perceived as such by many. Once again, Lansdowne adhered to the law, and income tax was paid in the ensuing years in varying amounts from 1930 to 1932 of £21 6*d*., £15 9*s*., and £10 3*s*. That the matter was overtly political was seen in the defeat of proposed amendments for extending the exemption to other sports in the Finance Acts of 1930 and 1931.[55]

The victory of Fianna Fáil in the 1932 General Election held out even less hope of such an extended exemption. A proposal from the Senate for the removal of a new 'Entertainment Tax' from the 1932 Finance Bill was defeated in the Dáil by sixty-eight votes to fifty-four. The vote occurred at the end of a lengthy debate on the matter in which it was pointed out on numerous occasions that the tax was unfair because of the exemption granted to the GAA. Others were more explicit in saying that the purpose of the tax was to penalize so-called 'foreign' games such as rugby and soccer. Others advocated for the removal of the tax from all sports, and that instead the government should be providing financial support for sporting organizations. The reality was however that non-GAA clubs and organizations were going to have to pay more money to the state. For Lansdowne, that meant that in the first year of this new tax regime the Club had to pay income tax of £13 13*s*. plus the new tax on Club membership subscriptions of £35 6*s*. from a gross income of £385 10*s*., and a further levy of £84 14*s*. 10*d*. on gate receipts of £393 4*s*. 7*d*. However, as the honorary treasurer mused, 'the amusement tax' put him to much trouble, 'but I suppose we are lucky to have gates that can contribute to the up keep of the state'.[56] The Leinster Branch were not as forgiving, noting at the time that they had to pay £499 in Entertainment Tax, which was 'a most unfair, unsportsmanlike, and unjust tax' and that all they desired was to 'be put on the same basis as any other sport, and they asked for no privileges'. After one more round of the Entertainment Tax, at a cost of £113 16*s*. 7*d*. to Lansdowne, political pressure resulted in the re-imposition of the exemption for all sporting organizations that had been granted in 1925.[57]

This febrile political atmosphere within the new Free State was also seen at that time in relation to the flying of flags at international rugby matches. Having looked to get around the issue of two different national jurisdictions on the island by purchasing the Ravenhill ground in Belfast and proposing to split international games between there and Lansdowne Road, the IRFU had tried to avoid the question of flying a national flag of any ilk in Dublin by designing an IRFU flag in 1925. Yet national sentiment in the Free State, spurred on by the flying of the Union Jack in Ravenhill, meant the matter came back to haunt the IRFU in January 1932 when both University College Galway FC and UCD FC complained about the matter. When the government also became involved, the IRFU backed down and in February agreed to fly the Irish Tricolour alongside the IRFU flag at internationals in Lansdowne Road thereafter.[58]

Election candidates Eugene Davy and Ernie Crawford at half-time during a Lansdowne versus Wanderers match, *Irish Times*, 1 Feb. 1932. Crawford has his touch judge flag tucked under his arm and appears to be giving instructions to Davy and O'Reilly, while also smoking a cigarette.

It was also within this wider political context of the early years of the Free State that the decision of both Eugene Davy and Ernie Crawford to run in the General Election of 1932 must be understood. Their decision demonstrated a core component of associational culture as a central part of civil society – fulfilling one's civic duty within the community – as well as the evident politicization of Irish society at the time. Davy stood for Cumann na nGaedheal in Dublin South, having been selected at a party convention at the Royal Hibernian Hotel in January 1932. Crawford, who had just been awarded the Silver Medal of Honour by the French Minister for Sports and Physical Education, ran as an Independent in Dublin County, having been asked by 'a large number of ex-Service men, to go forward'. Both men polled well but were ultimately unsuccessful, with Davy achieving 3,478 first preferences and Crawford 3,194, but neither picking up enough transfers thereafter.[59]

International developments also affected the Club. Increasing poverty in Ireland as a result of the worsening global economic depression led in turn to a greater demand for charitable donations by those who could afford it. Increasing membership and an improving balance sheet during the 1920s had seen Lansdowne develop a tradition of making annual donations to various charities as part of its endeavours to support the wider non-rugby community.

One of the main charities supported was St Vincent de Paul (SVP), who launched a major national appeal in October 1932 to assist the increasing numbers of Irish people driven into poverty. Lansdowne responded with a substantial donation of £10 10*s*., which was itemized in a printed list of such donations in the *Irish Times*. In an associated economic context, the influence of de Valera's policy of 'protectionism' was seen the following month when the Club decided to only use rugby balls and other Club necessities that were 'guaranteed Irish manufacture'.[60]

It is also important to recognize that all of these issues were played out against an ongoing growth in the popularity of the game. By early 1932 there were 147 clubs affiliated with the IRFU in comparison to only forty-six in 1921. More importantly, it was a country-wide phenomenon. The greatest increase was in Munster, where numbers had gone from only six clubs in 1921 to forty-nine in 1932. In Leinster growth had been from nineteen to forty-three, in Ulster from twenty-one to forty-four, and in Connacht from zero to eleven. In the same period crowds attending international matches had increased from 15,000 to a capacity of 35,000 at Lansdowne Road, with the demand for tickets greatly exceeding availability.[61]

Increased interest also brought closer scrutiny of how the game was played. The spectator's enjoyment mattered. So, not surprisingly, the 1932–3 season saw an IRB rule change aimed at trying to speed up the time taken to set and complete scrums, where increasing specialization of forwards in given positions was deemed to be decreasing the entertainment value of games. Undaunted by such matters, and in a season when Davy became captain of Ireland, Mick Dunne captained Lansdowne to an eleventh Leinster Cup, and a sixth in seven years. Having first beaten Wanderers 13–7 and then Clontarf 12–3 in the semi-final, UCD were overcome 6–4 in the final. Two brothers originally from Presentation College Bray, Aidan and Jack Bailey, played against each other on the day, with Aidan kicking a penalty for Lansdowne and Jack getting UCD's only score with a dropped goal (still worth four points at that time). Aidan would go on to win thirteen caps for Ireland between 1934 and 1938.[62]

The Bateman Cup was cancelled that year owing to fixture congestion, but even still, it had again been a hugely successful season for Lansdowne.

Leinster Senior Cup, 1932–3. Standing: W.E. Crawford, D. Moran, M.E. Bardon, M.A. Sheehan, V.V. Drennan, A.E. Thompson, A. Bailey, J.C. Powell, F.A. Ross (Vice-Pres.). Seated: J.J. Coffey (Hon. Sec.), F. Conroy, E.J. Lightfoot, J.E. Arigho, M.J. Dunne (Capt.), J.G. Robertson, T. Sinnott, P. Quinn, J.J. Warren. On Ground: T.A. O'Reilly, E.O'D. Davy.

The Third XV, captained by Michael Murphy, had won the Minor League for a second time, beating Suttonians 16–3 in the final in February, while the Second XV under Tishy Byrne only lost out on winning the Junior League after extra-time in the final against Dublin University. The season had also seen a better arrangement put in place for the junior teams in terms of a ground. A one-season rental of the Riverside grounds adjacent to Lansdowne Road in 1931–2 had been abandoned owing to the excessive cost. Instead, for 1932–3 a deal was struck with Monkstown FC for use of their nearby grounds for £25 rent and 10*s*. per match for teas, towels and attendance, an arrangement which was deemed successful enough to warrant renewal for the 1933–4 season.[63]

In the annual accounts for the 1932–3 season printed in September 1933, it was noted that 'some of our players are getting to a veteran age'. It was an unintentionally prophetic statement, as substantial player turnover often leads to a drop in performance, and so it was to be for Lansdowne for the remainder of the 1930s and into the 1940s as the Leinster Cup eluded the

Club for the following sixteen years. The changing of the guard got underway as the cohort of players who had done so much to establish the legacy of six Leinster Cups in seven seasons retired or moved on and the rebuilding process commenced. But a tradition of open, entertaining rugby had also been established, and would continue to flourish at the Club regardless of short-term results.[64]

Central to rebuilding was of course the existing junior team players. The occasional resurfacing of concerns over the lack of attention shown by the Club committee to the playing ability of those turning out for the junior teams had resulted in a decision being taken to record the weekly selection of the First, Second and Third XVs in the Club minutes from 1933 onwards. The first full season for so doing was 1933–4, when the name of Con Murphy appeared as a new regular starter at fullback on the Second XV, with the occasional appearance on the First XV. Like Sarsfield Hogan before, Murphy had come from CUS, and was part of another evolving tradition of Dublin schools with strong Lansdowne connections over generations. By the following season Murphy was the starting fullback for the First XV, a position he would hold for fourteen seasons.[65]

A second factor in the rebuilding process was the culmination of the search for a long-term solution to the Junior ground issue. In November 1933 two grounds, in Milltown and Terenure, had been inspected for suitability. The latter ground, soon being described in Club minutes as 'Terenure Kimmage', proved best suited and was quickly moved upon, with a lease being agreed and temporary changing facilities installed with plans for a more permanent pavilion. The whole process was driven by the honorary treasurer, Leslie Heaney. The new ground was called Kimmage Grove, or the Polo Grounds as it was also known, which would be home to Lansdowne Junior rugby for many years to come, and was presided over by the doyen of Third As, Bs and Cs rugby, Eddie Carthew, who had been quietly managing the task of getting junior teams out each week since 1928. Having a permanent home gave added impetus to Junior rugby at the Club, creating a real sense of belonging and camaraderie among generations of Junior team players. And as more players joined the Club, so more pitches were laid out and facilities improved. Located

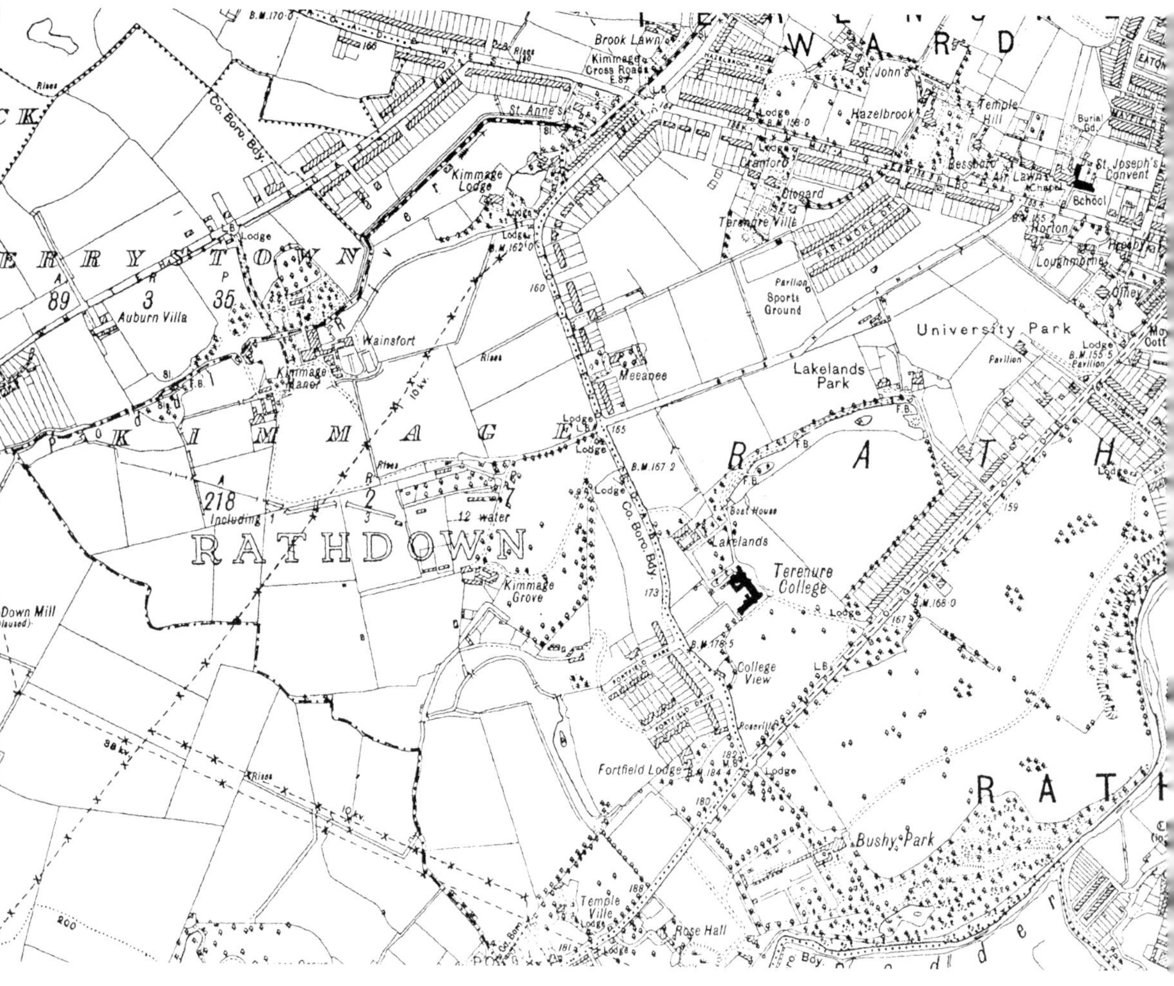

Kimmage Grove, 1937. OS Dublin 6inch map, Sheet 22, 1937. © Ordnance Survey Ireland/ Government of Ireland Copyright Permit No. MP 000122. All rights reserved. Courtesy of UCD Library.

on the outskirts of south-west Dublin, Kimmage Grove was an area of farmland leased by many sporting organizations in the 1930s–40s, including women's hockey and camogie as well as other rugby clubs, most notably St Mary's. The grounds were at the top of Green Lane (modern-day Greenlea Road) on the west side of Fortfield Road. This greenfield site was synonymous with the pressures of an expanding city on sporting activity as junior grounds had to be sourced further afield, with players having to trek out to where the city met the countryside for weekend games. In time, even these pitches would be consumed by an ever-increasing urban sprawl that gobbled up older satellite villages as demand for suburban housing constantly increased.[66]

Central to both the nurturing of connections with secondary schools and with the quest for a junior ground had been Ernie Crawford. It was appropriate then that he was honoured by the Club at the April 1934 General meeting. The President, F.A. Ross, noted how Crawford had 'few equals' as a fullback, but that they were honouring him first and foremost as a 'Lansdowne man' because of all he had done for the Club. Pointing out that his work with schools 'had borne good fruit', Ross also thank Crawford's wife, Florence, for her 'great assistance … in the tea pavilion on all occasions'.[67]

The investment in the junior grounds also bore fruit in the following years, with the Third XV winning the Minor Cup for a third time in 1935, under the captaincy of E.J. Montgomery. The team's 3–Nil victory over Blackrock in the final was described as 'a keen, strenuous game' with Lansdowne worthy winners because 'their backs showed more cleverness, and their forwards … were always superior'. The season overall had seen nineteen victories out of twenty games, with 415 points for and only forty-seven against, and that included three games played with only fourteen players throughout. The failure of the fifteenth man to turn up on those three occasions was balanced by one match when there were eleven substitutes in attendance. Not to be outdone, the Second XV claimed their fifth and sixth Junior League titles in 1941 and 1945. Captained in 1941 by Brendan Matthews at fullback, CYMS were beaten 7–Nil in the final, while in 1945 the captain was Harry Tunney, with Railway Union being overcome 13–3 in the final.[68]

Despite the lack of further success in the Leinster Cup during the later 1930s and early 1940s, Lansdowne continued to be one of the top clubs in the province, usually ranking among the genuine contenders at the start of the season. It was therefore unsurprising that quality players continued to gravitate towards the Club, as in September 1938 when it was reported that Lansdowne had 'captured' some top-class players, including the Irish wing, Charles Vesey Boyle, from Dublin University. Boyle also toured South

(left) The front cover of the Lansdowne FC Annual Dinner Menu Card, April 1938.

(opposite page) Con Murphy's notification of his selection for the Ireland team to play Wales on 11 March 1939.

Africa with the Lions in 1938 and went on to serve in the RAF during the Second World War, being awarded the Distinguished Flying Cross for his endeavours. Club membership also remained buoyant during this time, with on average 360 pavilion members, 175 playing members, and twenty-five schoolboy members per year in the mid-1930s, while there was also an evident increasing emphasis upon the importance of training sessions and physical fitness for all levels of competition in the Club. And despite the regular poaching of new players for the First XV, the Seconds and Thirds continued to be extremely competitive in their own leagues year-on-year.[69]

TELEGRAPHIC ADDRESS, "FOOTBALL, DUBLIN." TELEPHONE No 21984.

IRISH RUGBY FOOTBALL UNION,
14, WESTMORELAND STREET,
DUBLIN.

Date 27/2/39

DEAR SIR,

I have pleasure in advising that you have been selected to play for :—

Ireland v. Wales

At Belfast

On 11/3/1939

and shall be glad to receive your **early** acceptance.

The team will travel in reserved accommodation *via* .... by 9 A.M. train leaving Amiens Street Station on 10/3/39

You are requested to be present at Station to receive Travelling Ticket.

Headquarters .... Hotel .... where programme of final arrangements will be issued.

Your jersey will be supplied, and must be returned immediately at the conclusion of the game.

The Irish Union provide transportation and pay Hotel Expenses, including gratuities to servants, but do not hold themselves responsible for personal tips, telegrams, 'phone calls, etc., etc., given by Members of the Team. Should you, however, incur any other legitimate expenses, please furnish on attached Form to Hon. Treasurer.

Yours truly,

RUPERT W. JEFFARES, *Secretary.*

Bring training togs for use afternoon of arrival also Dinner jacket

As ever, the demands of careers took players away, not least as international tensions heightened and the road to world war was embarked upon once again. In 1936 W. Cummins, a junior team player with Lansdowne and a Leinster cricketer, left Dublin to join the Royal Air Force, a path already taken by a stalwart of the Lansdowne Second XV, Paddy Bennett, an ex-CUS pupil who was then stationed in Cairo. In July 1938 another ex-Lansdowne player in military service, John Anthony Law, son of Claud Law who had died while in office as President of Lansdowne, was killed in action in Palestine while serving as an officer with the Royal Ulster Rifles. He was posthumously awarded the Military Cross.[70]

The outbreak of the Second World War in September 1939 brought an end to international rugby once again. The President of the IRFU at that time was Lansdowne's J.J. Warren, and he was to remain in the post for the duration of the war until his death in December 1944. The home nations matches in 1939 had seen the first three caps in the fledgling international career of the young Con Murphy. Unfortunately, as with Ernie Crawford before, world war would steal many potential caps from a Lansdowne fullback. The absence of formal international matches was in part replaced by five games between an Irish XV and the British army in Belfast between 1942 and 1945. All but the last match were lost, but they proved important opportunities for Lansdowne players Con Murphy, Colm Callan, William 'Bill' Moynan, Kevin O'Flanagan and Don Hingerty. Charity matches also offered an opportunity for variety. A game in January 1941 to raise money for the SVP was likened to a final Ireland trial, while Con Murphy's play in particular was said to make 'one almost believe that another W.E. Crawford was in the land'. Another Press article in 1944 deemed Murphy 'possibly the best Irish full-back since W.E. Crawford'.[71]

However, unlike during 1914–18, there was much more opportunity during the Second World War for playing rugby in Ireland. With a new Constitution and name in 1937, the twenty-six-county Éire was able to remain neutral during the conflict, which in turn facilitated the continuation of domestic rugby at provincial, club and schools levels, to the evident relief of club officials and players alike. It was also the case that cross-border games continued between Lansdowne and Belfast Collegians, NIFC and Instonians, though in the 1939–40 and 1940–1 seasons the latter two clubs fielded a combined side, presumably in light of the very significant recruitment of over 20,000 soldiers by November 1941 within Northern Ireland. But thereafter both clubs were able to field their own full sides for the following four seasons impacted by the ongoing war, while Malone also came back into the fixture list from 1942–3 onwards and Queen's University reappeared in 1944–5 as well.[72]

The war clearly impacted negatively upon the game in a number of ways. Reduced transport facilities due to shortages of fuel resulted in fewer teams being able to travel for away games in other counties or provinces. As a result, Lansdowne First XV had no fixtures against Munster or Connacht clubs from 1941 through to 1945. Such restrictions also put a final end to the Bateman Cup. The game more generally also experienced a slump in the standards of play during those years with much greater emphasis on defence and a decline in backline play in particular. Such problems were associated with a variety of causes, including the reduced levels of competitiveness owing to less variety in fixture lists which led to a degree of over-familiarity with the opposition, reduced spectator attendance, the absence of international rugby, and the enlistment of players and supporters into both the Irish and the British armed forces. Rationing also led to less opportunity for conviviality and sociability, which remained crucial aspects of successful associational and club culture. Blackout curtains on the bar and pavilion windows and black paint on the changing-room windows at Lansdowne Road were also a constant reminder of war not far away. The war also resulted in reduced Club income owing to less spectators and a decline in membership at all levels. To help alleviate the financial pressure, and to ensure some sociability, the junior committee undertook to run several dances per season in the pavilion, which saw fruitful returns of £69 7*s*. 3*d*. in 1940–1, £100 5*s*. in 1941–2, £147 15*s*. 2*d*. in 1942–3, £110 14*s*. in 1943–4, and £116 3*s*. 3*d*. in 1944–5, all of which served to place the Club in a healthy financial position through the war years.[73]

Like many other Irish people, some Lansdowne members chose to join the British armed forces, while others chose to join the Irish defence forces during the 'Emergency', as the war was termed in Éire. Harold 'Harry' Vard, who joined Lansdowne in 1937 after finishing school at Wesley College,

Minor League, 1934–5. Standing: T.C. Fox, W.J. Smith, P.A. Tobin, G.P. Bennett, J.J. Coffey (Hon. Sec.), R.D. Lambert, M. Bell, W.T. Robertson, E.W. Garland. Seated: C.J. Delaney, T. Donaghy, L.F. Scott, E.J. Montgomery (Capt.), A.N. Murray, A.B. Johnston, J.I. Fitzpatrick. On Ground: J.J. Byrne, W. Cummins.

did both. Following the outbreak of war he joined the Irish defences forces before shifting to the tank corps of the British army and serving in the Italian campaign. After the war he returned to play in the junior levels of Lansdowne before segueing into refereeing at Kimmage Grove on the weekends. Eventually in 1974–5 he served as Club President. The Mitchell family did both as well, but through different family members. Noel Mitchell, who had played on the First XV prior to the First World War and had then served in the Royal Navy during 1914–18, returned to service in the Navy during the Second World War. Then in 1948–9, he served as President of Lansdowne. His son, Bobby, also a First XV player in the 1930s and early 1940s including being Club Captain in 1942–3, took a different route to his father and served in the

Irish defence forces. As a family, they belied the simple and false dichotomy of Irish and British national loyalties. They demonstrated on the one hand the continuing sense of connection with Britain that many Irish people of all religious denominations still maintained, and which led to possibly as many as 40,000 of them volunteering for service in the British armed forces during the Second World War, and on the other, the evident commitment of those same people to the Free State, to Éire and, in time, to the Republic. It was also of note that the Lansdowne members who served in the Irish defence forces during the war were exempted from having to pay their annual membership and the Club undertook an annual fixture against the Curragh army camp during that time.[74]

Despite the absence of international matches during the war years, Lansdowne had seen fifteen players capped for Ireland between 1924 and 1939. With a variety of caps between one and thirty-four, the players were: J.E. Arigho; A.H. Bailey; M.E. Bardon; C.V. Boyle; W.E. Crawford; M.P. Crowe; E. O'D. Davy; M.J. Dunne; N.H. Lambert; E.J. Lightfoot; C.J. Murphy; T.O. Pike; V.J. Pike; H.J. Sayers; and J.S. Synge.[75]

The end of the Second World War heralded another changing of the guard at Lansdowne FC, as the preceding years had seen the death of a number of long-serving members of the Club, including R.G. Warren in November 1940, G.P. 'Blucher' Doran in April 1943 and J.J. Warren in December 1944. Within several months of the war's end, J.J. Coffey passed away, while still serving in the office of honorary secretary to the Club. Just as the players in the great teams of the late 1920s–early 1930s had retired and moved on, so the great administrators and stalwarts of Lansdowne, Leinster and Irish rugby in the first four decades of the twentieth century had passed on. Yet they, like the retired players, had helped to establish a lasting legacy of a commitment to entertaining, running rugby above all else and a tradition of nurturing the game at all levels, from secondary schools through to all grades of junior and senior rugby, and an ethos of offering a home-from-home to players from all over Ireland and beyond.[76]

Chapter 4

Home-From-Home

1946–1972

The immediate post-Second World War years offered new challenges and opportunities for Lansdowne FC. Re-establishing the traditional variety of fixtures both within Ireland and overseas was high on the Club's agenda, while the pressures of an expanding cityscape began to focus minds upon the need to purchase a junior ground as a more long-term replacement of the leasing arrangement at Kimmage Grove. It was also the case that increasing socio-economic mobility and population growth in Dublin in particular meant that Lansdowne's long-standing tradition of offering a friendly home-from-home for people from all over Ireland and beyond would become even more evident as more players from Connacht and Munster joined the Club.

One of the priorities for Lansdowne in the 1945–6 season was to honour two of its stalwarts, J.J. Warren and J.J. Coffey, who had passed away during and just after the Second World War respectively. To that end a memorial was

Lansdowne FC portrait of A.W. Campbell (one of six portraits of members commissioned by the Club). Lansdowne FC junior match secretary in the 1940s and 1950s, Campbell was synonymous for hundreds of players with life at the Kimmage Grove grounds. A life-long member of the Club, he served as President in 1973–4.

unveiled in the tea pavilion in March 1946. The evident sense of a changing of the guard was also seen in the stepping down of Eddie Carthew as junior honorary or match secretary and his replacement by Art Campbell, who was already making a name for himself in organizing and managing all of the Club's junior fixtures and teams. It was also a time of re-birth, and after a lull in activity at schoolboy level in the Club during the war years, in January it had been reported that over fifty boys had turned out and several fixtures had been fulfilled. Revitalized by Kevin Kelleher, a future leading Irish referee and headmaster of the nearby St Conleth's College, the Christmas vacation schoolboy rugby was part of the Club's ongoing commitment to nurturing rugby at grass-roots level. For example, in January 1949 it was reported in the *Irish Times* how Lansdowne Schoolboys were continuing their winning ways by defeating Palmerston 8–3.[1]

The restrictions imposed by the war on both international and regional rugby also began to lift quite quickly. In 1946 international rugby was back on the agenda, but unofficially and without caps being awarded. Lansdowne were represented by Con Murphy, who captained the Ireland XV for all four such matches in 1946; by Colm Callan, who also played in all four; and by Don Hingerty, who played in three. Murphy went on to win his last two formal caps as captain of Ireland the following year in the Home Nations games against France and England, who were famously defeated 22–Nil. On both occasions he was accompanied in the team by Hingerty and Callan. Those two caps also ensured that Murphy became the only person to have played for Ireland both before and after the Second World War. The re-opening of international society more generally also allowed for both Murphy and Callan to take part in a four-match Barbarian FC tour in Wales during Easter 1946, playing against Penarth, Cardiff, Swansea and Newport in a five-day period from 19 April to 23 April. Among the instructions issued to the players was that they were 'asked to be in bed by 11 p.m. on the night prior to playing; and not to play more than nine holes of golf on the morning of a match'.[2]

The war had also put on hold matches against overseas clubs and reduced the opportunities to travel around Ireland, but such activity was also quick to resume after 1945. In December 1946, Headingley, who had first started playing fixtures against Lansdowne in 1937–8, made the journey once again across the Irish Sea only to lose out 12–3, while the following season Lansdowne paid a return visit to Yorkshire, winning 6–Nil by 'playing ideal football under adverse weather conditions'. Towards the end of the 1947–8 season, Glasgow Academicals were defeated 13–9 at Lansdowne Road. In late 1948 the annual fixture with Heriots FP made a welcome return to the calendar, while the first post-war tour to France occurred at the beginning of the 1949–50 season with games against Stade Toulousain and Romans-Péage. That season also saw the return of occasional fixtures against London Irish. The Lansdowne Third As also became the first Dublin Junior team to go on tour, playing in Anglesey against an RAF team in 1948, which in turn heralded a regular fixture against Bangor University in the same part of North Wales for many years thereafter. Regional seasonal fixtures had also returned by then, with annual matches against both Dolphin and Cork Constitution reappearing from 1946–7 onwards.[3]

The later 1940s also saw a revival in Sunday rugby fixtures for the Club as petrol rationing eased and more distant travel became possible again, an occurrence which facilitated the adoption once more of the earlier endeavours by Ernie Crawford to spread the game around the country. Recommencing in the 1946–7 season in response to an appeal to that effect from the Leinster Branch, Lansdowne started sending teams to various 'country clubs, thereby helping to revive the game in country towns'. As a result, Provincial Towns' rugby also revived. Arranging an interesting variety of fixtures each season

TELEGRAPHIC ADDRESS, "FOOTBALL, DUBLIN." TELEPHONE No. 21984.

IRISH RUGBY FOOTBALL UNION,
14, WESTMORELAND STREET,
DUBLIN.

Date 14th January, 1946

DEAR SIR,

I have pleasure in advising that you have been selected to play for:—

An Irish XV ~~Ireland~~ v. A French XV

At Lansdowne Road, Dublin

On Saturday 26th January, 1946

and shall be glad to receive your **early** acceptance.

The team will travel in reserved accommodation *via*........................ by........................ train leaving........................Station.

You are requested to be present at........................ to receive Travelling Ticket.

Headquarters Shelbourne Hotel Dublin where programme of final arrangements will be issued.

Your jersey will be supplied, and must be returned immediately at the conclusion of the game.

The Irish Union provide transportation and pay Hotel Expenses, including gratuities to servants, but do not hold themselves responsible for personal tips, telegrams, 'phone calls, etc., etc., given by Members of the Team. Should you, however, incur any other legitimate expenses, please furnish on attached Form to Hon. Treasurer.

Yours truly,

RUPERT W. JEFFARES, *Secretary.*

Please bring one pair clean white knicks.
Report for training in College Park at 4 p.m. on 25/1/1946, and please advise other players in Shelbourne Hotel. Escort French Team to Theatre Royal in evening Bring Dinner Jacket.

(Above and opposite page) Con Murphy's official notification of selection for Ireland's unofficial international matches against France in January 1946 and Wales in March 1946.

TELEGRAPHIC ADDRESS,
"FOOTBALL, DUBLIN."
TELEPHONE No 21984.

IRISH RUGBY FOOTBALL UNION,
14, WESTMORELAND STREET,
DUBLIN.

Date 25th February, 1946

DEAR SIR,

I have pleasure in advising that you have been selected to play for:— An Irish XV v A Welsh ~~Ireland v.~~ XXXXXXX

At Cardiff

On 9.3.46

and shall be glad to receive your **early** acceptance.

The team will travel in reserved accommodation *via*................ by................ train leaving................Station.

You are requested to be present at................ to receive Travelling Ticket.

Headquarters Esplanade Hotel Penarth where programme of final arrangements will be issued.

Your jersey will be supplied, and must be returned immediately at the conclusion of the game.

The Irish Union provide transportation and pay Hotel Expenses, including gratuities to servants, but do not hold themselves responsible for personal tips, telegrams, 'phone calls, etc., etc., given by Members of the Team. Should you, however, incur any other legitimate expenses, please furnish on attached Form to Hon. Treasurer.

Yours truly,

RUPERT W. JEFFARES, *Secretary.*

Please bring one pair clean white knicks.

Meet party at Westland Row Station at 8 a.m. on Thursday 7th March, 1946

Please bring soap and towel with you.

at all levels was always a priority for Lansdowne and was one of the many reasons why such a diverse and broad range of players from around Ireland were attracted to, and joined, the Club.[4]

With regard to normal domestic club fixtures, the start of the 1946–7 season was postponed for two weeks owing to the need for volunteers for harvest time around Ireland. An appeal to that effect at the Lansdowne General Meeting on 20 September provoked 'a good response' among members. But such concerns were temporary and clearly did not worry Lansdowne's players too much, as that season the Second XV, captained by Paul Warren, claimed their seventh Junior League title, beating Old Wesley 18–4 in the final. In a dominant display at Donnybrook, Lansdowne were deemed 'devastating in their attacks' and scored four tries, including one by Garry Redmond, who many years later went on to write the Lansdowne Centenary volume published in 1972. The Second XV followed up a year later in 1948 by winning the Metropolitan Cup under the captaincy of Eamonn 'Bull' Lanigan, another player to come via CUS and UCD.[5]

The late 1940s and early 1950s were a golden period in Irish rugby, with Ireland's first ever Grand Slam achieved in 1948, followed by a fourth Triple Crown in 1949 and the Five Nations Championship in 1951. Second-row Colm Callan, who won ten international caps, was the only Lansdowne player in the 1948 team that clinched Ireland's third Triple Crown and first Grand Slam in a 6–3 victory over Wales at Ravenhill, though Michael O'Flanagan had played in the earlier victory over Scotland. Callan, described in a 1974 *Irish Times* retrospective as 'tough and uncompromising', was originally from County Louth and had served as Lansdowne captain in 1946–7. Along with his Irish team captain, Old Belvedere's Karl Mullen, he also played in November 1948 on the R.V. Stanley invitational XV against Oxford University.[6]

The 1948–9 season commenced with the election of Lansdowne's Sarsfield Hogan as President of the IRFU, at a time when the poacher-turned-gamekeeper, Ernie Crawford, was in the middle of a first term as an Ireland selector and IRFU committee man. It was noted at the time that Crawford and Lightfoot, two of the five selectors of the Irish team in both 1948 and 1949, were Lansdowne members, a fact the Club happily chose to consider to be a major contributing factor to Ireland's great achievement in those years.[7]

Leinster Senior Cup, 1948–9. Standing: M.J. Dunne (Hon. Sec.), E. Connellan, K. Kennedy-O'Brien, T.D. McNally, R.N. Mitchell (Pres.), C. Callan, F. Johnston, W. O'Neill, L.J. Heaney (Hon. Treas.). Seated: J. O'Neill, J.C. Dawson, R. Carroll, J.F. Coffey (Capt.), W.J. Moynan, P. Warren, M. O'Flanagan. On Ground: G.A. Aherne, C. Crowley. Inset: J. Flood, P.L. Gibson.

In the Leinster Senior Cup the war years had been dominated by Old Belvedere with seven titles in a row, even though they had only gained Senior Club status in the 1937–8 season. In the mid-1940s they had become Lansdowne's nemesis, ending the Club's interest in the Cup in 1945, 1946 and 1948. Nothing lasts forever, and in the 1948–9 season Lansdowne's luck changed. Captained by J.F. 'Jack' Coffey, son of the late J.J. Coffey, Lansdowne first defeated Wanderers 9–3 and then beat UCD 5–3 in a replayed semi-final, before going on to an 11–9 victory over Old Belvedere in the final. In so doing, a twelfth Leinster Cup title was secured. In a game in which Old Belvedere were said to have sat on a narrow 9–6 half-time lead, Lansdowne were deemed fitting victors. Callan, having been injured in the mid-week semi-final replay, did not get the chance to put one over on his international captain, Mullen. However it was Callan's replacement, John Flood, who had only recently returned on leave from Singapore, who got to score the winning try ten minutes from

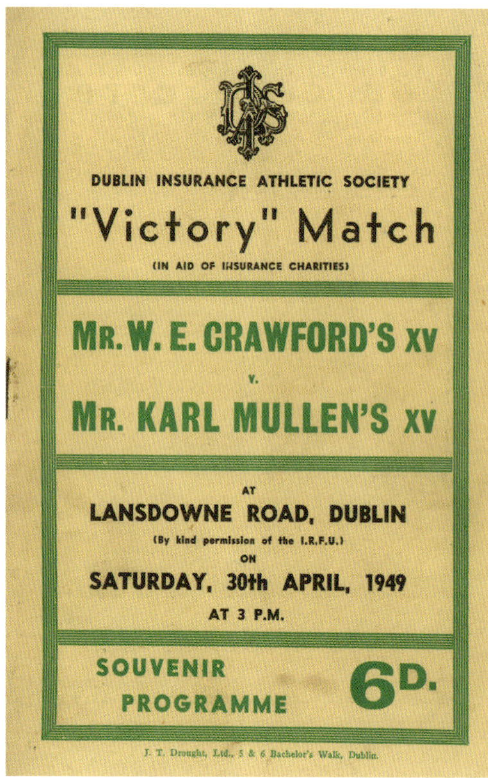

'Victory' Match Programme, 30 April 1949.

the end of the match. The move started when a kick through from O'Flanagan was collected at speed by Gerald 'Gerry' Aherne who found half the forwards in support. Passes from Ken O'Brien, Leo Gibson and Tom McNally culminated in Flood touching down to the right of the posts. The conversion was kicked by Frank Johnston and despite immense Old Belvedere pressure in the closing minutes, victory was sealed therewith.[8]

The established traditions of Lansdowne membership were seen once again in the 1949 Cup-winning side. Johnston had followed a well-worn route to Lansdowne via UCD, while J.C. 'Jack' Dawson had come via CUS. Others, such as Aherne, who had previously played for Dolphin and been capped for Munster in the newly instigated Interprovincial Championship, had found a home-from-home at Lansdowne. Earlier in the 1940s the Connacht player, P.J. Horan, had played for several years on the Lansdowne First XV also, while the incoming hooker for the 1949–50 season was the Corkman, Joe Holloway. Others from around Ireland would follow suit in the coming years in increasing numbers at all levels of rugby at the Club.[9]

The 1948–9 season was concluded with a match at the end of April at Lansdowne Road between a Karl Mullen XV and an Ernie Crawford XV. Organized by the Dublin Insurance Athletic Society as a celebration of

Ireland's recent international rugby successes, including a fourth Triple Crown that season, the proceeds of the game went to Insurance Charities. For the game itself, the Ireland players were mixed and matched among both teams, with Jack Kyle playing outhalf for the Crawford selection along with Lansdowne's Aherne and W. O'Neill. Mullen's XV included Ken O'Brien and John Flood, still on leave from service in Singapore. Ham Lambert refereed, and Eugene Davy ran one of the touchlines. The large crowd were properly entertained as both teams eschewed kicking and ran up a 40–32 final score in favour of the Mullen XV.[10]

Such rugby camaraderie was less evident early in the 1949–50 season when Lansdowne became embroiled in a controversy that reflected ongoing concerns about both the rules of the game and the ways in which play had changed in recent years. In the aftermath of a match between Lansdowne and NIFC in November, the *Sunday Independent* rugby correspondent, known as 'Rugger', quoted from a letter ascribed to a 'well-known Dublin rugby follower who prefers to remain anonymous', but who took issue with Lansdowne's apparent targeting of NIFC's winger, Des McKee, during a game. In light of 'Rugger's' recent highlighting of a similar tactic deployed by Munster against Ulster's Jack Kyle, the nameless correspondent bemoaned that Lansdowne's 'tacticians' had apparently decided that 'whenever there was a chance of the ball reaching McKee, his opposite Lansdowne wing ran up and worried him, not with any idea of a tackle, but simply to prevent the centre from passing out'. The correspondent went on to claim that 'Lansdowne men were obviously playing to instructions and "slammed" him to such purpose that we may lose his services for the remainder of the season. Personally I consider this particular late tackle, long after the ball had crossed the touchline, called for a penalty'. For his part, 'Rugger' believed that 'the Lansdowne winger's destructive role in "blotting out" McKee' was obstruction, and therefore should have been penalized: 'Such tactics are to be deplored and referees should punish offenders severely. We see so little attractive, open club rugby … [because of] destructive and obstructionist players [who] should be given short shrift. Club committees could and should give a desirable lead in this connection with a view to discouraging this type of play'.[11]

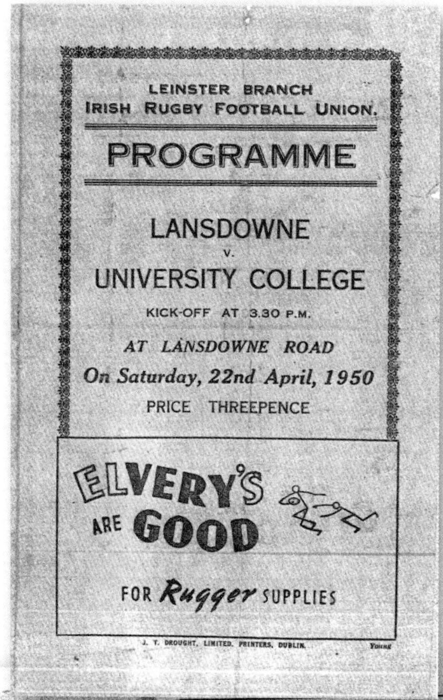

LEINSTER BRANCH
IRISH RUGBY FOOTBALL UNION.

PROGRAMME

LANSDOWNE
v.
UNIVERSITY COLLEGE

KICK-OFF AT 3.30 P.M.

AT LANSDOWNE ROAD
On Saturday, 22nd April, 1950

PRICE THREEPENCE

ELVERY'S ARE GOOD

FOR *Rugger* SUPPLIES

J. T. DROUGHT, LIMITED, PRINTERS, DUBLIN.

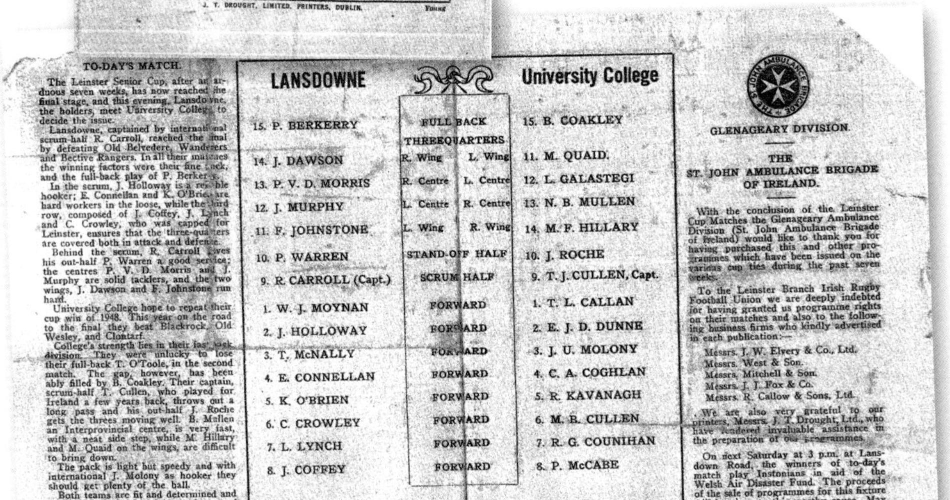

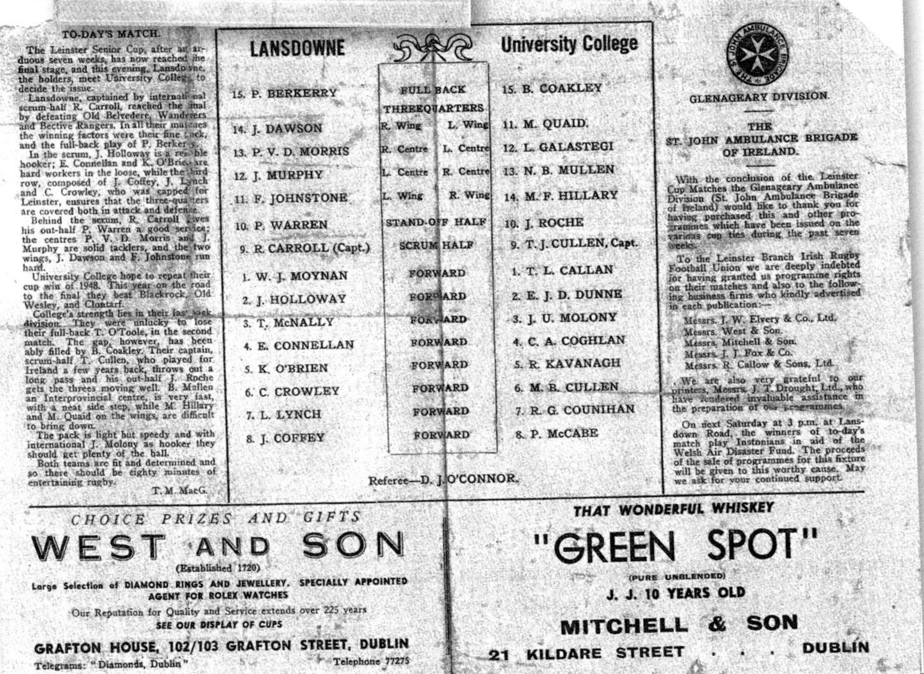

TO-DAY'S MATCH.

The Leinster Senior Cup, after an arduous seven weeks, has now reached the final stage, and this evening, Lansdowne, the holders, meet University College to decide the issue.

Lansdowne, captained by international scrum-half R. Carroll, reached the final by defeating Old Belvedere, Wanderers and Bective Rangers. In all their matches the winning factors were their fine back, and the full-back play of P. Berkery.

In the scrum, J. Holloway is a reliable hooker; E. Connellan and K. O'Brien are hard workers in the loose, while the third row, composed of J. Coffey, J. Lynch and C. Crowley, who was capped for Leinster, ensures that the three-quarters are covered both in attack and defence.

Behind the scrum, R. Carroll gives his out-half P. Warren a good service; the centres P. V. D. Morris and J. Murphy are solid tacklers, and the two wings, J. Dawson and F. Johnstone run hard.

University College hope to repeat their cup win of 1948. This year on the road to the final they beat Blackrock, Old Wesley, and Clontarf.

College's strength lies in their fast back division. They were unlucky to lose their full-back T. O'Toole, in the second match. The gap, however, has been ably filled by B. Coakley. Their captain, scrum-half T. Cullen, who played for Ireland a few years back, throws out a long pass and his out-half J. Roche gets the threes moving well. B. Mullen an Interprovincial centre, is very fast, with a neat side step, while M. Hillary and M. Quaid on the wings, are difficult to bring down.

The pack is light but speedy and with international J. Molony as hooker they should get plenty of the ball.

Both teams are fit and determined and so there should be eighty minutes of entertaining rugby.

T. M. MacG.

LANSDOWNE		University College
15. P. BERKERRY	FULL BACK	15. B. COAKLEY
	THREEQUARTERS	
14. J. DAWSON	R. Wing L. Wing	11. M. QUAID.
13. P. V. D. MORRIS	R. Centre L. Centre	12. L. GALASTEGI
12. J. MURPHY	L. Centre R. Centre	13. N. B. MULLEN
11. F. JOHNSTONE	L. Wing R. Wing	14. M. F. HILLARY
10. P. WARREN	STAND-OFF HALF	10. J. ROCHE
9. R. CARROLL (Capt.)	SCRUM HALF	9. T. J. CULLEN, Capt.
1. W. J. MOYNAN	FORWARD	1. T. L. CALLAN
2. J. HOLLOWAY	FORWARD	2. E. J. D. DUNNE
3. T. McNALLY	FORWARD	3. J. U. MOLONY
4. E. CONNELLAN	FORWARD	4. C. A. COGHLAN
5. K. O'BRIEN	FORWARD	5. R. KAVANAGH
6. C. CROWLEY	FORWARD	6. M. B. CULLEN
7. L. LYNCH	FORWARD	7. R. G. COUNIHAN
8. J. COFFEY	FORWARD	8. P. McCABE

Referee—D. J. O'CONNOR.

GLENAGEARY DIVISION.

THE
ST. JOHN AMBULANCE BRIGADE
OF IRELAND.

With the conclusion of the Leinster Cup Matches the Glenageary Ambulance Division (St. John Ambulance Brigade of Ireland) would like to thank you for having purchased this and other programmes which have been issued on the various cup ties during the past seven weeks.

To the Leinster Branch Irish Rugby Football Union we are deeply indebted for having granted us programme rights on their matches and also to the following business firms who kindly advertised in each publication:—

Messrs. J. W. Elvery & Co., Ltd.
Messrs. West & Son.
Messrs. Mitchell & Son.
Messrs. J. J. Fox & Co.
Messrs. R. Callow & Sons, Ltd.

We are also very grateful to our printers, Messrs. J. T. Drought, Ltd., who have rendered invaluable assistance in the preparation of our programmes.

On next Saturday at 3 p.m. at Lansdown Road, the winners of to-day's match play Instonians in aid of the Welsh Air Disaster Fund. The proceeds of the sale of programmes for this fixture will be given to this worthy cause. May we ask for your continued support.

CHOICE PRIZES AND GIFTS
WEST AND SON
(Established 1720)
Large Selection of DIAMOND RINGS AND JEWELLERY. SPECIALLY APPOINTED AGENT FOR ROLEX WATCHES
Our Reputation for Quality and Service extends over 225 years
SEE OUR DISPLAY OF CUPS
GRAFTON HOUSE, 102/103 GRAFTON STREET, DUBLIN
Telegrams: "Diamonds, Dublin" Telephone 77275

THAT WONDERFUL WHISKEY
"GREEN SPOT"
(PURE UNBLENDED)
J. J. 10 YEARS OLD
MITCHELL & SON
21 KILDARE STREET . . . DUBLIN

(left) The cover of the Match Programme for the Leinster Senior Cup final between Lansdowne and UCD in April 1950. (below) The team sheet for the Leinster Senior Cup final between Lansdowne and UCD in April 1950. Lansdowne won the game 6–Nil, thereby securing the Club's thirteenth Leinster Senior Cup title overall.

Understandably, Lansdowne took umbrage at the report, and it was agreed to write to the newspaper refuting the accusations. Accordingly, Mick Dunne, who had taken over from the late J.J. Coffey as honorary secretary, wrote of 'the unfair and completely unfounded allegations' against the Club and its players. He explicitly denied that any instructions had been given by either the team captain, the Club committee or any 'tacticians' regarding McKee, whether in relation to worrying, slamming or otherwise obstructing him. Dunne also sent in a letter from A.S. Pollock, the honorary secretary of NIFC, stating that the Club was 'emphatic that McKee was not obstructed or worried and that the particular tackle referred to was perfectly fair and not a late tackle and McKee himself says he was not unfairly tackled at any time during the game. The members of the [NIFC] Committee who were present refute the suggestion that McKee was harassed every time he was about to receive the ball'.[12]

Leinster Senior Cup, 1949–50. Standing: F. Conroy (Hon. Sec.), K. Kennedy-O'Brien, F. Johnston, J. Murphy, T.D. McNally, J. Holloway, L. Lynch, M.J. Dunne (Pres.). Seated: E. Connellan, C. Crowley, J.C. Dawson, R. Carroll (Capt.), J.F. Coffey, W.J. Moynan, P. Berkery. On Ground: P. Warren, J.P. Morris.

Despite such issues, the 1949–50 season brought success again for Lansdowne's First and Second XVs. In the Leinster Senior Cup, the First XV defeated Old Belvedere 6–5 in the first round, while Wanderers were beaten 8–6 in round two in a replay. The semi-final saw Bective Rangers dispatched 6–Nil, a score-line repeated in the final against UCD in a victory which secured for Lansdowne a thirteenth Cup title overall and constituted the third occasion upon which the Club had won the Cup twice in a row. The results throughout the 1950 competition were synonymous with the continuing dominance of defence and forward play in Irish rugby at the time. As the report on the final noted, it was a 'grim, keen struggle' littered with 'relentless tackling' and 'safety-first' tactics. Yet even still, the outstanding feature of the game was deemed to be the play of the young Lansdowne fullback, P.J. 'Paddy' Berkery. Once again, Lansdowne had found a future international fullback, with Berkery going on to win eleven Irish caps between 1954 and 1958. And, like Aherne before him, Berkery also hailed from Munster, having previously played with Old Crescent. He also played for Munster throughout his time at Lansdowne in the 1950s. Having started the 1949–50 season on the Lansdowne Seconds, Berkery had made such an impression that by January 1950 he had forced his way on to the First XV. For their part, the Second XV, under the captaincy of Don Fitzgerald, went on to defeat Dublin University 6–3 in the final of the Junior League, thereby securing the Club's eighth such title overall. It was also the Second's third Junior League title in six years, their fourth for the decade 1941–50, and their fifth trophy in total for that period also.[13]

Although the Bateman Cup had been a victim of the Second World War, its essence was briefly revived in a one-off match on 29 April 1950 between Lansdowne and Instonians as respective champions in their Senior Cup competitions that year. However, the purpose of the match was for more sombre reasons than celebrating Cup victories. The game was played in order to raise money for the Welsh Air Disaster Fund, set up following the death of eighty Welsh rugby supporters in a plane crash at Llandow Airport in the Vale of Glamorgan on their return from attending the Ireland–Wales match on 11 March 1950. In the game itself, Instonians were deserving 13–10 victors.[14]

During the 1950–1 season it was noted that Lansdowne had found another

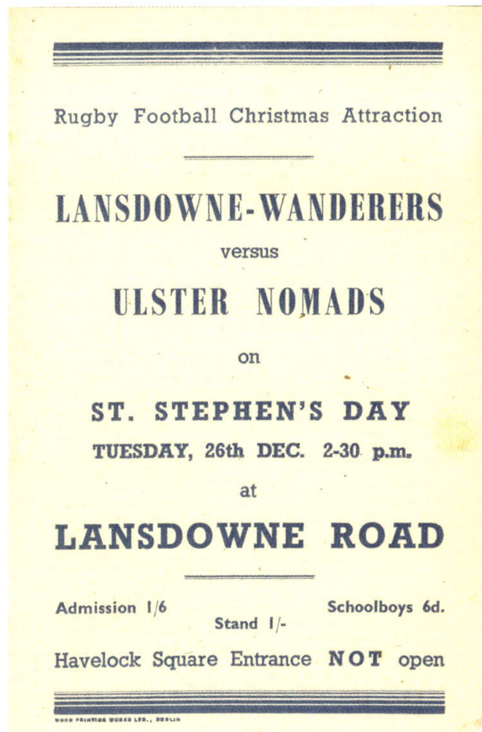
Rugby Football Christmas Attraction

LANSDOWNE-WANDERERS

versus

ULSTER NOMADS

on

ST. STEPHEN'S DAY

TUESDAY, 26th DEC. 2-30 p.m.

at

LANSDOWNE ROAD

Admission 1/6 Stand 1/- Schoolboys 6d.

Havelock Square Entrance NOT open

The notification for a St Stephen's Day combined Lansdowne-Wanderers XV versus an Ulster Nomads selection during the 1950–1 season. Such games were put on as a form of entertainment over the Christmas vacation.

attacking outhalf in Seamus Kelly. Having come straight to the Club from Clongowes College, Kelly had also played Gaelic football for Wexford before committing to eleven seasons as first-choice outhalf at Lansdowne, training alone and then travelling up from his native county each weekend to play matches. He would also go on to win five caps for Ireland, a haul that would have been much more had he not been in competition with the great Jack Kyle throughout the 1950s. Although Kelly's arrival at the Club was perceived to make Lansdowne 'among the strongest of the Irish club teams', the season did not yield any trophies at any levels within the Club. It was also the case that the issue of a junior ground was looming once more. At the April General Meeting in 1951 it was noted that a short-term renewal of the lease for the junior grounds at Kimmage Grove had been secured, but that in the longer-term new grounds would have to be found. The continuing pressures of the expanding urban landscape of Dublin once again forced the Club to look further afield for playing pitches.[15]

Yet overall the Club was in good stead as it entered into its eightieth year in existence. In that regard, in December 1951 the *Irish Independent* highly recommended to its readership *The History of Lansdowne Football Club*, compiled and edited by Michael J. O'Connor, as a publication which

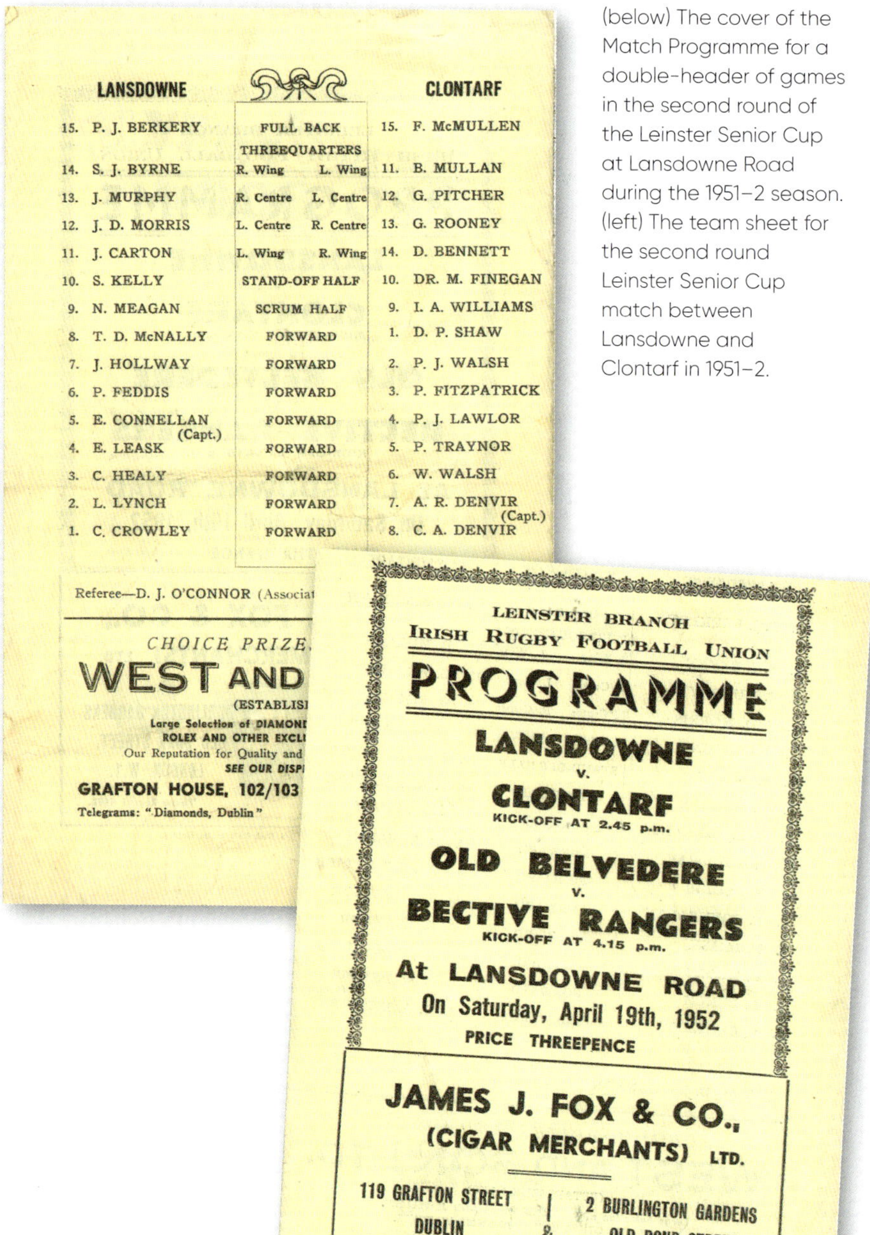

LANSDOWNE		CLONTARF
15. P. J. BERKERY	FULL BACK	15. F. McMULLEN
	THREEQUARTERS	
14. S. J. BYRNE	R. Wing L. Wing	11. B. MULLAN
13. J. MURPHY	R. Centre L. Centre	12. G. PITCHER
12. J. D. MORRIS	L. Centre R. Centre	13. G. ROONEY
11. J. CARTON	L. Wing R. Wing	14. D. BENNETT
10. S. KELLY	STAND-OFF HALF	10. DR. M. FINEGAN
9. N. MEAGAN	SCRUM HALF	9. I. A. WILLIAMS
8. T. D. McNALLY	FORWARD	1. D. P. SHAW
7. J. HOLLWAY	FORWARD	2. P. J. WALSH
6. P. FEDDIS	FORWARD	3. P. FITZPATRICK
5. E. CONNELLAN (Capt.)	FORWARD	4. P. J. LAWLOR
4. E. LEASK	FORWARD	5. P. TRAYNOR
3. C. HEALY	FORWARD	6. W. WALSH
2. L. LYNCH	FORWARD	7. A. R. DENVIR (Capt.)
1. C. CROWLEY	FORWARD	8. C. A. DENVIR

Referee—D. J. O'CONNOR (Associat

CHOICE PRIZE

WEST AND

(ESTABLISI

Large Selection of DIAMONI

ROLEX AND OTHER EXCL

Our Reputation for Quality and

SEE OUR DISP

GRAFTON HOUSE, 102/103

Telegrams: "Diamonds, Dublin"

LEINSTER BRANCH

IRISH RUGBY FOOTBALL UNION

PROGRAMME

LANSDOWNE

v.

CLONTARF

KICK-OFF AT 2.45 p.m.

OLD BELVEDERE

v.

BECTIVE RANGERS

KICK-OFF AT 4.15 p.m.

At LANSDOWNE ROAD

On Saturday, April 19th, 1952

PRICE THREEPENCE

JAMES J. FOX & CO.,

(CIGAR MERCHANTS) LTD.

119 GRAFTON STREET
DUBLIN
'Phone 70533/4.

&

2 BURLINGTON GARDENS
OLD BOND STREET,
LONDON, W.1.
'Phone Regent 4988.

John T. Drought, Ltd., 5/6 Bachelor's Walk, Dublin.

(below) The cover of the Match Programme for a double-header of games in the second round of the Leinster Senior Cup at Lansdowne Road during the 1951–2 season. (left) The team sheet for the second round Leinster Senior Cup match between Lansdowne and Clontarf in 1951–2.

was deemed to be 'as near as makes no difference to a history of rugby in Leinster'. The Club also continued to attract players from other parts of the country, such as Patrick 'Paddy' Joyce and James 'Jim' Murphy, both Connacht interprovincials who were on the Lansdowne First XV in the early 1950s.[16]

The Club also continued to balance the books in financial terms, not least as a result of bar profits, which were £110 for the 1951–2 season. Commenting on the matter at the General Meeting in April 1952, R.W. Jeffares, junior, said that 'it gladdened his heart to note the profit on the bar', but 'he shuddered to think of the Club's financial standing in the event of the country going "dry"'. By way of response, Tommy O'Reilly 'was of the opinion that the possibility of such a calamity was remote' and 'he hoped that drinking – within the law of course – would continue with undiminished vigour'. Humour aside, the exchange was a reminder of the centrality of conviviality and sociability to the associational nature of club life and sporting activity more generally.[17]

In the 1952–3 season, with the First XV captained by Conor Crowley, the Leinster Senior Cup was won for the fourteenth time and third time in five years. UCD were beaten in a first-round replay 16–Nil, while Old Belvedere were defeated 5–3 in a semi-final which was most notable for the pitch being 'churned up into a sea of mud' before the game had even started. In the final Wanderers were dispatched 16–3. With Crowley leading by example and ably supported by the Munster interprovincial, Gerald Reidy, the Lansdowne forwards were on top throughout. The dominant figure in the match, however, was Kelly at outhalf, with stand-out performances also from Berkery at fullback and Seamus Byrne on the wing, who scored the try of the match from a long pass by Crowley. Byrne had only recently marked his international debut for Ireland by scoring three tries against Scotland in Edinburgh, while Reidy had also won his first Irish cap in that season's match against Wales.[18]

While the General Meeting of April 1953 rightly celebrated these various successes, special mention was reserved for the Club Captain of 1950–1, Jack Dawson, who in the hour of need had stepped into the role of captain of the Second XV for the 1952–3 season at very short notice. In what was deemed an 'example of clubmanship … worthy of note', Dawson's actions were synonymous with the importance attached to the regular habit of ex-

(below) The cover of the Match Programme for a double-header of games in the second round of the Leinster Senior Cup at Lansdowne Road during the 1952–3 season. (left) The team sheet for the second round Leinster Senior Cup match between Lansdowne and UCD in 1952–3.

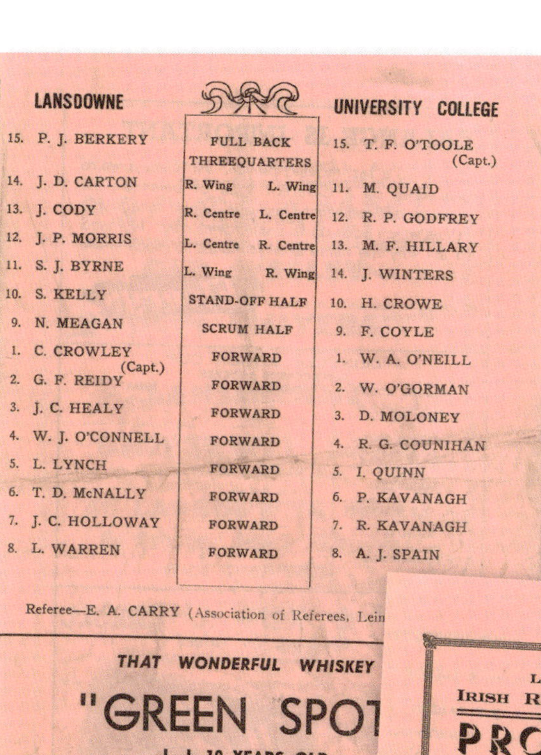

LANSDOWNE		UNIVERSITY COLLEGE
15. P. J. BERKERY	FULL BACK	15. T. F. O'TOOLE (Capt.)
	THREEQUARTERS	
14. J. D. CARTON	R. Wing L. Wing	11. M. QUAID
13. J. CODY	R. Centre L. Centre	12. R. P. GODFREY
12. J. P. MORRIS	L. Centre R. Centre	13. M. F. HILLARY
11. S. J. BYRNE	L. Wing R. Wing	14. J. WINTERS
10. S. KELLY	STAND-OFF HALF	10. H. CROWE
9. N. MEAGAN	SCRUM HALF	9. F. COYLE
1. C. CROWLEY (Capt.)	FORWARD	1. W. A. O'NEILL
2. G. F. REIDY	FORWARD	2. W. O'GORMAN
3. J. C. HEALY	FORWARD	3. D. MOLONEY
4. W. J. O'CONNELL	FORWARD	4. R. G. COUNIHAN
5. L. LYNCH	FORWARD	5. I. QUINN
6. T. D. McNALLY	FORWARD	6. P. KAVANAGH
7. J. C. HOLLOWAY	FORWARD	7. R. KAVANAGH
8. L. WARREN	FORWARD	8. A. J. SPAIN

Referee—E. A. CARRY (Association of Referees, Lein

THAT WONDERFUL WHISKEY

"GREEN SPOT

J. J. 10 YEARS OLD

MITCHELL & SO

21 KILDARE STREET . . .

'Phone 62377

LEINSTER BRANCH
IRISH RUGBY FOOTBALL UNION

PROGRAMME

OLD WESLEY
v.
DUBLIN UNIVERSITY
KICK-OFF AT 2.45 p.m.

LANSDOWNE
v.
UNIVERSITY COLL.
KICK-OFF AT 4.15 p.m.

At LANSDOWNE ROAD
On Saturday, March 28th, 1953
PRICE THREEPENCE

JAMES J. FOX & CO.,
(CIGAR MERCHANTS) Ltd.

We are now happy to supply Leather Cigarette Cases and Tobacco Pouches in Club and Regimental Colours.

119 GRAFTON ST., DUBLIN.

Telephone: Dublin 70533-4

2 BURLINGTON GARDENS, OLD BOND STREET, LONDON, W.1. Telephone: Regent 4968 | 60 PALL MALL, LONDON, S.W.1. Telephone: Whitehall 7573

John T. Drought, Ltd., 5/6 Bachelor's Walk, Dublin.

Leinster Senior Cup, 1952–3. T.C. Fox (Hon. Treas.), W. O'Connell, J.P.D. Morris, L. Warke, Col. J. Burke-Gaffney, MC (Pres.), P. Feddis, J. Carton, G.F. Reidy, N.J. Burke (Hon. Sec.). Seated: S. Kelly, P. Berkery, T.D. McNally, C.V. Crowley (Capt.), L. Lynch, J. Holloway, S.J. Byrne. On Ground: N. Meagan, V. Finnegan.

members of the First XV continuing to play on the Second and Third XVs in their later years, passing on their expertise and experience and bringing some battle-hardened know-how to affairs. Such continuity across the various teams at Lansdowne also helped to instil a sense of the Club's ethos of an open, running game. A particularly notable example at that time was the double Cup-winning hooker, Holloway, who went on to play for many years with the Seconds, Thirds and Third As. Such commitment of players to the greater good of the Club also demanded that the Club do all it could to provide long-term sustainability for junior rugby. Hence both the April and September General Meetings in 1953 also involved a lengthy discussion about the need to move on from leasing pitches at Kimmage Grove and bite the bullet on purchasing a junior ground.[19]

The 1952–3 season had been rounded off on 25 April with a celebratory match between a Dublin County XV and a Lancashire XV hosted by

LEINSTER BRANCH, I.R.F.U.

LANSDOWNE FOOTBALL CLUB

A COUNTY DUBLIN XV

versus

LANCASHIRE

SATURDAY, 25th APRIL, 1953

LANSDOWNE ROAD, DUBLIN

In 1873 there came the first visit of an English Team to Dublin. The visitors were the DINGLE FOOTBALL CLUB of LIVERPOOL and they had a very even match with Trinity in the College Park.

—(Whitehead, "The Marshall," 1925.)

The Match Programme for the Lansdowne FC-organised County Dublin XV versus Lancashire game in April 1953. The occasion was utilised to promote the Irish Blood Transfusion Board and to encourage people to become blood donors.

Lansdowne. Kelly, Byrne, Crowley, L. Warke and Leo Lynch all played for the Dublin team, with Crowley captaining the side. The Match Programme promoted the Irish Blood Transfusion Board, a connection that in November 1954 seems to have prompted fifty Lansdowne members to each give a pint of blood to the organization all at the same sitting at the Club pavilion. At the end of the 1953–4 season Lansdowne organized another Dublin County XV to play an English Midlands Counties team, with Warke, Lynch, Reidy, and McNally as captain turning out for the Dublin side. Another Dublin County fixture was organized against the Midlands Counties again for the end of April 1955, which resulted in a game of 'careless and gay rugby' with nine tries scored, all in 'fast, sweeping movements', as Dublin won 26–14. The *Irish Press* match report was penned by Lansdowne's in-house sports journalist, Garry

Redmond. Then in September a combined Lansdowne–Old Belvedere side defeated a visiting French Auvergne–Limousin team 19–3, with Kelly, who had only just returned from injury, shining once again alongside Berkery and a young Tony Twomey at scrumhalf who was in the first of his fourteen seasons on Lansdowne's First XV.[20]

These types of fixtures were in part an endeavour to replace the defunct Hospital Charity matches played in the first decade of the twentieth century, but they also served as a reminder of the continuing importance of tours and invitational matches as part of the Lansdowne rugby ethos. In that regard at Club level during the rest of the 1950s old overseas acquaintances continued to be renewed while new connections were made. At the start of the 1953–4 season, the famous Welsh club, Newport, came to Lansdowne Road and triumphed 20–14, though Kelly led Lansdowne to victory 9–6 the following season when Newport came calling once again. Then, when London's Harlequins arrived in October 1955 with four English internationals in their team, Lansdowne won 27–9 in a game of 'open football, with the emphasis on speed and entertaining back movements'. Lansdowne's forwards led the way, but both Kelly and Twomey were also said to have been 'in fine fettle'. Although the return fixture with Harlequins did not occur until October 1958, it was remarkable in that it was the first time an Irish club played at Twickenham. And, just for good measure, Lansdowne won the game 17–8.[21]

The evident importance of showcasing the best of rugby through invitational and foreign club fixtures led in the summer of 1956 to the establishment of the Wolfhounds Club. Drawing obvious comparisons with the Barbarian FC, the purpose of this new club was to grow the game around Ireland and to improve playing standards by putting out occasional invitational sides made up of international players from the Five Nations along with promising young uncapped Irish players. Proceeds from matches were to go to the Varsity Club of Ireland, described by Karl Mullen at the launch of the Wolfhounds as 'a thirty-two-county non-sectarian charity which specializes in looking after blind children'. Instrumental in the whole endeavour was Lansdowne's Ham Lambert. The first match in September 1956 at Donnybrook was against an invitational international team captained by France's Jean Prat. Lansdowne's Berkery and Lynch turned out for the Wolfhounds, while Crowley and Tom McNally played for Prat's side. A weather-affected game ended 11–10 to the Wolfhounds.[22]

With regard to domestic competition during the mid-to-late 1950s Lansdowne made it to the Leinster Cup final on three more occasions, in 1954, 1956 and 1959. Unfortunately, all three finals were lost: in 1954 to Wanderers in a replay by 12–15; in 1956 to Bective Rangers 6–11; and in 1959 to Wanderers once again, 6–13. But those losses did not undermine the fact that Lansdowne continued to demonstrate that they were, as ever, one of the top clubs in the country playing some of the most entertaining and high-scoring rugby, a fact demonstrated in October 1959 when Kelly became the first Irish player to score more than 1,000 points in senior and representative rugby.[23]

It was also the case that the ongoing investment in junior rugby at the Club, and the work of Art Campbell in particular, was truly starting to

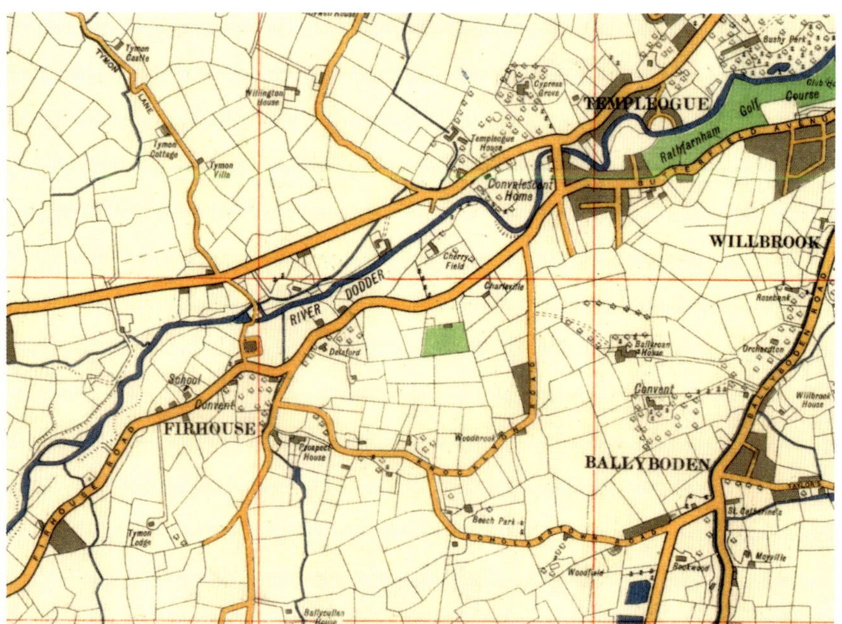

Templeogue Junior Grounds, 1950s. Source: *Dublin, Popular Edition*, by Ordnance Survey Office (Dublin, 1953). © Ordnance Survey Ireland/Government of Ireland Copyright Permit No. MP 000122. All rights reserved. Reproduced from the American Geographical Society Library, University of Wisconsin Milwaukee Libraries.

Albert O'Connell Cup, 1957–8. Standing: W.G. Sutherland (Hon. Sec.), T. Duggan, F. Keogh, J. Hoey, T.C. Fox (Pres.), J. Egan, F. O'Donovan, A. Moorhead, H. Vard. Seated: G. Donworth, W. McNally, M. Kennedy, A. McNally (Capt.), J. Holloway, J. Nestor, P. Ryan. On Ground: M. Begley, G. Cunniam.

pay off in the late 1950s and early 1960s. In 1954–5 the club purchased for £6,375 15*s*. 9*d*. a new junior ground in Templeogue, between the junction of the Knocklyon and Firhouse roads and Charleville Manor. Financed by an overdraft loan with Royal Bank of Ireland, a fund-raising campaign to repay the debt was initiated and by 1958 the outstanding amount had reduced to £3,053 4*s*. By August 1960, it had further reduced to £2,362 5*s*. 10*d*. The new ground had a pavilion and also provided a source of income during the summer months, when it was rented out. As had been the case at Kimmage Grove, the new ground was located on the outer limits of the expanding city, and was bordered by farmland. As a result, occasional issues arose over local cattle and horses entering the grounds to graze on the pitches at night-time.[24]

Such financial investment saw results on the playing fields. In 1958 the Third XV won the recently instituted Albert O'Connell Cup for the first time, while the Third As won the Moran Cup for the first time also. Not to be outdone, the Second XV won their third Metropolitan Cup title in 1959,

Moran Cup, 1957–8. Standing: W.G. Sutherland (Hon. Sec.), T. Hannigan, F. Aiken, F. Keogh, T.C. Fox (Pres.), B. O'Sullivan, D. Hayden, P. Kelly, A. Campbell. Seated: P. Kavanagh, G. Kilduff, A. Moorhead, N. Hayden (Capt.), J. Dempsey, N. O'Keefe, J. Kavanagh. On Ground: H. Murrin, D. Lynch.

beating Terenure 11–6 in extra-time in the final, with the captain, Patrick 'Paddy' Kirwan, scoring the winning try. Then, in 1960, the Third XV under the captaincy of Greg Cunniam went on to do the 'double', winning both the Minor League (for a fourth time overall) and the Albert O'Connell Cup. The team scored 333 points for and only conceded ninety-five against throughout the season. The 1960 Minor League title was in fact the first of three-in-a-row. In 1961 the title was retained under the captaincy of Dermot Lynch and was then won again in 1962 under the captaincy of Dave O'Riordan. Those two successes constituted the Club's fifth and sixth titles in that competition. The Third As, captained by John Maguire, also won a second Moran Cup title in 1962, while Patrick 'Paddy' Shortall's Second XV won a ninth Junior League title in 1963.[25]

The 1950s had also seen the passing of some old stalwarts of the Club, including one of the great IRFU administrators, R.W. Jeffares, in 1954 and, at the age of sixty-six, Ernie Crawford in January 1959, the year after he had served as President of the IRFU. His death had been sudden and unexpected, which somehow seemed in keeping with his rugby career. Owing to the First World War and a serious wound in 1917, his playing days almost ended before they had truly got going, only to be revived in earnest with Lansdowne and Ireland in the 1920s. He had given his all both as a player and administrator to his adopted club and to the game he loved in his evidently unique, unorthodox but yet compelling manner. Always one to surprise, he had done so to the end. As President of the IRFU in April 1958 he had received 'tremendous applause' at the after-match dinner in Paris when proposing the toast to the French team and FFR in their own language, which was apparently a first for IRFU presidents and was an action that prompted the official interpreter to declare in jovial mood that he had just lost his job.[26]

In the early 1960s the ongoing strong association of Lansdowne with Munster and Connacht rugby was further consolidated. Having moved to the Club in late 1959, the Garryowen, Munster, Ireland and Lions prop, Gordon 'Woody' Wood, was elected Club Captain for the 1960–1 season. Among his many achievements was a 1954 Comhairle na Muire Saile Certificate for Bravery, awarded for rescuing people from drowning that summer. Interviewed after his retirement from rugby in the 1960s, Wood noted how he was one of many rugby players who had played Gaelic football and hurling in his school days, but that 'when I appeared on a rugby team, I was brought under the [GAA 'foreign games'] ban, as were my colleagues'. Wood's 1960–1 Lansdowne First XV also included Noel Feddis, capped against England in 1956, and Joe Nesdale, both of whom had played for the Club during the 1950s but had thereafter spent time in America before returning to Ireland.[27]

The Cork-born and Limerick-raised Tom Reynolds, who was capped by Connacht in 1958, had also arrived at Lansdowne in the later 1950s. Involved on and off with the First XV, he played alongside Wood in the front-row in a resounding 27–5 first round Leinster Cup victory over Palmerston in March 1960. He later went on to captain the Second XV to a Junior League and Metropolitan Cup 'double' in 1965. He was still appearing for the First XV as late as 1968. In 1961 the Munster and future Irish player, Dave Kiely, joined

Minor League and Albert O'Connell Cup, 1959–60. Standing: S.T. O'Kelly, F. Aiken, P. Moorhead, P. Egan, F. O'Donovan, C. McDonnell, Dr H. Jack (Pres.), G. O'Mahony, M. Hickey, P. Kelly, H. Vard. Seated: J. Kavanagh, M. Kennedy, A. Kenna, G. Cunniam (Capt.), J. Holloway, W. Williams, P. Kavanagh. On Ground: H. Murrin, D. Lynch.

the Club, with his younger brothers Paddy and Eddie following suit during the decade, while in 1962 the Bohemians, Munster, Ireland and Lions outhalf, Michael 'Mick' English, also joined. The Connacht prop, Sean MacHale, also joined in the early 1960s, later changing his provincial allegiance to Leinster in 1964 and thereafter going on to win twelve caps for Ireland. Another to shift provincial allegiance was Noel Dwyer, who started playing on the Lansdowne First XV in 1963–4 and went on to play for Connacht in 1967–8 before being capped fourteen times for Leinster in 1969–73. Munster's next outhalf after Mick English, David Huddie, also came to the Club in 1964.[28]

The first half of the 1960s also saw the arrival of new players such as Noel Hoffman, Patrick 'Pat' Casey, Alan Duggan, Caleb Powell, Paul Van Cauwelaert and Sidney Minch, the Clongowes-educated son of the 1930s Kildare TD S.B. Minch and nephew of J.B. Minch, who had played for Ireland prior to the First World War. As for Van Cauwelaert, like others before and after him, his first contact with Lansdowne FC was as a schoolboy when, as a boarder in Glenstal Abbey in County Limerick, he would take part in the Christmas vacation training and games organized by Kevin Kelleher at Lansdowne Road. Friends made during those winter holidays returned to play for Lansdowne, some after formative years playing at university, a connection that also further strengthened the Club's links with the likes of UCD and Dublin University. That connection was also seen at that time in relation to Barry Bresnihan, the future Irish and Lions player in the 1960s, who as a schoolboy at Gonzaga College in the later 1950s had also taken part in the Lansdowne Christmas vacation rugby and, after playing at UCD, returned to Lansdowne for a short while before heading off to England and London Irish.[29]

The First XV in the 1960s also had a very international flavour to it, in keeping with the Club's tradition of welcoming players from far and wide. Alongside Van Cauwelaert, whose father had moved to Ireland from Belgium, the second-row Paul Boladz came from Poland, while the backrow forward George Patrikios hailed from Greece and had come to Lansdowne after studying at Dublin University. Another second-row, Miklos Kos, was of Hungarian origin and had attended secondary school at CBC Monkstown.[30]

All of these new players were quick to make their mark. In the ongoing fixtures with London Irish, Lansdowne achieved a 24–9 home victory in October 1961. With Wood, Nesdale and the Club Captain, Feddis, leading from the front, the young wing Van Cauwelaert scored two of Lansdowne's four tries, the first from a break by R.S. Kelly who fed the ball on to the centre Duggan who gave the scoring pass, and the second an intercept and sixty-yard sprint to the line. Unable to play in the 1961–2 seasonal fixture with 'the ancient enemy' Wanderers, 'Vanner' (as Van Cauwelaert was nicknamed) kept the score-board instead and thereby contributed psychologically to the result by displaying Lansdowne's score at one point as '61' instead of '16'. Wanderers apparently 'visibly wilted' thereafter and Lansdowne went on to win 33–12, scoring eight tries in the process. It was recorded in the Club minutes at the time that 'All is fair in love and W-A-N-D-E-R-E-R-S'. Two years later, a 24–6 victory over Palmerston in December 1963, with an Irish selector present, saw both Mick English and Duggan in impressive form. The latter was said to have 'carved out two of Lansdowne's scores with delightful running'. Duggan went on to win his first two caps for Ireland in 1964. As for English, even though he was coming to the end of his international career, he was in impressive form again in January 1964 when 'he made a series of dazzling breaks that caught everyone completely by surprise' in a 14–6 victory over UCD.[31]

It was also evident that the Club was refreshing its long-standing ethos of open, running, entertaining rugby. In an interview in June 1963 the recently retired Gordon Wood, when asked how he thought the game of rugby might be 'brightened up', referred to a friendly game that Lansdowne's Second XV had played the previous season against Nottingham University: 'We arranged beforehand that neither team should kick for touch except when in its own "twenty-five". And the wing forwards kept in the scrum until the ball was away from the scrum. The result was a splendid game of continual handling and passing by both backs and forwards. I must admit an exhausting one too'. Then in August 1963 at a luncheon in McKee Barracks hosted by the incoming Lansdowne President, Major Sean Collins-Powell (a nephew of Michael Collins), a public commitment was made to playing 'attractive football'. At the same time, the incoming Club Captain, Dave Kiely, stated that 'it behoved them to play good rugby. They intended to do some hard training ... to be fit for their first game against Racing Club de France, on September 15. They hoped to play open rugby, not rashly, but intelligently, making use of their backs from the rucks, which would give them better opportunities than from the set scrums, where the marking was so tight'. This commitment also included further investment in the junior grounds at Templeogue, with 'levelling and re-surfacing to produce a really good full-sized pitch and a somewhat smaller one for their junior players'.[32]

True to his word, Kiely introduced a more focused training regime for the First XV, commencing with pre-season runs around the roads surrounding the Templeogue grounds in Knocklyon. As had also been notified in August 1963,

Lansdowne FC portrait of W.G. Sutherland. Club President for 1964–5, Sutherland had been Club Captain for two seasons in 1940–2. He also served as honorary secretary from 1957 to 1970 and honorary treasurer from 1978 to 1983, as well as being a long-time Trustee for the Club.

Lansdowne's constant quest for finding new and transformative fixtures with overseas clubs had resulted in the 1963–4 season commencing with a match against the famous Racing Club de Paris. It was the commencement of a long-standing annual reciprocal fixture between the two clubs. The first game, played in Paris, went the host's way 19–11. That outcome was reversed in the return fixture at Lansdowne Road at the beginning of the 1964–5 season by three tries to one, a result which turned out to be a good omen, as the First XV once again embarked upon the road to success in the Leinster Senior Cup.[33]

Lansdowne's President for the 1964–5 season was W.G. 'Billy' Sutherland, who had been Club Captain in 1940–2 and was in the middle of a lengthy period of service as honorary secretary as well, having taken up that role in 1957. The Club Captain for the 1964–5 season was Caleb Powell, who was originally from Nenagh in County Tipperary and had been educated at The King's Hospital School and Dublin University. He had previously won Munster Senior Cup medals with Bohemians in 1957 and 1958, and he would in time go on to serve as President of Lansdowne in 1993–4, of the Leinster Branch in 1997–8, and of the IRFU in 2010–11.[34]

Considered one of the favourites for the Cup in 1965 and with strength in depth with the likes of Connacht's David Coen competing with English for the fullback berth, Lansdowne's traditional strength up front was also recognized.

Yet it was not an easy road to victory. A below-par performance in a 9–9 draw with Dublin University in the first round was put to one side in the replay 26–3. Bective Rangers were defeated 3–Nil in the second round, before Old Belvedere were beaten 6–Nil in the semi-final. Clontarf awaited in the final, which resulted in a 3–3 draw, with Lansdowne surviving 'by the skin of their teeth'. Trailing 3–Nil with one minute of injury time left, Powell's comrade-in-arms in the second-row, Miklos Kos, who was known for his long-range kicks at goal, marked a Clontarf drop-out and proceeded to kick the required three-pointer from almost fifty yards out. In the replay, and exemplified by Powell, Feddis, Dwyer and John Barry, a goal-kicking New Zealander, Lansdowne's strength up front won the day 9–6. With a dropped goal by the outhalf David Huddie and a penalty from Barry, Lansdowne's try came from a blindside break from a scrum by Twomey who put Duggan over for the score.[35]

Leinster Senior Cup, 1964–5. Standing: J.P. Barrett, S. MacHale, P. Kavanagh, P. Casey, C.J. Murphy, M. Kos, N. Dwyer, J. Barry, J.C. Dawson. Seated: N. Hoffman, N. Feddis, C. Powell (Capt.), W.G. Sutherland (Pres.), A. Duggan, M.A. English, S. Healy. On Ground: D. Hannigan, A. Twomey, D. Huddie, B. Reddan. Inset: S. Minch.

While a fifteenth Leinster Senior Cup title had been secured in 1965, the season was even more notable for the level of success once again within the junior ranks of the Club. Tom Reynolds' Second XV did the 'double', winning both the Junior League, for the tenth time, and the Metropolitan Cup, for the fourth time, with a 6–3 victory over Blackrock in the final of the latter. The Third As, captained by Dermot Murphy, had also won the Moran Cup for a third time. Further success followed in 1966 when the Third As captained by J. Hoey won the inaugural Junior 3A League. In the same season the Third Bs, under the captaincy of the honorary junior match secretary, Colm Madigan, won the recently inaugurated Winters Cup, named in honour of Colonel J.J. Winters, who had played on the Lansdowne Cup-winning side in 1927 and had been President of the Leinster Branch in 1953–4.[36]

Junior 1 League and Metropolitan Cup, 1964–5. Standing: C.J. Murphy, W. Pike, P. Kavanagh, T. Barry, B. Reddan, W.G. Sutherland (Pres.), N. O'Keefe, P. Dowse, P. Egan, H. Vard. Seated: J. Casey, N. Hoffman, R. Kelly, T. Reynolds (Capt.), W. Williams, E. Byrne, D. Hannigan. On Ground: B. O'Rafferty, C. Flanagan, B. Brereton, P. Van Cauwelaert. Inset: P. Ward, M. Rafferty, D. Ennis.

Moran Cup, 1964–5. Standing: M. Nestor, G. Danaher, P. Kavanagh, W.G. Sutherland (Pres.), J. O'Connor, B. O'Neill, P. Henry, A. Campbell. Seated: D. Hayden, J. Hickey, J. Hoey, D. Murphy (Capt.), P. O'Reilly, A. Healy, R. Palmer. On Ground: A. Adair, D. Lynch.

With a slight hiatus during the 1966–7 season, the junior teams got back to winning ways in the following three seasons. In 1968 a fifth Metropolitan Cup was secured by Colm Flanagan's Second XV with a 6–3 victory over Terenure in the final, while the Third As under M. Nestor won the Junior 3A League for the second time. They proceeded to back up that success in 1969 under Wyndam Williams as part of a 'double' with a fourth Moran Cup. The Junior 3A League was then won again in 1971 under Marcus Hunt, giving the Club four titles in the first six years of that competition. In the interim, the Third XV under Tommy O'Reilly had won the Albert O'Connell Cup in 1969 and did so again in 1971 under Peter Kiernan.[37]

During that time, other older Lansdowne members were also continuing to leave their mark. In 1967 Eugene Davy was elected President of the IRFU for the 1967–8 season, during which Kevin Kelleher entered the hall of fame as the only referee to have the nerve to send off New Zealand's enforcer extraordinaire, Colin 'Pinetree' Meads, in a Test match against Scotland at Murrayfield. As Kelleher himself recalled many years later, the reaction in

New Zealand 'was akin to JFK's assassination in Dallas. They all remembered where they were when news filtered through of the great "Pinetree's" dismissal'. Kelleher had already formally cautioned Meads before he swung his boot at Scotland's David Chisholm. Despite missing, Kelleher did not hesitate to dismiss Meads for the intention to injure. The affair was such that the match whistle has ended up in the All Blacks' Museum in Palmerston North. While others were slow to forgive, Meads and Kelleher went on to exchange Christmas cards every year.[38]

As the 1960s drew to a close, the Club also turned its attention to its upcoming centenary in 1972. In October 1968 plans were put in place for financing a series of centenary events, including a Club history. The sense of continuity with the past was also seen in January 1969 when a collection from among 240 members resulted in a presentation to Mary Kavanagh of £301 7*s.* 6*d.* to honour the fact that she had been presiding over the tea pavilion for

Junior 3A League, 1965–6. Standing: J. Holloway, P. Henry, K. du Plessis, B. Hand, J. O'Connor, M. Hunt, B. O'Neill. Seated: B. O'Rafferty, N. Cotter, J. McEnery (Pres.), J. Hoey (Capt.), J. Wynne, J. Hickey, F. Keogh. On Ground: D. Lynch, A. Adair.

fifty years, ever since she came to the Club following the First World War. But the Club was also, as ever, looking to the future. Having agreed in October 1968 to open a new bank account for a proposed fund for building a new clubhouse, in February 1969 the detailed discussions got under way with initial plans and costings being entered into. In April 1970, an Extraordinary General Meeting was convened on the matter as well. It would be eight more years however before that plan came to full fruition.[39]

The 1960s also saw the passing of a number of long-term Club supporters and personalities. The First World War veteran and ex-Lansdowne President Billy 'Ludendorff' Young passed away in 1960, the same year in which Mervyn Bell died during his term in office as Senior Vice-President of Lansdowne. He had played for the Club in the 1920s and had also served for a time as auditor to the IRFU. In March 1964 R.W. 'Billy' Jeffares, junior, died. Having had his playing career at Lansdowne ended early by a knee injury, Jeffares had gone on to a successful career as an international referee, including the unique claim to fame of having to step in at short notice to referee Ireland against New Zealand in December 1935 when the appointed Scottish match official was unable to travel owing to fog. Jeffares went on to serve as President of Lansdowne in 1945–6 before taking up the role of assistant to his father, Rupert, who was secretary of the IRFU. He then succeeded his father as secretary of the IRFU in 1951, serving in that role until his death. Another ex-President and long-serving treasurer of Lansdowne, Arthur Sibthorpe, died in November 1965, when it was noted in his obituary that he had played on the Lansdowne First XV when forty years old, in the 1920–1 season. Then in February 1967, the Irish and Lions international Mick Dunne passed away at the age of sixty-one. He had been both honorary secretary and President of the Club, and in his later years had revived an earlier Club tradition of taking issue with the running of the IRFU and arguing for new people and ideas on its management committee, as well as proposing a county championship in Leinster. Immediately following his death, a Leinster County Competition was established with the winners receiving the Michael Dunne Cup. In its first year in 1967 the Cup went to County Meath. In 1975, it was changed into a Provincial Towns Junior 4 competition. The later 1960s also saw the passing of two other long-serving Club administrators, Noel Burke, who had served as honorary secretary from 1952 to 1957, and Tom Fox, who had been in the office of Club Treasurer from 1951 to 1965. The Tom Fox Cup for Third Ds in the Dublin area was established in the 1970–1 season in his honour.[40]

It was also the case, however, that Lansdowne's continuing success as a club in the 1960s, and indeed all of Irish rugby activity during that decade, occurred in the shadow of a growing international anti-apartheid movement that was increasingly looking toward sporting boycotts of South Africa and

Winters Cup, 1965–6. Standing: J. McEnery (Pres.), P. Henry, F. O'Connell, J. Hurley, M. Dorcey, B. Hand, J. Molloy. Seated: M. Cotter, N. Cotter, K. du Plessis, C. Madigan (Capt.), B. White, A. Adair, S. O'Donovan. On Ground: D. Feddis, J. Veale.

its touring players and teams. Few people in Ireland in the 1950s knew what apartheid was, but that began to change following the arrest in 1963 of Nelson Mandela and the other leaders of the Umkhonto we Sizwe, the armed wing of the African National Congress. In response, activists established the World Campaign for the Release of South African Prisoners, and in 1964 the Irish Anti-Apartheid Movement (IAAM) was formed by Kader Asmal, a Dublin University law lecturer and third-generation member of South Africa's Indian community.[41]

It was therefore not surprising that the visit of the South African rugby team to Lansdowne Road in April 1965 was objected to in certain quarters. Dublin University students protested at the use of College Park for training purposes by 'the racially selected South African rugby team', while in the Dáil the Labour TD, Noel Browne, unsuccessfully pressed the Fianna Fáil government to order its ministers to boycott the match. The IAAM also organized a protest march and picket of the grounds on match day. The game went ahead regardless and resulted in Ireland's first victory in six attempts, with a winning margin of 9–6. Sean MacHale was the only Lansdowne player to play in the match. Three years later in 1968, a similar protest was organized for a game between Wanderers and Cape Town University at Lansdowne Road.[42]

It was early days for anti-apartheid protests in Ireland, but the efforts of those activists in 1965 and 1968 gathered both momentum and wider support in the coming years. When the IRFU invited South Africa to visit again in January 1970, the protests were much more significant. Against a backdrop of increasing tensions, pitch invasions and protests in England in late 1969, the pressure on the IRFU intensified. With hunger-striking clerical students, protests at interprovincial games, pressure from Trade Unions and TDs, and anti-apartheid slogans painted on the walls and gates of Lansdowne Road, it was evident that the level of public discontent had increased greatly since the 1960s. The security measures for the match demonstrated that rugby had ventured into a very different and troubled arena. Garda leave was cancelled in Dublin during the tour and an additional 400 police were drafted in from around the country. On match day, barbed-wire surrounded the pitch and the terraces behind the goalposts were empty of spectators for security reasons.

Junior 3A League and Moran Cup, 1968–9. Standing: J.D. Spoor, P. Whelan, J. Hoey, J. Molloy, J. O'Connor, N. Deasy, D. Thompson, A. O'Beirne, A. Campbell. Seated: D. Murphy, T. Reynolds, I. Brown, W. Williams (Capt.), T. McKenna, M. Nestor, D. O'Donohoe. On Ground: B. O'Rafferty, P. O'Reilly, K. Hanley, J.M. O'Neill.

A 6,000-strong protest march from Dublin's city centre arrived at Lansdowne Road forty-five minutes before the game, with protesters remaining in the area throughout the afternoon. The match resulted in an 8–8 draw, with Lansdowne's Duggan scoring Ireland's only try. The Irish team also included Munster's Barry McGann, who had spent the previous season playing with Lansdowne. Despite the dramatically increased protests, growing international condemnation, and the fact that the Scottish Rugby Union had already cut its links to South Africa, the IRFU along with other leading rugby unions proved more stubborn in adhering to out-dated arguments regarding

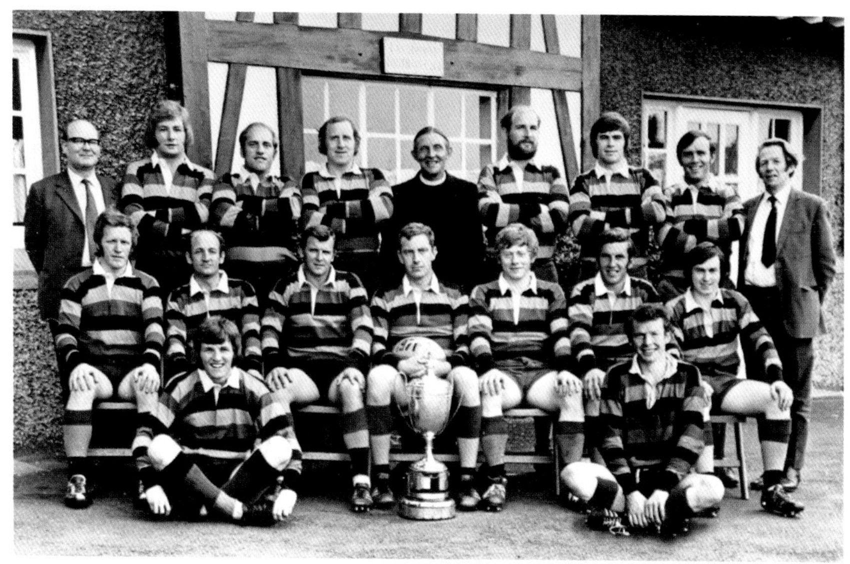

Leinster Senior Cup, 1971–2. Standing: P.J. Moore (Hon. Treas.), D. Power, J. Mitchell, N. Dwyer, Rev. W. Moynan (Pres.), C. Feighery, P. Inglis, J. Craig, P. Berkery (Hon. Sec.). Seated: J. Flanagan, B. O'Rafferty, A. Duggan, E. Kiely (Capt.), V. Becker, J. Kerin, E. Meredith. On Ground: M. Quinn, R. Cooke.

the game's amateur ethos and not mixing sport with politics. As a result, in the 1970s and early 1980s Irish rugby players, including some from Lansdowne, would at times be placed in very difficult and unenviable positions.[43]

Such considerations were for the future, however. For Lansdowne the late 1960s and early 1970s saw the emergence of another tranche of leading senior players at the Club. Once again, Munster and Connacht provided new blood in the likes of Henry Blake, Larry Cheevers and Richard 'Dickie' Cooke, while the Seconds and Thirds nurtured new young talent such as John Kerin (who went on to play for Connacht in 1972–5), Michael 'Mick' Quinn, Eric Meridith, Barry O'Rafferty and Vincent 'Vinny' Becker, the latter of whom, like Barry Bresnihan before him, had attended Gonzaga College for a while. Becker however had also spent time at Mungret College in Limerick.[44]

The dynamic combination of youth and experience was to come to fruition in the 1971–2 centenary season. The Club Captain for the year was Eddie Kiely, who, like his older brother Dave, was a doctor from a Cork medical dynasty. In later years he would become best known for leading the Great Ormond Street surgical team in 2010 that successfully separated the conjoined Cork twins, Hassan and Hussein Benhaffat. Under Kiely's captaincy in 1971–2, and alongside longer-established First XV players such as Noel Dwyer, Alan Duggan and Paul Inglis, who like Van Cauwelaert had attended Glenstal Abbey, the younger crop of new talent helped to ensure that the Leinster Senior Cup was regained by Lansdowne. The season also saw the initiation of the Leinster Senior League, with Lansdowne making it to the inaugural final, where they faced the much-fancied St Mary's. In what was deemed a thrilling game, Lansdowne only lost out to a late controversial penalty goal with a final score-line of 6–4. Undaunted, Lansdowne turned attention to the Leinster Cup thereafter. Monkstown were beaten 16–15 in a very closely contested first round, followed by victory over Dublin University 15–10 in round two, with Mick Quinn kicking 11 points alongside a try from Cooke. An early opportunity for revenge for the League final defeat then came in the Cup semi-final meeting with St Mary's, which Lansdowne won 16–10, a victory credited to the Lansdowne forwards, with Inglis 'head and shoulders' above all others. In the final, UCD were defeated 6–3. In a rain-affected game, 'only a great tackle … on the line' by Vinny Becker at the end of the match prevented a UCD victory at the death.[45]

Lansdowne's sixteenth Leinster Senior Cup title was a most fitting way to commence the centenary year. A range of celebrations ensued in the following months, including three official centenary games in September. The first was against the Wolfhounds. With Quinn out ill, Barry McGann made a guest appearance for his old club at outhalf, while the Wolfhounds included ten international players from France, Wales, England and Ireland, including Tom Grace, Ken Kennedy, Sean Lynch, Kevin Mays, Fergus Slattery, Joe Maso, Christian Carrere and Max Wiltshire. The ensuing 56–23 victory for the Wolfhounds, with four tries by Grace, was considered a game of 'vintage' running rugby, which was most apposite for Lansdowne as a club steeped in that tradition. A week later the second centenary game against Racing Club de Paris went Lansdowne's way 17–15, with first-half tries from Johnny Mitchell and Duggan giving Lansdowne a half-time lead of 17–3. The third centenary

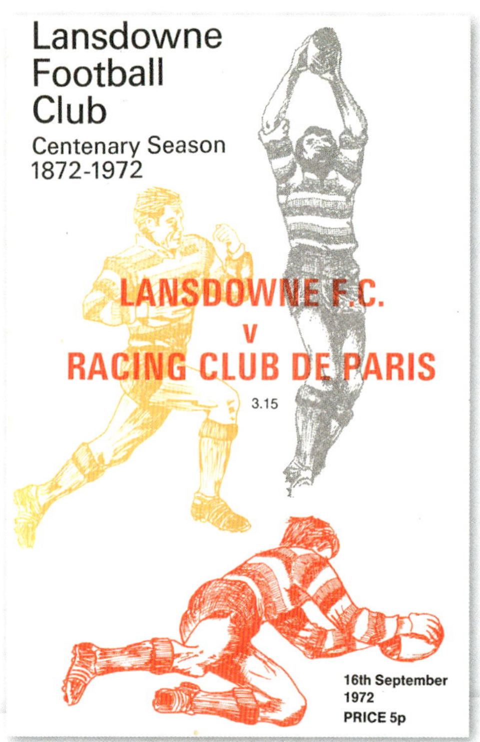

(left) The cover of the Match Programme for the Centenary game between Lansdowne FC and Racing Club de Paris on 16 September 1972.
(below) The team sheet for the Centenary match between Lansdowne and Racing Club de Paris.

LANSDOWNE F.C. **RACING CLUB DE PARIS**

KICK-OFF 3.15 P.M.

	LANSDOWNE F.C.			RACING CLUB DE PARIS	
FULL BACK	15. B. O'RAFFERTY			15. GERARD LAVIE	FULL BACK
THREEQUARTERS	14. A. DUGGAN	*Right Wing*	*Left Wing*	11. MARC CHEVALLIER	THREEQUARTERS
	13. E. MEREDITH	*Right Centre*	*Left Centre*	12. MICHEL TAFFARY	
	12. J. KERINS	*Left Centre*	*Right Centre*	13. PAUL CIEPLY	
	11. B. O'NEILL	*Left Wing*	*Right Wing*	14. PIERRE JANSSENS	
HALF BACKS	10. M. QUINN	*Stand-Off*	*Stand-Off*	10. PIERRE BASSAGAITS	HALF BACKS
	9. R. COOKE	*Scrum*	*Scrum*	9. JEAN-MARC GAIGNIER	
FORWARDS	8. P. INGLIS			8. RENE BONNEFONT	FORWARDS
	7. G. SHEEHAN			7. PATRICE PERON	
	6. J. CRAIG			6. JACQUES VIOLLE	
	5. E. KIELY			5. FRANCOIS ZLIGARIC	
	4. G. FEIGHERY			4. ERIC AUGUST	
	3. N. DWYER			3. GEORGES MAGENDIE	
	2. J. MITCHELL (Capt.)			2. ARMAND CLERC	
	1. D. POWER			1. BERNARD CARET	

REFEREE : DAVID BURNETT
(Association of Referees, Leinster Branch)

RESULT :
LANSDOWNE .... Pts.
RACING CLUB DE PARIS .... Pts.

(right) The cover of the Match Programme for the Centenary game between Lansdowne and Munster on 23 September 1972. (below) The team sheet for the Centenary match between Lansdowne and Munster.

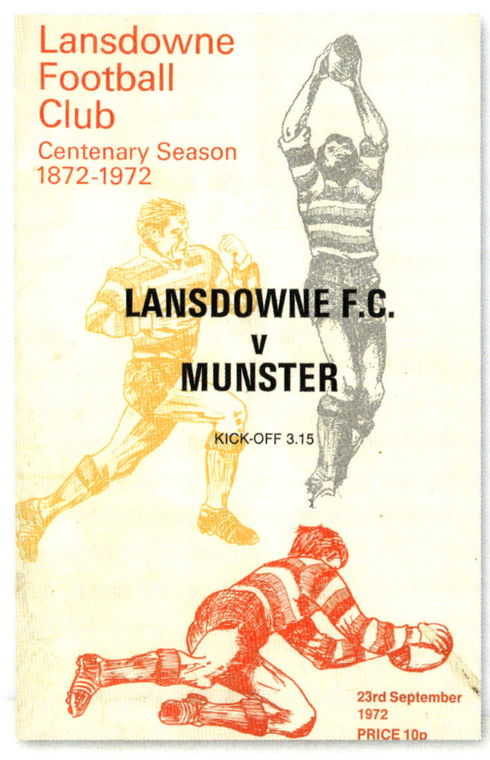

LANSDOWNE F.C. | **MUNSTER**

KICK-OFF 3.15 P.M.

	LANSDOWNE F.C.			MUNSTER	
FULL BACK	15. B. O'RAFFERTY			15. T. KIERNAN	FULL BACK
THREEQUARTERS	14. A. DUGGAN	*Right Wing*	*Left Wing*	11. J. BARRY	THREEQUARTERS
	13. E. MEREDITH	*Right Centre*	*Left Centre*	12. L. MALONEY	
	12. J. KERINS	*Left Centre*	*Right Centre*	13. P. PARFREY	
	11. B. O'NEILL	*Left Wing*	*Right Wing*	14. D. COTTER	
HALF BACKS	10. M. QUINN	*Stand-Off*	*Stand-Off*	10. B. McCANN	HALF BACKS
	9. R. COOKE	*Scrum*	*Scrum*	9. D. CUNIFFE	
FORWARDS	8. P. INGLIS			8. T. MOORE	FORWARDS
	7. G. SHEEHAN			7. N. MURPHY	
	6. J. CRAIG			6. N. ELLIOTT	
	5. E. KIELY			5. E. MOLLOY	
	4. C. FEIGHERY			4. C. MURRAY	
	3. D. COYLE			3. J. BRESLANE	
	2. J. MITCHELL			2. P. WHELAN	
	1. D. POWER			1. P. O'CALLAGHAN	

REFEREE : KEVIN KELLEHER
(Association of Referees, Leinster Branch)

RESULT : LANSDOWNE .... Pts.
MUNSTER .... Pts.

game, against Munster, was lost 23–10, though it once again highlighted the long-standing connection for Lansdowne with Munster rugby.[46]

The centenary celebrations also included the publication of Garry Redmond's *Lansdowne Football Club, Centenary 1872–1972: A Club History*. The book was rightly recognized in the press as setting a very high standard for Club histories, and for shining a light on the administrators and the junior teams that also make up such a huge part of any successful rugby club. The book was launched by the Club President, Jack Coffey, in November 1972 in the Lansdowne pavilion. The event was attended by many former players and members, as well as Eric Dunlop, son of the Club's founder, H.W.D. Dunlop. Eighty years younger than his father, Eric had reminisced in September 1972 in the *Irish Times* about his formative years as a child attending Lansdowne matches in the late 1920s and watching players such as Eugene Davy, Ned Lightfoot and Tommy O'Reilly, all three of whom were also in attendance at the book launch that November. As such, the event offered a perfect continuity from the founding of the Club all the way through to its centenary.[47]

At one hundred years old, Lansdowne FC was venerable, assured and true to its long-standing traditions and ethos. Described by Sean Diffley at the time as 'one of the world's most famous rugby clubs', the years 1946–1972 had seen the Lansdowne First XV win the Leinster Cup on five more occasions as well as a further twenty-one players being capped for Ireland. With a variety of caps between one and twenty-nine, they were: P.J. Berkery; S.J. Byrne; C. Callan; P. Casey; R. Carroll; A.T.A. Duggan; M.A.F. English; N. Feddis; C. Feighery; D. Hingerty; S. Kelly; M.D. Kiely; L. Lynch; B. McGann; S. MacHale; C.J. Murphy; W. O'Connell; M. O'Flanagan; G.F. Reidy; Revd R. Roe; and B.G.M. Wood. The total number of players capped from the foundation of the Club in 1872 to 1972 was sixty-six.[48]

The years 1946–72 had also seen the Club consolidate and build on its success at junior levels. The benefits of leasing a junior ground at Kimmage Grove had been built upon in the 1950s with the purchase of a permanent ground in Templeogue. Combined with the trojan work of Art Campbell and his successors as junior match secretaries, these endeavours had been rewarded with unprecedented success on the pitch and the winning of twenty-two junior titles in those years. As had happened before, however, the continuing expansion of Dublin in the early 1970s was putting pressure on the Club with regard to the Templeogue grounds, owing in particular to plans for a new road to be driven straight through the middle of it. So a buyer for Templeogue and another new junior ground would need to be found, all at a time when the Club was also putting a clearer and more defined coaching structure in place for the junior teams, with a lead being taken in the matter by Tom Reynolds and with others such as Tony Twomey, Mick English, John Barry, Brian Loughney, Tom McNally, Sidney Minch and Tom McKenna stepping into the role in the early years. Alongside the plans for a new clubhouse, such matters served as a reminder that despite having successfully survived one hundred years in existence, new challenges always lay around the corner – and also new opportunities.[49]

GILBERT

Chapter 5

A Dream and a Plan

1973–1995

In the Foreword to the Lansdowne FC Centenary publication in 1972, Judge J.C. Conroy had concluded his remarks by stating that the Club 'start their 101st year as holders of the Leinster Senior Cup, and go into their second century with a dream and a plan'. The dream was for the creation of the most modern purpose-built clubhouse yet seen in Ireland, and the plan was to make that clubhouse the focal point for 'an even finer and stronger club than at present'. The journey to fulfilling both of those aims would come with serious challenges and obstacles, but ultimately Lansdowne delivered on both fronts – and in some style.[1]

The Centenary celebrations that had commenced in later 1972 continued during the first half of 1973. In February a formal dinner was held at Lansdowne Road with 400 guests, the Army Number One Band and a large team of Aer Lingus catering staff. In the absence of a clubhouse capable of

Lansdowne FC portrait of J.F. Coffey. Club President in 1972–3, Coffey had captained the Lansdowne Leinster Senior Cup-winning side in 1948–9 and would go on to serve as President of the IRFU in 1977–8.

accommodating such numbers, a marquee tent was erected for the purpose behind the West Stand. The weather cooperated, and though a tight squeeze for all, the night was deemed a great success. Presided over by the Centenary year Club President, Jack Coffey, the dinner guests included H.W.D. Dunlop's son, Eric, as well as Lansdowne players from the 1920s onwards, such as Sarsfield Hogan, Harry Jack, Sir Theodore Pike and Tommy O'Reilly, and Ireland players of the ilk of Tom Kiernan and Willie John McBride. Then, in March, a special viewing was arranged in the pavilion of a Centenary film presented to the Club by P.J. Carroll and Company. As well as extracts from the three Centenary games played in the autumn of 1972, the film comprised interviews by RTÉ's Fred Cogley with fifteen ex-Lansdowne players whose careers stretched back over seventy years, including O'Reilly, Eugene Davy, Ham Lambert, Jack Arigho, Morgan Crowe and Ned Lightfoot. The latter, musing that forwards had become much more involved in the passing game since the early 1930s, concluded that 'In my day, if you passed the ball to a forward in a game, he most likely wouldn't speak to you that night'. The year's celebrations concluded in the Spring with a Centenary Ball at Lansdowne Road. Once again, a marquee tent was erected for the purpose, though on this occasion on the main pitch.[2]

On the playing field, the Centenary season did not result in any trophies, though it did see Mick Quinn get the first of ten Ireland caps in the Five Nations game against France in April 1973. The season was also notable in that the Club Captain Johnny Mitchell was following in his father Bobby's footsteps in that regard, while his grandfather, Noel, had played on the First XV prior to the First World War. Whether the ongoing celebrations had undermined on-field performance remains unknown, but an injury in February 1973 that brought Alan Duggan's rugby career to an abrupt halt was certainly considered at the time to have put the season in jeopardy for the First XV. Duggan sustained a broken leg in training when he 'was practising a move with his three-quarters and awaiting Eric Meredith, the full-back, to come into the line … Just as Duggan was about to release the ball to Meredith he was tackled by a couple of forwards and he fell in pain'. Duggan was unable to return to playing for Lansdowne until 1975.[3]

The start of the 1973–4 season seemed to offer a bit of a mixed bag for Lansdowne, though the signs of future success were there for those who wished to see. An early season 'laboured win' by 12–4 over a touring Canadian side from Alberta was most notable for the performance of Lansdowne's new recruit, Moss Keane, whose 'power in the rucks and out of touch stamped him as the most effective forward on either team'. Originally from Currow in County Kerry, Keane, like so many others before him, had moved to Dublin for work reasons, being employed in the Department of Agriculture. By choosing to play with Lansdowne, Keane continued that strong connection between the Leinster Club and Munster players. In an eleven-year international career that commenced in 1974, Keane was capped fifty-one times for Ireland and once for the Lions, against New Zealand in 1977. He had only taken up rugby in 1970 when in his early twenties, having prior to that excelled at Gaelic football, representing Kerry at under-21 level and captaining UCC. It was at university that he first took to rugby in 1970 though his first game was under a pseudonym owing to the GAA ban on 'foreign' games. Once the ban was lifted in 1971, Keane began to play rugby more regularly, and quickly rose to interprovincial and international levels as an outstanding and formidable second-row and one of Lansdowne's and Ireland's great players and characters. His move to Lansdowne facilitated his greater education in the game, with Con Murphy, ever-present to assist the First XV in both training and on match-days, providing Keane with invaluable advice. Keane also quickly became a key figure within a new golden era of achievement for Lansdowne's First XV in the 1970s and 1980s, an era fit to rival that of the late 1920s and early 1930s.[4]

With Keane on board as well as the Connacht interprovincial hooker Brendan Troy, the First XV for the 1973–4 season, captained by Dermot Power, went on to win the Club's first Leinster Senior League title in the third year of the competition. The final in December 1973 was against the defending champions, Wanderers, a match that went Lansdowne's way 13–4. With six interprovincials in the forwards, alongside the Irish international second-row Conleth 'Con' Feighery, Lansdowne finally wrapped up the game in the seventy-fifth minute with a push-over try. Once again, Moss Keane was noted as looking 'increasingly of international calibre'. Not surprisingly, the Irish selectors thought likewise, and in January 1974 Keane won the first of his fifty-one caps for Ireland in the Five Nations game against France, a match which also saw Vinny Becker win the first of two Irish caps.[5]

The end of the 1973–4 season also saw the undertaking of a Club tour to Canada in May 1974. The tour, which in the end took in both Canada and the US and had been planned since early 1973, was deemed a success, with three wins from six games. Mick Quinn missed the first three games, having been touring in Bermuda with the Penguins FC invitational side, and his arrival in Canada bolstered the travelling squad for the remaining three matches in which he scored forty-one points. With the first game in Seattle, the remainder were played in Western and Central Canada, in Vancouver and Victoria in British Columbia, in Calgary in Alberta and in Winnipeg in Manitoba. Playing attractive, running rugby throughout, Lansdowne commanded big attendances at the matches, with the final game in Winnipeg televised live. Vinny Becker was hailed as the 'star back' of the tour, scoring eight tries and touching down

Vinny Becker in action for Lansdowne FC. Source: Des Daly Private Collection. Courtesy of UCD.

in all six games, including what was deemed 'one of the greatest tries of his career' when he received the ball from Quinn just outside his own twenty-two and proceeding to beat 'the entire defence *en route* to the line'. The tour was also notable for reviving the 1970 Leinster Schools Senior Cup-winning Newbridge College partnership of Quinn and scrumhalf Stephen Tunney, while the final game also marked the culmination of Noel Hoffman's long service on the Lansdowne First XV, which had commenced back in the 1959–60 season.[6]

Change was very much in the air at that time, as the summer of 1974 also saw the retirement of Mary Kavanagh, after over fifty years of service to the Club. As for the development of the game itself, a significant step was taken by the IRFU in September 1974, on the back of an IRB ruling, to allow for the use of substitutes at all levels of rugby in Ireland. In the first iteration of the idea, substitution was only allowed for players deemed by a doctor to be injured. Although different levels and competitions could have from three to five substitutes in attendance, only two were allowed to be substituted on for injured players.[7]

The winds of change were also blowing in the direction of more structured and expert coaching and training. Like the wider rugby world more generally at that time, the late 1960s and early 1970s had seen an increasing focus by Lansdowne upon the importance of proper coaches and training for all teams. To that end, Lansdowne players participated in the annual Leinster Branch Coaching Scheme held in Mosney, which ran from 1965 to 1974. Early Club adopters of the scheme included the likes of Tom Reynolds, while in 1973 the Club looked to increase the number of current players across all levels who were interested in learning the intricacies of coaching. Thereafter during the 1970s the Club continued to look to develop its coaching structures at all levels. Lansdowne's involvement in the development of proper coaching standards at that time was also seen in the key roles played by Caleb Powell, who served as Chief Instructor at Mosney for a time and then along with Kevin Kelleher took over running courses in the 1970s for schools' coaches. Both Sarsfield Hogan and Kelleher also contributed to the training programmes at Mosney.[8]

On the international front, the issue of Apartheid in South Africa continued to loom large. In early 1973 the Leinster Branch canvassed the rugby clubs as to views on the upcoming 1974 Lions tour to South Africa. The Lansdowne committee concluded that they did not 'have any strong views to be put forward'. The matter also arose in March 1973 when four Irish players, including Mick Quinn, were invited to take part in the Penguins RC invitational tour to South Africa. But during 1974 the pressure on the IRFU increased in relation to the pending Lions tour. The IAAM looked to the IRFU to make a statement reassuring any invited Irish player that they would not be detrimentally affected in relation to future Irish selection if they withdrew from the tour on moral grounds. Such concerns highlighted the types of pressures players faced. A small IAAM protest at IRFU HQ in Lansdowne Road in March included a letter referring to the government's known disapproval of the IRFU's continued involvement in the upcoming tour, as expressed by the Minister for Foreign Affairs, Garret FitzGerald. As a result, in pronouncing its continuing commitment to the tour in April, the IRFU confirmed in explicit terms that all Irish players selected for the Lions had been informed that they could decline the invitation 'without any

Junior 2 League, 1975–6. Standing: M. English (Coach), D. Forbes, P. Dunne, R. Walsh, M. Kearney, J.C. Dawson (Pres.), D. Coyle, B. Ennis, J. Morrissey, P. Berkery (Hon. Sec.). Seated: K. Roche, C. White, B. Farrell, J. Byrne (Capt.), R. Becker, P. O'Reilly, K. Nuzum. On Ground: C. Flanagan, M. Dawson.

fear of being pressurized or penalized'. The tour went ahead as planned and resulted in an historic first-ever Test series victory for the Lions over South Africa. Captained by Ireland's Willie John McBride, the only other Irish players in the Test side were Fergus Slattery and Dick Milliken. There were no Lansdowne players among the Irish tourists, though Mick Quinn was one of the unsummoned reserve out-halves.[9]

With regard to domestic competitions, the next trophy secured by Lansdowne was when the Third XV won the Junior 2 (formerly Minor) League for a seventh time in the 1975–6 season, defeating Old Belvedere in the final on 30 March 1976. Captained by Jim Byrne and coached by Mick English, the team included the likes of David Coyle, Ken Nuzum, Michael 'Mick' Kearney and Michael 'Mick' Dawson – a son of Jack Dawson, and the third generation of the family to play for Lansdowne. The following season both Dawson and Kearney appeared regularly for the First XV, and continued to do so in future years, while Nuzum would become a mainstay of the Lansdowne front-row, first at tighthead prop and thereafter as loosehead from 1978 through to the mid-1980s. Both Dawson and Kearney would also in time go on to senior roles in Leinster and Irish rugby as well: Kearney, who had followed in a long line of Castleknock pupils who joined Lansdowne, served as team manager of the Ireland Under-20s and the Senior Ireland team while also fitting in a year as President of Lansdowne in 1999–2000; and Dawson, one of many generations of CUS students who also joined the Club, after serving as Director of Rugby for three years with Lansdowne in 1998–2001, was appointed to the post of Chief Executive of the Leinster Branch in which role he oversaw an extended period of dramatic transformation, development and advancement in the provincial team's success in the professional era.[10]

In the 1976–7 season the Lansdowne First XV also returned to winning ways. Having moved to Lansdowne for the start of the 1974–5 season, the Munster interprovincial scrumhalf Donal Canniffe captained Lansdowne to a second Senior League title in January 1977 with a 15–3 victory over the defending champions, Wanderers, in the final. Lansdowne were said to have 'steam-rolled' Wanderers with a wholly dominant display up front led by Keane and Patrick 'Paddy' Gahan in the second-row, and with a backrow of Patrick 'Paddy' 'Basher' Boylan, John Flanagan and Basil Conroy playing with 'tremendous verve'. The only try of the game came in injury time and was scored by the Lansdowne wing and Connacht interprovincial, Brian Sparks, who latched on to a loose ball, kicked ahead and won the race for the line. The victorious team also featured James Crowe, who had been capped for Ireland against New Zealand in 1974 while at UCD and was the son of Morgan Crowe, who had been part of Lansdowne's great backline of the late 1920s and early 1930s. The Crowes were just one example of the many multi-generational Lansdowne families such as the Coffeys, Jeffares, Mitchells, Dawsons and others, a tradition that continues at the Club in the twenty-first century. The 1976–7 season also saw the Third As under the captaincy of Eddie O'Connor win the Moran Cup for the fifth time. Two other finals were reached that season, with the Second XV beaten 7–6 by Blackrock in the Metropolitan Cup final and the Third XV losing out to Seapoint in the final of the Junior 2 League.[11]

At the close of the season, in May 1977, Kevin Kelleher made history by being the first representative from the Leinster Schools section to be elected President of the Leinster Branch, serving in the role for the 1977–8 season, at the same time that Jack Coffey was President of the IRFU.[12] Given Kelleher's focus on schoolboy and youth rugby, it was appropriate that back in the 1970–1 season the Leinster Branch had initiated a competition for under-19 club teams and Blackrock RFC had donated a cup for the purpose in honour of a former President of their club, Charlie McCorry. Establishing an under-19 team in a club could be a challenge. In advance of the 1972–3 season, Lansdowne ran a newspaper ad to get players down to the Club in late August, having only thirteen names confirmed at that stage. But already the requirements for future success were being put in place by Colm Flanagan and Ron Wynne, not least in having Mick English as coach for the team that year. The continuing success of Lansdowne's Christmas vacation schoolboy rugby through the work of Colm Madigan and Dougie Spoor offered an ongoing connection to potential future under-19 players in this regard, with thirty-six boys taking part in the December–January games in 1972–3, most of whom came from CUS, Templeogue College, King's Hospital and Castleknock College. Maintaining contact with such players thereafter was also pursued as a strategy for recruitment.[13]

All of the hard work and effort at Under-19s level finally paid off in December 1977 when Lansdowne won the McCorry Cup for the first time, defeating Clontarf 11–Nil in the final. Leading 3–Nil at the end of a closely contested first half, thereafter Lansdowne adapted better to the wet conditions with the forwards playing a major role in the ensuing victory. While the captain Eugene Sheehan, Mark MacWhite and Andy Corcoran were singled out for particular praise in the press, it was Peter Veale who benefited from the power of a close-in maul in order to drive over the line for Lansdowne's first try. The second came from a kick-ahead by MacWhite who was then tackled without the ball, though the Lansdowne centre, Brian Winckworth, 'with a tremendous turn of speed', managed to touch the ball down inches from the dead-ball line.[14]

Such continuing success on the field was also mirrored in the committee-room in relation to securing the best possible future for the Club. While the

Mc CORRY CUP FINAL

DONNYBROOK - 17th DECEMBER, 1977 - KICK-OFF 2.30.

	CLONTARF		LANSDOWNE	
FULL BACK	15. R.T. Green	Full Back	15. D. Cowman	FULL BACK
THREEQUARTERS	14. J.J. McDevitt	Right Wing	14. J. Kearney	THREEQUARTERS
	13. O.F. Halpin	Right Centre	13. C. Walsh	
	12. J.D. Dillon	Left Centre	12. B. Winkworth	
	11. B.N. Sheridan	Left Wing	11. O. Fennell	
HALF BACKS	10. M.J. Owens	Out Half	10. J. Gallagher	HALF BACKS
	9. K.S. Curran	Scrum Half	9. A. Quirke	
FORWARDS	1. S.P. Houlihan	Loose Head Prop	1. C. O'Reilly	FORWARDS
	2. L.D. Dexter	Hooker	2. E. Sheehan (Capt.)	
	3. K.B. Moroney	Tight Head Prop	3. P. Kinsella	
	4. C.J. Cawley	Second Row Lock	4. W. Shaw	
	5. D.H. O'Driscoll	Second Row Lock	5. P. Kearney	
	6. C.L. O'Leary	Wing Forward	6. M. MacWhite	
	7. E.F. Tucker	Wing Forward	7. P. Veale	
	8. N.F. Gaffney (Capt.)	No. 8	8. A. Corcoran	

REPLACEMENTS:
K.C. Mooney
I.N. Carthy
P.P. O'Loughlin

REFEREE
Mr. P. Farrell
(Assoc. of Referees Leinster Branch)

TOUCH JUDGES
Mr. B. Kirwan Mr. S. Mallin
(Assoc. of Referees Leinster Branch)

REPLACEMENTS:
S. Murphy
P. Conroy
T. Carton

Match Programme team sheet for the McCorry Cup final, 17 December 1977.

considerations for building a new pavilion had commenced in the late 1960s, the practical process of raising the required funds was more drawn out. By September 1971 £20,000 had been subscribed by 200 members, though a great deal more was needed with builders' quotes at that stage ranging between £93,000 and £119,000. In light of the expanding city-scape, consideration was also being given to whether to sell the Templeogue ground and purchase a new site further out of the city, which would in turn help to raise money for the new pavilion. Revised plans resulted in a more competitive quote of £75,000 in September 1972. The emergence in early 1973 of the potential for sharing the cost of purchasing a new ground with Old Wesley FC offered another option on spreading the financial burden. At the same time, the first suggestion of a possible ground in Sandyford arose as well, on the dairy farm of Frank Aiken, a mainstay of Irish political life for much of the twentieth century. In March 1973 planning permission was secured for the revised pavilion plan, though the cost continued to creep upwards with a quote of £80,000 during the following months. Royal Trust Bank were prepared to provide bridging finance for the project on the premise that Templeogue was to be sold as well. In that regard, negotiations had been ongoing with Old Wesley for a shared new ground at Cherryfield in Templeogue, at a cost of £90,000, for which the bank was also willing to provide a bridging loan. Time was clearly of the essence, yet further complications arose over the provision of onsite parking for the new pavilion, while a failure to get planning permission held up the proposed sale of Templeogue so that the purchase of the new ground stalled also. In June 1974 agreement was finally reached for the co-purchase with Old Wesley of eleven acres on Kilgobbin Road in Sandyford for a total price of £81,500. With Lansdowne paying fifty percent of that price, the total outlay for the Club when proposed additional costs for building a pavilion and laying out pitches were included was projected at £80,000, though over time this amount crept up towards £86,000.[15]

The purchase and development of the new ground at Kilgobbin went ahead in 1975, though the sale of Templeogue was held up owing to objections to planning permission being sought for the site. Work on Kilgobbin continued regardless and with changing facilities and a tea-room completed by September 1976, a Club management committee was put in place for the grounds comprising the outgoing Club President Jack Dawson alongside Eddie O'Connor and Maurice M. Hayden. The sale of Templeogue was finally completed in October–November 1976, with a purchase price of £152,000. It is of note that the housing estate later built on the old Templeogue grounds is called Lansdowne Park. Once outstanding liabilities had been cleared in relation to Kilgobbin, the Templeogue sale left a sum of £100,000 for investment in the proposed new pavilion at Lansdowne Road. By January 1977, Club junior matches had commenced taking place at Kilgobbin.[16]

In the interim, having been stalled for a while, the matter of the pavilion had regathered momentum in September 1976 when a new committee was appointed to manage the whole process. Under the guidance of Sean MacHale, a series of sub-committees were established in early 1977 to look after a range of matters with different members taking overall responsibility for each.

(left) Lansdowne FC portrait of J.C. Dawson. Club President in 1975–6, Dawson had been a Leinster Senior Cup winner in 1948–9 and Club Captain in 1950–1. A life-long servant to the Club, he went on to be a Lansdowne FC Trustee from 2007 to 2012.

Tony Twomey took on finance, Michael Quinn was responsible for design and planning, John Craig had control of Club re-organization, Thomas O'Reilly looked after any legal issues, and David O'Keeffe was tasked with communications. The overall honorary chairmen of the project were the long-serving Jack Coffey and Eugene Davy, with the latter also being one of five senior members who were the official Trustees for the project, the others being Lt. Col. J.J. Burke-Gaffney, Morgan Crowe, Ned Lightfoot and Billy Sutherland.[17]

The project was initially costed at £235,000, though in the end came in at £275,000 when completed in late 1978. With £100,000 from the sale of Templeogue and over £20,000 raised from members already, the plan was to raise a further £110,000 from members, £25,000 from company donations, and to source the remainder by way of a loan from Allied Irish Banks (AIB). The member donations were to be facilitated by means of individual term loans with AIB guaranteed by the project's Trustees and repayable over either three or five years. When the project was completed, member donations in all shapes and forms had accounted for £130,000 of the total cost. However, by October 1979 there still remained a deficit with the bank of £74,500 on which weekly interest was accruing of £200. With over 300 members having contributed to the cost by that stage, the new plan was to appeal to the

New Pavilion Fund-raising Brochure, 1977.

remaining 400 members for contributions while also running a number of fund-raising activities, including a series of teenage dances and a Lansdowne poker classic. A new building fund committee to oversee the fund-raising was set up under Wyndam Williams.[18]

Construction took place during 1978, commencing in December 1977 with the ceremonial turning of the first sod by Jack Coffey, then serving as President of the IRFU, and John Barrett, the Lansdowne President for the 1977–8 season. As Edmund Van Esbeck said of the project, it would 'provide ultra-modern facilities for one of Ireland's oldest, biggest and most distinguished clubs'. The architect was Don Henihan, the consulting engineers Ove Arup and partners, and the contractor was A. McDonald and Sons. The whole process was a major, and exceptional, undertaking for an Irish rugby club at that point in time, and was in keeping with the dream and plan highlighted in 1972 by Judge J.C. Conroy. More importantly, it was a testament to the belief, commitment, selflessness and drive of the many Lansdowne members who had given of their time and effort over the preceding years to make that dream a reality – both those leading the various sub-committees and the members thereof, including the likes of David Noble who acted as project manager; Hugh Governey who early in the 1977–8 season stepped into the role of honorary secretary in light of the incumbent, John Driscoll, moving to Wales for employment reasons; and Bryan O'Neill and David Glynn. In March 1979, the journal *Architecture in Ireland* featured the new Lansdowne pavilion, noting how exceptional it was for an Irish rugby club to assume 'the role of patron of architecture' in the manner that Lansdowne had.[19]

The official opening of the new pavilion took place on 18 October 1978 and was presided over by the Club President for 1978–9, Aidan McNally. It had been preceded two days earlier by the first Club committee meeting in the new pavilion, by which time the move from the old pavilion had been completed. The opening ceremony was undertaken by Kevin Quilligan, President of the IRFU, while other guests included the lord mayor of Dublin Patrick Belton, government ministers of state Jim Tunney and David Andrews, Eric Dunlop, Ronnie Dawson, Sarsfield Hogan, and the Lansdowne Trustees Davy, Lightfoot, Burke-Gaffney, Crowe and Sutherland, as well as representatives from all of the senior clubs in Leinster and many from the other provinces. A small group of senior members had underwritten the cost of the event.[20]

The new pavilion also heralded a new management structure for the Club to match its new premises and ambitions for the future. The official press release at the time stated that 'the construction of the new pavilion is part of an overall plan by Lansdowne for development of the Club on and off the field of play'. To that end the new management structure had four clearly defined areas of responsibility, with Jack Dawson appointed as Controller of Rugby, Bryan O'Neill as Controller of Clubhouse, Hugh Governey as Controller of Administration, and Billy Sutherland as Controller of Finance. The whole process had commenced with a report in January 1977 from an executive sub-committee chaired by Sean MacHale and comprising Dick Butler, John Driscoll and Gerry Sheedy. On the back of that initial report, a Reorganization Committee had been set up, chaired by John Craig and comprising Bryan O'Neill, Miklos Kos, Martin Rafferty and Paddy Shortall. The new management structure was the end result of their deliberations.[21]

The new pavilion was also of course a fundamental component of the associational nature of club life. Since the foundation of the Club, conviviality and sociability had been a key part of its purpose. That it remained so in 1978 was evident in the concluding statement of the press release for the official opening: 'Lansdowne's aim is to provide for its members and ... families a rugby football and social environment in which the Club will go from strength to strength in the future.'[22]

In relation to the rugby component of that aim, the new pavilion brought good fortune almost immediately on the playing field. The Club Captain for the 1978–9 season was the future Labour TD, Party leader, government minister and Tánaiste, Dick Spring. Hailing from Kerry, Spring had already been capped for Munster before moving to Lansdowne in the 1977–8 season, having also played club rugby for London Irish before then. He also went on to win three caps for Ireland at fullback in 1979. With the likes of MacWhite and Ken Nuzum graduated from the junior ranks in the Club, the First XV won the Leinster Senior Cup for the seventeenth time. Having already defeated Palmerston 11–3, in the quarter final Lansdowne secured a 6–3 victory over Old Belvedere thanks to a Quinn dropped goal. A 3–3 draw with Blackrock in the semi-final meant a mid-week replay, which went down as one of the games of the century. A final 15–9 score-line belied the drama. Before the game, concern had been expressed about Lansdowne's prospects owing to injuries to second-row Paddy Gahan and ball-playing number 8, Michael Gibson, who had won the first four of his ten Ireland caps that season. By half-time Lansdowne were losing 9–Nil, with the likes of Blackrock's Willie Duggan, Brian McLoughlin and Kevin Mays dominating the forward exchanges. Yet in the second half, with the elements finally on their side, Lansdowne were a team transformed. Moss Keane led by example, while the re-jigged backrow of Conroy, Boylan and MacWhite were magnificent. By the seventieth minute the scores were tied at 9–9 following two penalties by Spring and one by Quinn. The match went to extra-time and was decided in the final minute when from a scrum

LEINSTER BRANCH I.R.F.U.

SENIOR CUP FINAL

LANSDOWNE v TERENURE COLLEGE

KICK OFF 4.00 p.m.

PRECEDED BY:

CULLITON (Under 17) CUP FINAL

NAVAN v OLD KILCULLEN

KICK OFF 2.00 p.m.

LANSDOWNE ROAD

SATURDAY 28th APRIL 1979

PROGRAMME: 10p

(left) The cover of the Match Programme for the final of the Leinster Senior Cup between Lansdowne and Terenure College in April 1979, a game which was won 24–3 by Lansdowne. (below) The team sheet for the final of the Leinster Senior Cup between Lansdowne and Terenure College in April 1979.

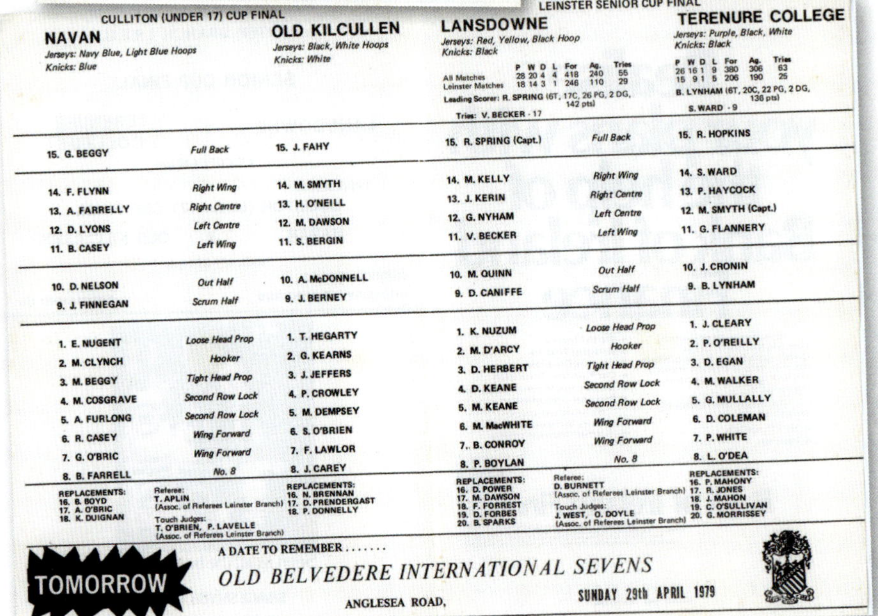

CULLITON (UNDER 17) CUP FINAL

NAVAN *Jerseys: Navy Blue, Light Blue Hoops* *Knicks: Blue*		OLD KILCULLEN *Jerseys: Black, White Hoops* *Knicks: White*
15. G. BEGGY	*Full Back*	15. J. FAHY
14. F. FLYNN	*Right Wing*	14. M. SMYTH
13. A. FARRELLY	*Right Centre*	13. H. O'NEILL
12. D. LYONS	*Left Centre*	12. M. DAWSON
11. B. CASEY	*Left Wing*	11. S. BERGIN
10. D. NELSON	*Out Half*	10. A. McDONNELL
9. J. FINNEGAN	*Scrum Half*	9. J. BERNEY
1. E. NUGENT	*Loose Head Prop*	1. T. HEGARTY
2. M. CLYNCH	*Hooker*	2. G. KEARNS
3. M. BEGGY	*Tight Head Prop*	3. J. JEFFERS
4. M. COSGRAVE	*Second Row Lock*	4. P. CROWLEY
5. A. FURLONG	*Second Row Lock*	5. M. DEMPSEY
6. R. CASEY	*Wing Forward*	6. S. O'BRIEN
7. G. O'BRIC	*Wing Forward*	7. F. LAWLOR
8. B. FARRELL	*No. 8*	8. J. CAREY
REPLACEMENTS: 16. B. BOYD 17. A. O'BRIC 18. K. DUIGNAN	Referee: T. APLIN (Assoc. of Referees Leinster Branch) Touch Judges: T. O'BRIEN, P. LAVELLE (Assoc. of Referees Leinster Branch)	REPLACEMENTS: 16. N. BRENNAN 17. D. PRENDERGAST 18. P. DONNELLY

LEINSTER SENIOR CUP FINAL

LANSDOWNE
Jerseys: Red, Yellow, Black Hoop
Knicks: Black

	P	W	D	L	For	Ag.	Tries
All Matches	28	20	4	4	418	240	55
Leinster Matches	18	14	3	1	246	110	29

Leading Scorer: R. SPRING (6T, 17C, 26 PG, 2 DG, 142 pts)
Tries: V. BECKER - 17

TERENURE COLLEGE
Jerseys: Purple, Black, White
Knicks: Black

P	W	D	L	For	Ag.	Tries
26	16	1	9	380	306	63
15	9	1	5	206	190	25

B. LYNHAM (6T, 20C, 22 PG, 2 DG, 136 pts)
S. WARD - 9

LANSDOWNE		TERENURE COLLEGE
15. R. SPRING (Capt.)	*Full Back*	15. R. HOPKINS
14. M. KELLY	*Right Wing*	14. S. WARD
13. J. KERIN	*Right Centre*	13. P. HAYCOCK
12. G. NYHAM	*Left Centre*	12. M. SMYTH (Capt.)
11. V. BECKER	*Left Wing*	11. G. FLANNERY
10. M. QUINN	*Out Half*	10. J. CRONIN
9. D. CANIFFE	*Scrum Half*	9. B. LYNHAM
1. K. NUZUM	*Loose Head Prop*	1. J. CLEARY
2. M. D'ARCY	*Hooker*	2. P. O'REILLY
3. D. HERBERT	*Tight Head Prop*	3. D. EGAN
4. D. KEANE	*Second Row Lock*	4. M. WALKER
5. M. KEANE	*Second Row Lock*	5. G. MULLALLY
6. M. MacWHITE	*Wing Forward*	6. D. COLEMAN
7,. B. CONROY	*Wing Forward*	7. P. WHITE
8. P. BOYLAN	*No. 8*	8. L. O'DEA
REPLACEMENTS: 16. D. POWER 17. M. DAWSON 18. F. FORREST 19. D. FORBES 20. B. SPARKS	Referee: D. BURNETT (Assoc. of Referees Leinster Branch) Touch Judges: J. WEST, O. DOYLE (Assoc. of Referees Leinster Branch)	REPLACEMENTS: 16. P. MAHONY 17. R. JONES 18. J. MAHON 19. C. O'SULLIVAN 20. G. MORRISSEY

TOMORROW

A DATE TO REMEMBER . . . .

OLD BELVEDERE INTERNATIONAL SEVENS

ANGLESEA ROAD,

SUNDAY 29th APRIL 1979

Leinster Senior Cup, 1978–9. Standing: H. Governey (Hon. Sec.), D. Canniffe, M. Keane, A. McNally (Pres.), D. Keane, C.J. Murphy (Manager), D. Herbert, M. D'Arcy, K. Nuzum, P. Berkery. Seated: M. Kelly, G. Nyhan, P. Boylan, R. Spring (Capt.), V. Becker, J. Kerin, D. Conroy. On Ground: M. Quinn, M. MacWhite.

forty-five metres out the ball was transferred from Canniffe to Quinn to John Kerin to Spring, who burst through the Blackrock defence and ran forty metres to score. For Boylan, at any rate, it was one of the best games of rugby he had ever played in.[23]

In the final, Terenure College RFC were comprehensively beaten 24–3. With Gibson and Gahan still out injured, MacWhite and Derek Keane continued to perform impressively in a game where the Lansdowne forwards dominated throughout. The only try of the match was scored by Kerin in the dying minutes, with the points otherwise coming from penalties and a Mick Quinn dropped goal. Overall, the First XV had lost only four out of twenty-nine matches all season, amassing 442 points for and only 243 against. To add to the season's success, the Third XV won the Junior 2 League for the eighth time.[24]

Securing the Leinster Senior Cup in 1979 was the start of an extended period of success for the Club to rival that of the late 1920s and early 1930s. For the 1979–80 season, with Tony Twomey as Club President, Boylan took over the captaincy of the First XV while also featuring more often in the second

LEINSTER BRANCH I.R.F.U.

1879 – 1979

Leinster Centenary Senior Cup
FINAL

BLACKROCK COLLEGE
V
LANSDOWNE

KICK OFF 4.15 pm

PRECEDED BY

CULLITON (Under 17) CUP FINAL

Kilkenny v Navan

KICK OFF 2.15 pm

LANSDOWNE ROAD,
SATURDAY, 26th APRIL, 1980.

Programme: 20p

(left) The cover of the Match Programme for the final of the Leinster Senior Cup between Lansdowne and Blackrock College in April 1980, a game which was won 16–4 by Lansdowne.
(below) The team sheet for the final of the Leinster Senior Cup between Lansdowne and Blackrock College in April 1980.

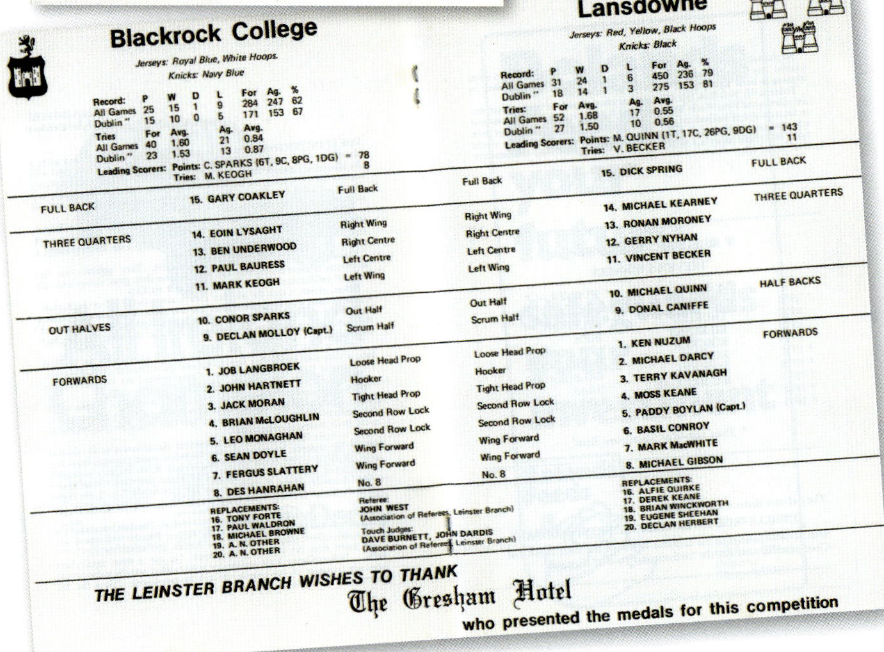

Blackrock College

Jerseys: Royal Blue, White Hoops.
Knicks: Navy Blue

Record:	P	W	D	L	For	Ag.	%
All Games	25	15	1	9	284	247	62
Dublin "	15	10	0	5	171	153	67

Tries	For	Avg.	Ag.	Avg.
All Games	40	1.60	21	0.84
Dublin "	23	1.53	13	0.87

Leading Scorers: Points: C. SPARKS (6T, 9C, 8PG, 1DG) = 78
Tries: M. KEOGH 8

Lansdowne

Jerseys: Red, Yellow, Black Hoops
Knicks: Black

Record:	P	W	D	L	For	Ag.	%
All Games	31	24	1	6	450	236	79
Dublin "	18	14	1	3	275	153	81

Tries:	For	Avg.	Ag.	Avg.
All Games	52	1.68	17	0.55
Dublin "	27	1.50	10	0.56

Leading Scorers: Points: M. QUINN (1T, 17C, 26PG, 9DG) = 143
Tries: V. BECKER 11

	Blackrock College			Lansdowne	
FULL BACK	15. GARY COAKLEY	Full Back	Full Back	15. DICK SPRING	FULL BACK
THREE QUARTERS	14. EOIN LYSAGHT	Right Wing	Right Wing	14. MICHAEL KEARNEY	THREE QUARTERS
	13. BEN UNDERWOOD	Right Centre	Right Centre	13. RONAN MORONEY	
	12. PAUL BAURESS	Left Centre	Left Centre	12. GERRY NYHAN	
	11. MARK KEOGH	Left Wing	Left Wing	11. VINCENT BECKER	
OUT HALVES	10. CONOR SPARKS	Out Half	Out Half	10. MICHAEL QUINN	HALF BACKS
	9. DECLAN MOLLOY (Capt.)	Scrum Half	Scrum Half	9. DONAL CANIFFE	
FORWARDS	1. JOB LANGBROEK	Loose Head Prop	Loose Head Prop	1. KEN NUZUM	FORWARDS
	2. JOHN HARTNETT	Hooker	Hooker	2. MICHAEL DARCY	
	3. JACK MORAN	Tight Head Prop	Tight Head Prop	3. TERRY KAVANAGH	
	4. BRIAN McLOUGHLIN	Second Row Lock	Second Row Lock	4. MOSS KEANE	
	5. LEO MONAGHAN	Second Row Lock	Second Row Lock	5. PADDY BOYLAN (Capt.)	
	6. SEAN DOYLE	Wing Forward	Wing Forward	6. BASIL CONROY	
	7. FERGUS SLATTERY	Wing Forward	Wing Forward	7. MARK MacWHITE	
	8. DES HANRAHAN	No. 8	No. 8	8. MICHAEL GIBSON	

REPLACEMENTS:
16. TONY FORTE
17. PAUL WALDRON
18. MICHAEL BROWNE
19. A. N. OTHER
20. A. N. OTHER

Referee:
JOHN WEST
(Association of Referees, Leinster Branch)

Touch Judges:
DAVE BURNETT, JOHN DARDIS
(Association of Referees, Leinster Branch)

REPLACEMENTS:
16. ALFIE QUIRKE
17. DEREK KEANE
18. BRIAN WINCKWORTH
19. EUGENE SHEEHAN
20. DECLAN HERBERT

THE LEINSTER BRANCH WISHES TO THANK
The Gresham Hotel
who presented the medals for this competition

Leinster Senior Cup, 1979–80. Standing: K. Nuzum, M. MacWhite, B. Conroy, M. Keane, M. Gibson, M. D'Arcy, R. Moroney, T. Kavanagh, H. Governey (Hon. Sec.). Seated: A. Twomey (Pres.), D. Canniffe, M. Quinn, R. Spring, P. Boylan (Capt.), V. Becker, M. Kearney, G. Nyhan, C.J. Murphy (Manager).

row with Keane, with MacWhite playing in the backrow alongside Conroy and Gibson. The First XV also featured the young centre Rory Moroney, who would go on to win three caps for Ireland in 1984–5. As defending champions, Lansdowne proceeded to secure back-to-back Leinster Senior Cup titles, and the Club's eighteenth overall. Having defeated Dublin University 28–9 in the second round with second-half tries from Moroney, Becker and Winckworth, St Mary's were beaten 15–9 in the quarter-final before Clontarf were dispatched 22–6 in the semi-final. Then, contesting their thirtieth Senior Cup Final overall, Lansdowne defeated Blackrock 16–4. On the back of another dominant display from the forwards with Keane and Boylan to the fore, the match-clinching try was scored by the hooker, Michael D'Arcy, who in the seventy-seventh minute had followed up on a break by Quinn and ran the ball in from twenty metres out. Having been trailing 4–3 at half-time, Lansdowne's first try had been scored early in the second half by Gibson and had in reality already put the game beyond Blackrock's reach.[25]

With the Club going from strength-to-strength on the pitch, and following another successful summer tour to Canada, the 1980–1 season resulted in not only a third Leinster Senior Cup title in a row and nineteenth overall, but also a 'double' with the winning of the Leinster Senior League as well. Under the captaincy of Moss Keane and with the Irish international Donal Spring, younger brother of Dick, moving from Dublin University and adding to the competition in the backrow, Lansdowne continued to field a formidable pack of forwards. In the League final in December 1980, Wanderers were defeated 24–6 at a packed Donnybrook stadium. Lansdowne's forward dominance throughout set the platform for the backs to prosper with four tries, two by the veteran Becker and one a piece for Moroney and Donal Spring, all of which were converted by Quinn. As was noted in the *Evening Echo* at the time, four of the victorious Lansdowne team hailed from Munster – Keane, Moroney, Donal Spring and the centre Gerry Nyhan.[26]

In the Leinster Senior Cup in April 1981, Lansdowne commenced their campaign with a 21–15 victory over Blackrock. The game was most notable for Quinn's seventeen-point haul from the boot, which took his seasonal tally to 231 from three tries, forty-two conversions, thirty-six penalty goals and nine dropped goals. His closest rival in Leinster was the Old Wesley fullback, Stephen Hennessy, with 208 points. After a 3–3 draw in the quarter-final with Greystones RFC, Lansdowne won a closely contested replay 13–9 with the result only sealed in the seventy-eighth minute with a try from Moroney. Palmerston were then defeated 8–3 in the semi-final through tries by Becker and the prop, Declan Herbert. In the final Lansdowne's opponents from their 1949 Cup victory, Old Belvedere, were once again defeated, on this occasion by the slimmest of margins, 7–6, with the only try of the game coming once again from Becker. It was of note that Lansdowne's fullback on the day, John Aherne, was the son of Gerald Aherne, who had also been on the victorious side in the 1949 final.[27]

The junior levels of the Club also experienced significant success in the 1980–1 season. Under the captaincy of Alan Ryan, the Second XV ultimately lost out on winning the Junior League to Blackrock, but proceeded to win the Metropolitan Cup in a replay in the final against Old Wesley, thereby securing the Club's seventh such title. The Third XV under Donal Forbes brought the Albert O'Connell Cup back to the Club a decade on from the last success,

(right) The cover of the Match Programme for the final of the Leinster Senior Cup between Lansdowne and Old Belvedere in April 1981, a game which was won 7–6 by Lansdowne.
(below) The team sheet for the final of the Leinster Senior Cup between Lansdowne and Old Belvedere in April 1981.

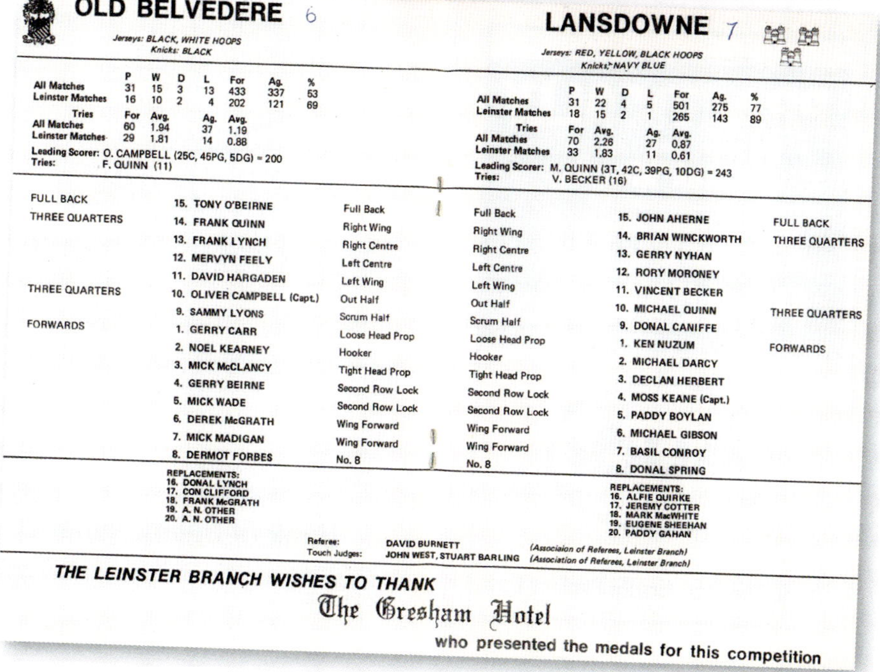

OLD BELVEDERE 6

Jerseys: BLACK, WHITE HOOPS
Knicks: BLACK

	P	W	D	L	For	Ag.	%
All Matches	31	15	3	13	433	337	53
Leinster Matches	16	10	2	4	202	121	69

Tries	For	Avg.	Ag.	Avg.
All Matches	60	1.94	37	1.19
Leinster Matches	29	1.81	14	0.88

Leading Scorer: O. CAMPBELL (25C, 45PG, 5DG) = 200
Tries: F. QUINN (11)

LANSDOWNE 7

Jerseys: RED, YELLOW, BLACK HOOPS
Knicks: NAVY BLUE

	P	W	D	L	For	Ag.	%
All Matches	31	22	4	5	501	275	77
Leinster Matches	18	15	2	1	265	143	89

Tries	For	Avg.	Ag.	Avg.
All Matches	70	2.26	27	0.87
Leinster Matches	33	1.83	11	0.61

Leading Scorer: M. QUINN (3T, 42C, 39PG, 10DG) = 243
Tries: V. BECKER (16)

	Old Belvedere	Position	Position	Lansdowne	
FULL BACK	15. TONY O'BEIRNE	Full Back	Full Back	15. JOHN AHERNE	FULL BACK
THREE QUARTERS	14. FRANK QUINN	Right Wing	Right Wing	14. BRIAN WINCKWORTH	THREE QUARTERS
	13. FRANK LYNCH	Right Centre	Right Centre	13. GERRY NYHAN	
	12. MERVYN FEELY	Left Centre	Left Centre	12. RORY MORONEY	
	11. DAVID HARGADEN	Left Wing	Left Wing	11. VINCENT BECKER	
THREE QUARTERS	10. OLIVER CAMPBELL (Capt.)	Out Half	Out Half	10. MICHAEL QUINN	THREE QUARTERS
	9. SAMMY LYONS	Scrum Half	Scrum Half	9. DONAL CANIFFE	
FORWARDS	1. GERRY CARR	Loose Head Prop	Loose Head Prop	1. KEN NUZUM	FORWARDS
	2. NOEL KEARNEY	Hooker	Hooker	2. MICHAEL DARCY	
	3. MICK McCLANCY	Tight Head Prop	Tight Head Prop	3. DECLAN HERBERT	
	4. GERRY BEIRNE	Second Row Lock	Second Row Lock	4. MOSS KEANE (Capt.)	
	5. MICK WADE	Second Row Lock	Second Row Lock	5. PADDY BOYLAN	
	6. DEREK McGRATH	Wing Forward	Wing Forward	6. MICHAEL GIBSON	
	7. MICK MADIGAN	Wing Forward	Wing Forward	7. BASIL CONROY	
	8. DERMOT FORBES	No. 8	No. 8	8. DONAL SPRING	

REPLACEMENTS (Old Belvedere):
16. DONAL LYNCH
17. CON CLIFFORD
18. FRANK McGRATH
19. A. N. OTHER
20. A. N. OTHER

REPLACEMENTS (Lansdowne):
16. ALFIE QUIRKE
17. JEREMY COTTER
18. MARK MacWHITE
19. EUGENE SHEEHAN
20. PADDY GAHAN

Referee: DAVID BURNETT *(Associaion of Referees, Leinster Branch)*
Touch Judges: JOHN WEST, STUART BARLING *(Association of Referees, Leinster Branch)*

THE LEINSTER BRANCH WISHES TO THANK
The Gresham Hotel
who presented the medals for this competition

Leinster Senior League and Cup, 1980–1. Standing: E. Byrne (Coach), B. Conroy, J. McGeady, M. Gibson, D. Spring, R. Moroney, M. D'Arcy, C.J. Murphy (Manager). Seated: G. Nyhan, D. Herbert, M. Quinn, R. Carroll (Pres.), M. Keane (Capt.), V. Becker, D. Canniffe, P. Boylan. Inset: J. Aherne.

thereby bringing the Club's fifth title in that regard with a great performance in the final against St Mary's. Coached by Johnny Mitchell, the team included the likes of Brian Sparks, Michael Daly, Martin Deasy, James Meenan, James Crowe, and the brothers Mick and Geoffrey Dawson. Not to be outdone, the Third As won the Junior 3 League (formerly the Junior 3A League) under the captaincy of Kevin McAvinchy, beating Terenure in the final, while the Third Cs under Peter Branigan won the James O'Connor Cup for the first time, defeating Old Belvedere in the final.[28]

Lansdowne's great success at junior level and in securing the Club's first ever Senior League and Cup 'double' in 1980–1, following on from the Senior Cup wins of 1979 and 1980, was a remarkable achievement. However, internationally 1980 and 1981 were dominated once again by the question of the sporting boycott of Apartheid South Africa, with Lansdowne players drawn into the maelstrom. By the mid-1970s the tide of public and political opinion had turned decisively and the IAAM had secured a number of victories in their opposition to tours by South African sports teams. In 1979, following a campaign by the IAAM, the Irish government thwarted the IRFU by banning a proposed tour of Ireland by the South African Barbarians. However, the IRFU stood firm in their support for the 1980 British and Irish Lions tour to South Africa. A number of Irish players made known to the Lions selectors that they were unavailable to tour for either personal or professional reasons. Fergus Slattery, a hot favourite to captain the touring side, said the ten-week tour was too long 'for business reasons' but that he would, 'in all probability, have been available' if the touring period was shorter. Donal Spring, then still playing for Dublin University, likewise was unavailable for 'business and personal reasons', as was Paul McNaughton.[29]

Particular focus at the time fell on Moss Keane, given that he worked in the Department of Agriculture and the Irish government were by then wholly opposed to any sporting contact with South Africa. Like Spring, Keane also declared himself unavailable for selection owing to personal reasons. Yet he also rejected speculation that his employer had intervened, stating 'I must emphasize that I got no directive whatsoever from the Department of Agriculture in relation to undertaking this tour. I did not seek leave of absence, my reasons for not going on tour are purely personal and I came to the decision after I had given the matter a great deal of thought'. He also looked to avoid being further drawn into the fraught and tense public debate on the issue by stating that 'There were no political considerations' in his decision. He explained that he had been on tour to Australia in the summer of 1979, and after only a month off had been back training and playing in Ireland in the autumn and that he did not wish to spend another ten weeks in the summer of 1980 away from home before heading back into the next season: 'it would mean almost three years without a break from the game … [which] really is too long'. Keane's explicit denial of any political consideration in his decision hinted at the intense pressure that senior players felt at the time, being wary of displeasing the IRFU and thereby undermining their international career ambitions while also being conscious of the true evil of Apartheid.[30]

In the end, no Lansdowne players were selected for the 1980 Lions tour, but the difficulties were only beginning given that at the same time the IRFU agreed to undertake a tour of South Africa in the summer of 1981. As before, the Leinster Branch consulted with the clubs and after much discussion a majority of the Lansdowne executive committee agreed to support the tour, though it was evident there was disagreement on the matter. The official announcement of the tour was met with widespread anger and disgust and drew opposition from the IAAM, politicians, trade unions and the wider public. Even before the official announcement was made, Edmund van Esbeck reported in November 1980 that the IRFU would struggle to select a touring side given that at least two international players had already stated that they would refuse to travel 'on the grounds of principle'. Other players were also expressing grave reservations about the tour. When the IRFU contacted players in January 1981 to ascertain availability, four immediately declared they would not tour. Paul McNaughton cited the fact that he was moving to America in April as his reason, while Donal Spring, Moss Keane and Tony Ward all refused because of the amorality of Apartheid. The recently capped Hugo MacNeill would also do likewise. Both Ward and Spring had toured in South Africa before. Spring had gone in 1977 with London Irish, and stated that his experiences then convinced him that 'on grounds of principle I do not want to go back'. Ward had been with the Lions in 1980, and again cited his experiences as the reason he could not go back 'on moral grounds'. Moss Keane likewise was on this occasion explicit in declaring his opposition to the tour on moral grounds also.[31]

In South Africa, the news of the players' refusal to travel was praised by Hasan Howa, President of SACOS (South African Council on Sport), the country's anti-Apartheid sports movement. Howa had named Spring in particular, and the Irishman followed up with a more detailed explanation of his decision in *FLAC File*, a magazine produced by the Free Legal Aid Centres. A practicing solicitor, Spring argued that the South African legal code was 'so severe as to make the infamous Penal Laws that once existed in Ireland seem liberal'. He also acknowledged that even though he had opposed the 1974 Lions tour, he had toured with London Irish in 1977 'to see the facts of the case for myself', but realized in retrospect that he should not have gone. While agreeing in principal that sport and politics should not be mixed, he believed the reality was that 'when the evil involved is so fundamental a part of society that it transcends all aspects of human life ... one cannot hide behind a banner labelled sport, trade or tourism'.[32]

By March four more senior players had declared themselves unavailable for 'business and domestic reasons'. But despite growing pressure including a high court case, protests marches and public opposition from religious and youth leaders as well as all political parties and trade unions, the IRFU persisted with the tour, asserting *ad nauseum* that it would assist desegregation in sport, a claim that long-since had been proven untrue. Within Black South Africa, the IRFU's decision was seen as a betrayal. The challenges for the IRFU were seen when the tour squad was announced with ten uncapped players among the twenty-six selected. Such a situation was unprecedented, as was the tour itself.[33] As the journalist Eamonn Sweeney noted many years later, 'There was nothing routine about this tour, Ireland hadn't toured South Africa since 1961, ... [and was] the second-last official international team to travel to the Apartheid state'.[34]

Not surprisingly, the tour was widely condemned. Both the African National Congress and the UN Special Committee against Apartheid condemned it, while Denis Hurley, archbishop of Durban, commented, 'Be quite clear about it. Both white South Africans and the black majority of people in South Africa clearly interpret the tour as an acceptance of the policy of Apartheid'.[35] The reality was that white South Africa saw the tour as 'white solidarity' for Apartheid. Reflecting both the national and international condemnation of such attitudes, RTÉ took the unprecedented decision not to cover the tour, a decision informed by public opinion and by 'the almost unanimous opposition to the tour voiced by elected representatives of every major party, by the official position adopted by the Government ... [and] by the attitude of the United Nations'.[36]

Last minute appeals by the Taoiseach, Charles Haughey, and a picket on several Madigan's pubs in Dublin in an attempt to get the tour manager, Patrick 'Paddy' Madigan, to change his mind, had no effect. Yet the protests and fear of trade union obstruction at Dublin Airport led to the touring side effectively sneaking out of the country in early May, travelling in groups of twos and threes from Dublin and Belfast, before assembling in London. The IAAM commented that the team had 'skulked out of the country'. The initial touring squad had included only one Lansdowne player, Michael Gibson, who ultimately did not travel owing to injury, but two future Club members, Des Fitzgerald, then with Dublin University and originally a product of De La Salle College, Churchtown, and Michael Kiernan, then with Dolphin, were among the uncapped players. During the tour Mick Quinn was called out to replace the injured Ollie Campbell.[37]

Van Esbeck, who covered the tour for the *Irish Times*, concluded that regardless of how 'rugby administrators in Ireland, South Africa and elsewhere may protest about keeping politics out of sport, the structure of South African life is such that the politicians and the laws they frame and keep on the statute books are the biggest single impediment to meaningful multiracial rugby'. Ultimately, from what he saw first-hand in South Africa, he believed 'the weight of evidence indicates that this tour should not have taken place'.[38] In time, many of those involved realized the same thing. John Robbie, one of those who had resigned from his job in order to avail of the ultimate rugby prize of playing for one's country, and who thereafter settled in South Africa, acknowledged in 2020 that it was 'a stain which will never leave me'. In his own words, Robbie stated that his 'desire to be treated like a professional rugby player for a few months and play at the highest level' in 1981 was a decision 'I have lived to regret … my whole life'.[39]

Other controversies began to arise in Irish rugby in the early 1980s as well, in particular with regard to the payment of players by sporting goods manufacturers. The decade would see increasing pressure coming to bear on the amateur ethos of the game that would lead eventually in 1995 to the emergence of the professional game. However, such concerns could not dampen the excitement regarding Ireland's Triple Crown success in 1982, thirty-three years on since that title had last been won by an Irish side. Moss Keane was at the heart of a tremendous pack of forwards in all three victories over Wales, England and Scotland that year at the start of another golden era for Irish rugby. In 1983 the Five Nations Championship title was shared with France in Keane's penultimate season on the Irish team, while in 1985

Metropolitan Cup, 1981–2. Standing: B. Roche (Manager), T. Kavanagh, P. Boylan, P. Gahan, L. Lynch (Pres.), G. Cotter, K. Roberts, A. Ryan, F. Forrest (Coach). Seated: J. Crowe, B. Winckworth, C. Quinn, M. Dawson (Capt.), J. Meenan, J. Flanagan, E. Sheehan.

a Triple Crown and Championship was won once again, with Lansdowne's newest Munster recruit, Michael Kiernan, playing in the centre and kicking the points.[40]

But such lofty concerns did not trouble the vast majority of club players, toiling away in the junior levels. For Lansdowne, that ongoing endeavour bore further fruit in the 1981–2 season when the Second XV under the captaincy of Mick Dawson won the Metropolitan Cup for the second year in a row and eighth time in total, with the Under-19 Charlie Quinn, younger brother of Mick, in the side. Then, at the beginning of the 1982–3 season, tragedy struck the Club on 4 October when one of the new Under-19 players, Brian McGovern, collapsed and died at the end of a fitness training session on the back pitches at Lansdowne Road. McGovern was a talented second-row with Gonzaga College and had just joined the Club along with a number of school friends, all keen to reconnect with their old classmate, Peter Purcell, who had joined Lansdowne the year before and was captain of the Under-19s for 1982–3. Despite being unsuccessful in their pursuit of the McCorry Cup that season,

Moran Cup, 1982–3. Standing: D. Noble (Manager), J. Conmee, P. Austin, M. MacMahon, B. Woods, J. Carney, J. Murray-Hayden, C.I. McGrath, E. Byrne (Coach). Seated: K. Carey, D. Coyle, R. MacMahon, S. MacHale (Pres.), A. Delany (Capt.), P. Bell, J. Meenan, D. Walshe. On Ground: P. Costigan, P. Purcell, J. Lombard, C. Smith.

Greenlea Cup, 1984–5. Standing: J. Flanagan, A. Pinder, M. O'Dwyer, C. O'Keefe, P. Cooke, D. Sheehan, C. Shaw, D. Glynn, F. Kenny, R. Godson, M. Keogh, D. Nolan, D. Spoor. Seated: F. Byrne, N. Gaskin, J. Tuffy, K. Kelleher (Pres.), R. Keevey (Capt.), P. Halpenny, H. McGouran, P. Doyle. On Ground: M. Gaskin (Mascot).

the Under-19s were noted in Club minutes 'as an excellent example of the importance of team spirit' following a mini-tour to Wales at the beginning of March 1983 in which they won both of their fixtures. Although at that time the intention was for the Under-19s to play the remainder of their season with the Third Bs, that year a number of them progressed onto Aidan Delany's Third As and helped to secure a sixth Moran Cup title for the Club – the victorious team included the likes of Purcell, Jack Carney and Rory MacMahon, who thereby got to play on a Cup-winning side with his older brother Mark.[41]

Continued success at junior levels was seen in the following years also. In the 1983–4 season the Third XV under James Meenan won the Albert O'Connell Cup for a sixth time in the Club's history. The following season, 1984–5, brought further trophies to the junior teams: the Third XV under the captaincy of Martin Deasy won the Junior 2 League for the ninth time; John Murray Hayden's Third Bs won the Junior 4 League; and the Third Es under Richard Keevey won the Greenlea Cup for the first time ever in the Club's history. Unfortunately, however, the First XV under Donal Spring were defeated by Wanderers in the final of the Senior League that year, on 'one of those days when everything went wrong'.[42]

For the 1985–6 season the Club Captain was Mark Ryan, son of Senator Eoin Ryan and grandson of Dr James Ryan, government minister and Irish revolutionary. When Mark was appointed to the position, he wryly noted that he was the first non-international captain at the Club in six years. However, as a senior Leinster interprovincial who had first joined Lansdowne in September 1982 having previously played with Dublin University after school in St Michael's and Roscrea, Ryan was well able for the job and had the distinction of being only the second Club Captain to lead the First XV to a Senior League and Cup 'double'. The 1985–6 First XV featured a range of established players such as Noel Downer, Andy Corcoran and Vincent 'Mano' Ryan as well as newer names such as Mano's fellow Connacht interprovincial, Tom Clancy, who would go on to play for Ireland on nine occasions in 1988–9, and the fullback, Philip Danaher, who came from a Munster GAA background and would go on to win twenty-eight caps for Ireland between 1988 and 1995 including captaining his country on three occasions in 1992. The succession from earlier Lansdowne Under-19

Leinster Senior League and Cup, 1985–6. Standing: P. Boylan, D. Canniffe (Coaches), D. Fitzgerald, V. Ryan, A. Corcoran, T. Clancy, J. Daly, R. Moroney, G. Dilger, H. Blake, H. Governey (Hon. Sec.). Seated: W. Burns, C. Quinn, P. Purcell, D. Spring, M. Ryan (Capt.), N. Hayden (Pres.), N. Downer, W. Dawson, P. Danaher, C.J. Murphy (Manager).

teams epitomized by players such as MacWhite, Corcoran and Downer was also evident by the presence in the senior squad of the likes of Peter Purcell, Willie Dawson and Charlie Quinn, who had moved from fullback to backrow. More recent arrivals from the Dublin universities included Willie Burns from UCD and Greg Dilger from TCD. It was also the first season since 1973 in which Moss Keane did not feature in the second-row, having retired from senior rugby at the end of the 1984–5 season.[43]

In the League final at the end of December 1985 Terenure were beaten 16–6, with Donal Spring, recently returned from injury, getting the only try of the match following a short-side break by Downer. It was Lansdowne's fourth Senior League success, which put them on level-pegging with old rivals Wanderers for most titles won. The quest for a twentieth Senior Cup title commenced in March with a first round 12–9 victory over Greystones. In the second round the holders Old Wesley were beaten 12–7, with victory secured in the seventy-fifth minute with a try in the corner from the Lansdowne wing, Purcell. The semi-final saw Bective Rangers beaten 15–10, while in the final Blackrock were defeated 15–9 in a try-less, forward-dominated contest, with Dilger kicking all of Lansdowne's points, including a dropped goal. Overall for the season the team had delivered on Ryan's promise at the start of the season to play Lansdowne's traditional open, running style of rugby. In twenty-nine games, of which twenty-three were won, the First XV scored 543 points and only conceded 290, with seventy-five tries including seventeen by Purcell. Demonstrating the importance of strength-in-depth for any club, a total of forty-five players got game-time on the Firsts that season.[44]

Although Moss Keane had not featured in the 'double' success of 1985–6, he had of course been the first Lansdowne captain to lead the First XV to the Senior League and Cup 'double' in 1980–1. Nor had he trotted off into the sunset. The development of more structured coaching systems since the late 1960s offered another means for older players to give back to the Club. To that end, Keane joined with Mick Quinn in taking over as the coaches of the Lansdowne Under-19s. When the new coaching team was first announced in April 1986, a jocular report in the *Irish Independent* noted that 'A Lansdowne source insists that Moss will concentrate on teaching the sidestep and that Mick will pass on his knowledge of scrummaging'. More seriously, the report also observed that 'it is good to note that the pair are not to be lost to the game. Too often highly talented and experienced players tend to be lost to the game as soon as they retire (Not that either has announced any intention of retiring)'. The new coaching ticket had an immediate effect, with the Under-19s winning the McCorry Cup in the 1986–7 season. With UCD having dominated the Cup for many years, Lansdowne's 12–9 victory over the students in the final in December 1986 was seen as a highly significant moment. In bitterly cold conditions, the game went to extra-time before Lansdowne's Aidan Fitzgerald, previously of De La Salle Churchtown, kicked the winning penalty. The after-match on-field celebration was most notable for the fact that Keane 'pinned at least three Lansdowne players in a bear-hug of delight that was hardly surpassed when Ireland won the Triple Crown' in 1982.[45]

The First XV were not to be outdone and, under the captaincy of Willie Burns, secured a back-to-back Senior League title. Although the 'double' was not repeated, the 1986–7 First XV were voted 'Team of the Season' by the Irish rugby sportswriters as Lansdowne's traditional ethos of open, entertaining running rugby came back to the forefront in thrilling style. With twenty-seven victories

Junior 1 League, 1986–7. Standing: J. Flanagan (Manager/Coach), K. Nuzum, M. MacMahon, A. Ryan, J. Malone, J. Kearney, D. McEvoy, E. Byrne. Seated: P. Ward, M. Dawson, R. MacMahon, J. Craig (Pres.), A. Quirke (Capt.), B. Winckworth, I. Finnigan, B. Conroy. Insert: C. O'Brien, A. McDermott, P. O'Connor.

in thirty-one games and 142 tries, including a Club record of thirty-five tries by Purcell and sixteen by Downer, the team scored a massive total of 872 points, 266 of which belonged to Dilger alone. The Senior League final against Dublin University, which took place in January 1987, was a closely contested game with the only try coming from Lansdowne's newest recruit from Dublin University, Paul Clinch, with the winning points being kicked by Danaher in the seventy-third minute. For good measure, Burns' side threw in a victory over a touring Fijian Barbarians team as well that season. Unfortunately, the Senior Cup was lost in the final. Having 'swept aside' Palmerston 45–12 in the quarter-final and beaten Old Wesley 19–15 with a 'late scoring burst' in the semi-final, Lansdowne lost out 12–13 in the final to St Mary's, who were said to have defied 'all the odds' in winning the tightest of games.[46]

The 1986–7 season also saw the Lansdowne Second XV under the captaincy of Alfie Quirke win the Junior 1 League for the eleventh time in the Club's history. It was twenty-two years since the title had last been secured and so was a particularly satisfying achievement by the team, which included the likes of Mick Dawson, Ken Nuzum, Brian Winckworth, Conor O'Brien, and the MacMahon brothers Mark and Rory, as well as emerging players such as Paul O'Connor and Patrick 'Pat' Ward. The Club was also honoured in March 1987 when Eugene Davy was one of the first two Irish rugby internationals to be inducted into the newly established Rugby Writers of Ireland Hall of Fame.[47]

Ongoing developments at international level driven by commercialization opportunities and wider financial considerations, especially in the Southern Hemisphere countries, saw the 1986–7 season conclude in May–June with the inaugural Rugby World Cup in New Zealand and Australia. Retrospectively perceived as part of the move towards the introduction of professional rugby, the Ireland squad for the first World Cup included both Des Fitzgerald and the flanker Paul Collins, who was formerly of UCC and had come to Lansdowne in the 1986–7 season. Collins was also the incoming Lansdowne Club Captain for the forthcoming 1987–8 season.[48]

Leinster Senior League, 1987–8. Standing: P. Boylan (Coach), N. Downer, C. O'Brien, V. Ryan, T. Clancy, P. O'Connor, D. Spring, M. Ryan, C. Quinn, K. Roberts, B. Poland, W. Burns, P. Purcell, D. Canniffe (Coach). Seated: P. Danaher, D. Moore, P. Clinch, J. Maguire (Pres.), P. Collins (Capt.), C.J. Murphy (Manager), M. Dawson, W. Dawson, G. Dilger.

Having become the most successful team in the Leinster Senior League in 1986–7 with five titles in total, Lansdowne went one better in the 1987–8 season by winning the competition for a sixth time while also becoming the first club to win it three times in a row. In March 1988 the Lansdowne First XV were voted the *Irish Times* team of the month for February for winning the Senior League, having 'scorned adversity' by first defeating the front-runners St Mary's 16–6 in order to force a play-off, and then winning the play-off in extra-time against the same opposition. With Clancy unavailable owing to a pending first cap for Ireland, hooker Willie Burns out with a broken leg, and tighthead Des Fitzgerald a late cry-off with a back injury, Ken Roberts, Mick Dawson and Conor O'Brien stepped into the breach for Lansdowne. The team also included the upcoming Paul O'Connor in the second-row. The score was 9–9 at full-time, but as extra-time ticked away with Lansdowne laying siege to the St Mary's line, a dart by Downer was followed by Mick Dawson forcing his way over to the left of the posts. Dilger added the points, and the League was won. It was a fitting end to the scoring, as Dilger went on that season to score a Club record of 276 points, including two tries, fifty-nine penalty goals, thirty-five conversions and six dropped goals.[49]

The season also proved very successful at the junior levels of the Club. Captained by John Wilson and coached by Terry Kavanagh, the Third XV, having suffered bitter defeat in the last minute of extra-time in the Junior 2 League final against St Mary's, bounced back to win the Albert O'Connell Cup. The Third Bs, coached by Gerry Cullen and captained by Michael 'Butch' Cassidy, a future Club President in 2017–18, won the Junior 4 League with a team that included another of the Dawson clan in Mark Dawson, younger brother of Mick and Geoffrey and a future Club President in 2009–10. Possibly most notable of all, however, was the winning by the Third Ds of the Tom Fox Cup, named in honour of a long-serving former member of the Club. Captained by Danny Doyle and coached by Paddy Gahan, in total the Third Ds had used sixty-eight players during the season. It was also the case that the Third Es under Paddy Halpenny won the Greenlea Cup for a second time, defeating Wanderers in the final. The season also saw Sarsfield Hogan become the second Lansdowne member to be inducted into the Rugby Writers of Ireland Hall of Fame on the second iteration of that award. It also meant that half of the players inducted to that point in time were from Lansdowne.[50]

At the beginning of the 1988–9 season, Dublin University provided two new Lansdowne recruits in John Sexton and Fergus Dunlea, previously a noted schoolboy player with Belvedere College. Sexton had already received the first of his five caps for Ireland in the Millenium match against England in April 1988, while Dunlea was on the cusp of winning three caps in the 1989 Five Nations. Fergus Aherne, having likewise won the first of his seventeen Ireland caps in the Millennium match, was also now on the Lansdowne playing roster having moved from Dolphin, a path taken previously by his father Gerald. It was also the case that Fergus' older brother, John, was already a Cup winner with Lansdowne in 1981, demonstrating once again the inter-generational familial attachments to the Club.[51]

Leinster Senior Cup, 1988–9. Standing: F. Aherne, D. Fitzgerald, T. Clancy, J. Collins, V. Ryan, P. Purcell, W. Dawson, C.J. Murphy (Manager). Seated: F. Dunlea, J. Dawson, P. Ward (Pres.), G. Dilger (Capt.), P. Clinch, C. Quinn, J. Sexton. Inset: P. Ward, D. Spring.

While the First XV did not manage to retain the Senior League title in 1988–9, success was found in the Leinster Senior Cup. In the first round Monkstown were defeated 10–6. Thereafter, the quarter-final against Bective Rangers went to a replay, with the Lansdowne captain, Dilger, kicking all the points in a 24–14 victory. In the semi-final, Old Belvedere were defeated 19–16 in a game in which Lansdowne were said to be 'living dangerously for the third tie on the trot'. Despite falling behind 13–3 at half-time, two tries from Purcell in the second half turned matters Lansdowne's way with Dilger kicking the winning three points ten minutes from time. There was no dangerous living in the final against Terenure, with Lansdowne convincing 29–Nil winners, with a twenty-five-point salvo in the second half. The score-line was the second biggest Cup final winning margin, only bettered by the Club's own 45–Nil victory over Monkstown in 1929. Back then Morgan Crowe had scored a hat-trick – in 1989 Purcell did the same, with both Aherne and Sexton getting one a piece as well. It was also the case that by winning Cup medals in 1989, Aherne and John Dawson, the Lansdowne hooker and younger brother of Mick, Geoffrey and Mark, emulated the success of both their fathers, Gerald Aherne and Jack Dawson, who had done likewise with Lansdowne forty years earlier in 1949. It was also ninety-eight years since Lansdowne had first won the Leinster Senior Cup, while the 1989 victory constituted the Club's twenty-first title, just one place behind Dublin University's title-topping record of twenty-two – a record which was now officially under serious threat.[52]

It was not surprising that once again Purcell was the Club's top try scorer for the season with twenty-four, while Dilger almost surpassed his own Club record points haul with 275. Not to be outdone, however, the Second XV, captained by Noel Downer and coached by the Flanagan brothers, John and Colm, did a Junior 1 League and Metropolitan Cup 'double' which had last been achieved by the Club back in 1965. Heralded as possibly the best Second XV to play for Lansdowne, the 1988–9 squad included both the Quinn and MacMahon brothers, with Mick Quinn pulling the strings at outhalf with Downer at scrumhalf. The 1988–9 season also saw the first competition for the Dunlop Memorial trophy, awarded each year to the winner of the First XV match between Lansdowne and Wanderers – the first iteration thereof ended in a draw. It was also the case that in April 1989 Jack Arigho was inducted into the Rugby Writers of Ireland Hall of Fame, meaning that three of the six people inducted to that point in time were Lansdowne players.[53]

The winning of the Leinster Senior Cup in 1989 marked the culmination of an exceptionally successful four years for the First XV, with five titles secured in total. While the 1989–90 season was unproductive in that respect, it was a key season with regard to qualification for the soon-to-be All-Ireland League (AIL). Considerations for an All-Ireland Senior League had commenced in earnest in the early 1980s. While not all clubs were initially supportive of the initiative, Lansdowne recognized the significance of the proposed plan and, having considered in detail the various options available, chose to support it from early on. It was therefore 'an overwhelming aim' of the Club in 1989–90 to ensure qualification for the top-flight of the new competition when it came on stream in the 1990–1 season. To that end, with Mano Ryan as captain and John Flanagan as coach, the 1989–90 First XV duly secured qualification for the Club to Division One of the AIL. The journey had included a brief return from retirement by Donal Spring to assist in the process, while Conor O'Shea, who was captain of the Under-19s that season, started showing his international potential playing at fullback for the First XV. The season also saw the Third As under the captaincy of Mark Dawson win the Moran Cup for the seventh time in the Club's history, though the trophy was rescinded owing to the inadvertent fielding of an ineligible player.[54]

On the international front in the later 1980s Apartheid continued to dominate world news. In September 1989 a 'heated discussion' had taken place at the Lansdowne AGM over the presence of Irish players and IRFU officials in South Africa at that point in time. The previous year, in the wake of a number of rebel tours to South Africa that made a mockery of IRB rules on amateurism and non-payment of players, most notably the New Zealand Cavaliers (or 'mercenaries' as they were also known), the IRFU had belatedly banned invitations to Irish players to partake in such activity. Although welcomed by the IAAM, Kader Asmal had pointed out that there was still a road to travel in terms of a complete break by international rugby with Apartheid South Africa.[55] However, rather than pursue such aims, the IRFU back-tracked in 1989 and allowed Irish players to take part in a World Rugby XV tour to South Africa in August as part of centenary celebrations in that country. The presence in South Africa of the IRFU President, Ronnie Dawson, alongside the fact that the tour manager was Willie John McBride and the Irish hooker S.J. Smith was part of the travelling team, ensured that there was huge outrage and anger across Ireland, including among a majority of the rugby community. A post-fact apology in September by the IRFU did little to quell the anger as Dick Spring publicly called for Dawson's resignation, having already had a go at the 'complacent gentlemen at the top of the IRFU' who instead of representing 'the players and supporters of an amateur game … ignores the views of players and treats the supporters with contempt'.[56]

While such considerations continued to challenge the IRFU and its membership, at grass-roots level playing club matches on a weekly basis remained the name of the game. For the First XV, the stakes had increased for the 1990–1 season with the first iteration of the AIL. In Division One, Lansdowne were joined by fellow Leinster clubs St Mary's and Wanderers alongside Ballymena, Instonians, Malone, Garryowen, Shannon and Cork Constitution. With emerging players such as Angus McKeen, formerly of King's Hospital School, and Brian Glennon, who was another to come to the Club from De La Salle Churchtown, and a new recruit in the Irish international Noel Mannion, the First XV was captained by Paul Clinch and coached once again by John Flanagan. In the AIL six out of eight games were won, the only two losses coming against Shannon and Cork Constitution, the eventual winners. Lansdowne finished third behind runners-up Garryowen. Better fortune however occurred in the Leinster Senior Cup. In the first round Old Wesley were beaten 22–18, with tries from wing Craig Whelan, Mannion and O'Shea, while Bective Rangers were dismissed 28–3 in the quarter-finals, with two tries from Whelan and one from Glennon, all scored in the second half. In the semi-final Wanderers were defeated 15–12, with all of Lansdowne's points coming from Fergus Aherne, including the clinching try in the seventy-fifth minute. In the final Terenure were defeated 13–9, with the only try of the match coming from a blind-side carry off a scrum by Mannion who gave the scoring pass to Aherne. Terenure laid siege to the Lansdowne line in the last ten minutes, with players held up and tackled short, prompting acting captain Mano Ryan to claim in his victory speech afterwards that 'it had been the most nerve-wracking match he had ever played in'.[57]

So it was that 100 years after first winning the Leinster Senior Cup, Lansdowne secured their record-equalling twenty-second title in the competition. The 1991 Cup was also the Club's sixth Senior title in six years. Combined with the four Senior titles won in 1979–81 and the earlier Cup and League wins in 1971–2, 1973–4 and 1976–7, a total of thirteen Senior titles had been won between 1972 and 1991, of which seven were Senior Cups. It certainly constituted a second golden era on a par with that of 1922–33, when eleven titles were won, with seven Leinster Senior Cups and four Bateman Cups. If there was a difference, it was that the earlier generation had taken less time to win those seven Senior Cups while also securing four 'doubles', three of which were back-to-back. The later generation had done the 'double' twice, in 1980–1 and 1985–6. But whatever way it was viewed, an era of great success had been witnessed from 1972 to 1991.

It was also notable that those two periods of exceptional success at Senior level in the 1920s–30s and the 1970s–80s had been sustained because of the Club's ongoing focus upon and similar successes at junior levels as well, including the endeavours ever since the 1920s to provide improved training and match-day grounds and facilities. The journey out of the debt incurred in building the new pavilion in 1978 took up much of the 1980s with huge efforts made by a range of members in that regard through fund-raising and other activities, including the introduction of the Annual Match Programme in 1985–6 which by the later 1990s had transformed into the very successful and informative annual Yearbook under the editorship of Michael Daly, who acted for many, many years as the Club's statistician and record-keeper. The increasingly complex financial demands of running such a large and successful club required the appointment in 1988–9 of Lansdowne's first general manager, John Geoghegan, while the task of making the Club 'financially fit' in the later 1980s was led by the treasurer, Louis MacSherry, along with Joseph 'Joe' Leddin, then the Controller of Clubhouse / Grounds, and Noel Feddis. By the late 1980s early plans for refurbishment and extension of the pavilion at a projected cost of £250,000 also began to be made as part of such ongoing investment and improvement, a process which also aligned with the increasing focus in the sporting arena on corporate sponsorship. Alongside various trade sponsors in the alcohol and sporting goods industries, at the beginning of the 1990s Lansdowne also commenced a very successful partnership with Eagle Star Insurance (from 1998 part of Zurich Financial Services Group) as the main Club sponsors, a relationship that continued into the 2020s. The ongoing importance of nurturing the game among young players was also seen as the Club established mini-rugby for boys and girls aged 6–14, a project initiated by Mick Quinn in the summer and autumn of 1989 and thereafter driven onward by Michael D'Arcy. Structural changes at national level also saw the beginnings of a shift in focus from Under-19s to Under-20s rugby as a key level of competition for players on leaving secondary school.[58]

The advent of the AIL also led to a new round of administrative restructuring within the Club with a view to better addressing the various new challenges and demands arising from the new national senior league competition. A move to a more transparent wider squad system for the First team was combined with new or revised administrative roles for a rugby director, or chairman or controller of rugby, as variously called, and a coaching director or co-ordinator, alongside the more formalized roles of team manager and senior coaches. The increasing focus on corporate sponsorship and fundraising also saw a dedicated portfolio in that area carried out by Joe Leddin, who arranged the original sponsorship deal in 1991 with Eagle Star. However, owing to a financial downturn caused by a temporary loss of the right to hold student discos in 1991 and the concurrent offer of a post at the Point Depot, the first Club general manager, John Geoghegan, moved on.[59]

The reality is, however, that success in sport is cyclical, and all teams and clubs experience troughs and downturns for a wide range of reasons. At such times, thoughts turn to rebuilding and renewal. So it had been in the later 1930s for Lansdowne, and so it was again in the early 1990s. For the First XV, the early 1990s offered such challenges, most notably in the second season of the AIL in 1991–2, which was one of serious disappointment as the First XV were relegated to Division Two after winning only two of their eight AIL matches.

With the captain, Willie Burns, out injured for much of the campaign, Mano Ryan once again deputized, with John Flanagan continuing as coach. Patrick 'Paddy' Madigan, son of the 1987–8 IRFU President of the same name, having played at Lansdowne as an Under-19 in both the 1982–3 and 1983–4 seasons before spending several years with Greystones RFC, had returned to the Club in the more recent past and held down the hooker role for much of the season, while his younger brother, David, previously of UCD, also featured for the First XV. The team also included at outhalf the Connacht interprovincial and future Irish international, Eric Elwood, in his first season with the Club.[60]

Lansdowne's commitment to regaining Division One status straight away was evident with the appointment for the 1992–3 season of the Club's first professional coach, the New Zealander Graham Taylor. With Fergus Aherne as captain, the First XV proceeded to win all nine of their league games thereby winning Division Two and securing the earnestly sought-after return to the top-flight. The rebuilding process continued thereafter, with Steve Dowrick succeeding Taylor as coach for the next two seasons until March 1995, with the Firsts being captained by John Sexton in 1993–4 and Fergus Aherne for a second time in 1994–5. New players included Stephen Rooney in the backrow, Mark McDermott at hooker, Enda Bohan at prop, Rody Corrigan in the centre and Michael Kearin on the wing and at fullback.[61]

Eric Elwood waiting behind a scrum at the old Lansdowne Road stadium. Source: Des Daly Private Collection. Courtesy of UCD.

Despite the vicissitudes of the First XV in the early years of the AIL, Lansdowne continued to experience success on the pitch at junior levels in the early 1990s. The Third Bs won the Winters Cup for the second time in the Club's history in 1990–1 under the captaincy of Roc Mehigan, another in the long line of CUS pupils to make their way to Lansdowne. The team also included the journalist Rory Godson, a former pupil of both Gonzaga College and Rockwell, who was then writing for the *Dublin Tribune* but would later go on to be the Irish and Business Editor of the *Sunday Times*. In 1991–2, the Third As under Bryan Noble and coached by Paul Clinch and David Coyle won the Junior 3 League for the sixth time. The following season, the Under-19s under Brian Grehan won the McCorry Cup for the third time in the Club's history, defeating Terenure 24–14 in the final in March 1993. The victory-clinching try was scored by the wing, Declan Fassbender, after a sweeping move involving Rory Kearns, Maurice Murphy and David O'Mahony. The team also included other future First XV players such as Enda Bohan, Marcus Dillon, Willie Clancy and the try-scoring Stephen O'Connor.[62]

Winters Cup, 1990–1. Standing: R. Godson, M. Deasy, B. Cooper, R. McDermott, M. Corcoran, J. Kilroy, D. Moran, S. McCoy, J. Kavanagh, J. Shortall. Seated: P. Quinn (Manager), R. Mulligan, R. Connolly, M. Quinn, R. Mehigan (Capt.), D. Treacy, C. Mehigan, T. McInerney, J. Maguire. On Ground: E. Byrne, C. Murtagh. Inset: M. Cassidy.

Junior 3 League, 1991–2. Standing: P. Clinch (Coach), D. Diskin, A. Long, J. Burke, B. Cooper, R. Corrigan, D. McEvoy, K. McDermott, R. Williams, C. Flanagan (Pres.). Seated: J. Tuthill, M. Corcoran, R. MacMahon, B. Noble (Capt.), G. Doyle, T. Riordan, M. Bagnall, P. O'Flynn. On Ground: J. Lombard, B. Conroy. Inset: D. Moran, D. Coyle (Coach), M. Walsh.

The 1992–3 season also saw the Third XV win the Albert O'Connell Cup for the eighth time in the Club's history. Coached by Kevin Moloney and captained by Rory MacMahon, they defeated St Mary's 17–9 in the final, with tries from Peter Purcell and Daniel Doody. The following season, again under the coaching of Moloney and with Seán Twomey, son of Tony, as captain, the Third XV retained the O'Connell Cup, beating Blackrock 9–8 in the final. Then in 1994–5, the Second XV under Gary Collins and coached by Mick Dawson won the Junior 1 League for the thirteenth time, defeating St Mary's in the final. The 1994–5 season was also marked by tragedy, however, when one of the Lansdowne Under-19 players, Tiernan Caffrey, died of a heart attack while guesting in a match for Ashbourne FC against Coolmine in April 1995. A product of Edenderry Rugby Club and a gifted backrow with a great playing future ahead of him, Tiernan had already captained the Leinster Youths team in 1994.[63]

At international level, the first half of the 1990s saw the second and third iterations of the Rugby World Cup. In 1991, it took place in Britain, Ireland and

France, when Lansdowne were represented in the Irish squad by Mannion, Fitzgerald and Aherne. In 1995, heralding the greatly altered world of rugby following the end of Apartheid, it took place in South Africa, when it was presided over most famously by that country's first black President, Nelson Mandela, who had spent twenty-seven years in prison under the previous regime. The Ireland squad included Elwood and former Club player Conor O'Shea as well as a future Lansdowne player, Gabriel Fulcher. Overall during the years 1973–95, a total of twenty-three Lansdowne players had played for Ireland. With a variety of caps between one and fifty-one, they were: L.P.F. Aherne; V. Becker; D.M. Canniffe; T.P.J. Clancy; P.C. Collins; P.P. Danaher; F.J. Dunlea; E.P. Elwood; D. Fitzgerald; M.E. Gibson; B.T. Glennon; M.I. Keane; M.J. Kiernan; B.J. McGann; A. McGowan; R.J. Moroney; D.P. O'Mahony; C.M. O'Shea; M.A. Quinn; M.J.A. Sherry; D.E.J. Spring; R.M. Spring; and J.F. Sexton.[64]

It was also the case that during the period 1973–95 a number of long-serving members of Lansdowne had passed away. At the AGM in April 1976 it was noted that Eddie Carthew, the long-serving junior match secretary, had died the previous year. In late 1976, another long-serving member of the Club, Ken O'Brien, also passed away. Harry Jack also died at the end of 1977, while Ned Lightfoot, one of the members of Lansdowne's great backline of the late 1920s and early 1930s, died in March 1981. He had been Club President in 1951–2, as well as President of the Leinster Branch in 1957–8, having served for over a decade as Lansdowne's Branch representative as well as an Irish Selector in the glory years of 1947–50. Then in May 1982 Gordon Wood died at the young age of fifty-one, while in 1985, the long-serving Mary Kavanagh passed away. At the end of 1987 Sir Ted Pike also died, while in November 1989 Sarsfield Hogan passed away. Considered one of the game's great administrators, both nationally and internationally, he had been a member of the IRB for twenty-five years, as well as serving as IRFU President, Leinster Branch President, President of both Lansdowne and UCD, and a founding father and President of the Irish Universities Rugby Union. Then, in quick succession in April–May 1993 Morgan Crowe and Tommy O'Reilly died – both players had graced the Lansdowne backline in the late 1920s and early 1930s.[65]

Albert O'Connell Cup, 1993–4. Standing: K. Maloney, L. McHale, R. Finnegan, M. Corcoran, J. Desparu, M. Broderick, A. Long, B. McCoy, M. Dawson. Seated: S. O'Connor, W. Clancy, J. Tuttle, R. MacMahon, S. Twomey (Capt.), P. DeLacey, D. McEvoy, D. Bradley, P. Flynn. On Ground: G. Collins, C. Sherwood, M. Bagnall, S. O'Connor.

None of these stalwarts of Lansdowne FC had lived to see the most seismic change in the world of rugby unfold following the 1995 World Cup. Given the seriously fraught and divisive splits caused over the matter back in the later nineteenth century, the advent of professional rugby in late 1995 caused little surprise in reality. In truth, the international rugby world had been heading that way for some time, though often through the back-door rather than openly and transparently. The implications for club rugby in particular, however, were to be both dramatic and traumatic. The playing and financial landscape for clubs like Lansdowne was about to change in a manner never before experienced since the foundation of the Club in 1872. Rising to the challenge while remaining at heart the Club that had survived and thrived for 123 years was the task ahead for Lansdowne FC as it headed into the twenty-first century. The Club's long-standing traditions, legacies and ethos would help it to weather the storm and steer a successful path in this new world.

canterbury
1872
LANSDOWNE F.C.
LANSDOWNE F.C.

Chapter 6

Rising to the Challenge: Being Lansdowne FC

1995–2020

While the decision in late August 1995 by the IRB in Paris to make rugby an 'open' game – a euphemism for professionalism – was greeted with dismay by many involved in the sport, unlike in the late nineteenth century it did not cause a split into two different codes. Unhappy or not, all those involved in Rugby Union remained united in some shape or form. But the new world of professionalism would offer great challenges as well as opportunities for all involved.[1]

The key challenge of professionalism was money. As was pointed out straight away in August 1995, clubs in Ireland did not have the kind of finance needed to pay players the expected £30,000 or £40,000 per annum being quoted in the market. The type of gate receipts, sponsorship and other income big

English and French clubs might command was far removed from the realities of the sport in Ireland. The most prescient observers recognized that the cash-cow in Irish rugby was the IRFU via broadcasting rights and the international team, and that the future for Irish professional rugby lay in a small core of centrally contracted professional players playing for the provinces and Ireland. Those players would also continue to be members of the traditional clubs, but their paymasters would ultimately have the last word as to who they played for, and when.[2]

The concern for clubs was immediate. In November 1995 the IRFU convened a meeting to address the realities of the new situation. The pecking order was clearly outlined as international, interprovincial, and then the clubs, with 'financial rewards' only for international players. In response, the Lansdowne President, Barry McGann, stressed the importance of ensuring that the AIL remained the premier club competition, with the newly re-branded Leinster Championship (formerly the Senior League) and Leinster Senior Cup of equal importance, and that there needed to be clarity on what the IRFU policy would be in relation to the loss of club income arising from the AIL structure and what financial support the IRFU was willing to offer to the clubs. At the same time, the executive committees of Old Belvedere, Wanderers and Lansdowne had entered into preliminary discussions with the IRFU about a theoretical pooling of resources, facilities and player rosters to form a Dublin 'superclub' as one means of addressing the new range of challenges being faced.[3]

Internationally, professionalism and the broadcasting money it attracted threatened to derail the Five Nations Championship during the 1995–6 season, while the exodus of Irish players overseas, especially to England, proved equally challenging for the clubs they left behind. At the same time, the demands laid down by the new monied owners of clubs in England in particular also threatened to derail the nascent European Cup competition as well as unhinge the Five Nations. At the heart of it all was control – of the money, the players, and ultimately the game itself. The teething problems of the transition to an elite professional rugby establishment at the top of a still predominantly amateur game would run on for a while.[4]

There were also a range of other, at times connected, challenges faced by Lansdowne in the second half of the 1990s. One concerned access to the pitches at Lansdowne Road. A key attraction for players in coming to the Club throughout the twentieth century had been the fact that they got to play at the headquarters of Irish rugby. The chance to play on the main pitch of the famous Lansdowne Road Stadium, where generations of international stars had plied their trade, was a very strong pull factor for the Club. But increasing usage by the IRFU and FAI along with focus on health and safety concerns which required the removal of one of the two back pitches led to protracted discussions. Within the Lansdowne committee-room consideration was even given – in theory at least – to the idea of amalgamation with another club with local grounds, especially for mid-week training when trips to Kilgobbin would place excessive demands on players and coaches.[5]

Another challenge related to finance. A growing deficit arose from a combination of factors including a decline in membership owing to a reduction in the number of international tickets available to the Club, separate gate charges for AIL matches, ongoing loss of income due to the restrictions on holding discos and increased expenditure on professional full-time coaching. A pavilion refurbishment was undertaken in 1997–8 as part of the plans for a grander extension, first envisaged in the late 1980s but put on hold in light of the growing financial pressures. The refurbishment included the creation of a mezzanine floor function room in the original two-story sports hall, with additional office space and bar and catering facilities that provided important additional sources of income for the Club.[6]

Declining numbers of spectators attending matches, especially those games that in the past drew large crowds such as the Leinster Senior Cup, was also seen as a problem. The AIL had already put some pressure on numbers in that regard, but the emergence of the professional provincial franchises with fixtures against top sides from Wales, Scotland, Italy, and especially England and France, added to that decline. Yet amateur rugby remained a game fundamentally for the player. As Moss Keane had famously put it when reflecting on his initial impression of the game, 'it was like a pornographic movie – very frustrating for those watching and only enjoyable for those

(left) Lansdowne FC portrait of Eugene Davy. A very active member of Lansdowne even after his playing days were over, Davy served as Club President in 1954–5 and later as a Trustee. He was also President of the IRFU in 1967–8.

participating'. As long as players wanted to play and associate, clubs would continue to exist. In that regard, the club game continued to rely fundamentally upon the commitment and time of volunteers as administrators, organizers and coaches, with the sociability and conviviality of the clubhouse central to survival.[7]

For some older Lansdowne stalwarts, all of these concerns were but drops in the ocean. In November 1996 Eugene Davy passed away at the age of ninety-two. One of the greats of Lansdowne and Irish rugby, he had continued throughout his life as an active and crucial member of the Club. That lifelong commitment to Lansdowne was the essence of what makes a club both survive and thrive, even in a professional era. However, in all the obituaries and appreciations written about him at the time of his death, what stood out most was the overriding sense that he was a man of humility, integrity and compassion. As such, he had served Lansdowne well. Three years later, in November 1999, Jack Arigho also died at the age of ninety-two, leaving only Ham Lambert from the legendary Lansdowne backline of the late 1920s and early 1930s. Lambert lived on till the grand age of ninety-six, passing away in October 2006. The late 1990s also saw the passing of other Club stalwarts and ex-presidents, including both Johnny Maguire and Harold Vard in 1996 and Bobby Mitchell in 1997.[8]

On the domestic competition front, in the 1995–6 season the Lansdowne Third Ds had kept the Club's trophy cabinet stocked by winning the Tom

Leinster Senior Cup, 1996–7. Standing: P. Clinch (Coach), J. Leddin, F. Thompson (Hon. Sec.), B. McCoy, W. O'Kelly, S. Rooney, C. McEntee, P. O'Connor, S. O'Connor, E. Bohan, A. McCullen, K. Lewis, V. Ryan (Asst. Coach), P. Inglis (Pres.), M. Dawson (Manager). Kneeling: E. Elwood, I. Murphy, A. Reddan, M. McDermott (Capt.), B. Glennon, M. Dillon, K. McQuilkin, R. Governey, R. Corrigan.

Fox Cup for the second time. At First-team level, for the 1996–7 season Paul Clinch entered into a second year as head coach, with Mano Ryan assisting once again. Under the captaincy of the hooker Mark McDermott, and with the brothers Paul and Stephen O'Connor paired in the second-row, Lansdowne got off to an excellent start in the AIL, winning six of the first seven matches and topping the table at the halfway stage. Of most note was a 42–15 away victory over Young Munster, when Richard Governey kicked seventeen points in the absence of Elwood, while wing Marcus Dillon scored a hat-trick to complement an earlier try by Angus McKeen and a penalty try. Two close defeats against Ballymena and Garryowen and a final day loss to Terenure meant that Lansdowne finished as runners-up to Shannon, who secured their third AIL title in a row that year.[9]

Better fortune awaited in the Leinster Senior Cup. Having defeated De La Salle Palmerston FC (DLSP) in an ill-tempered first-round game, the quarter-final was against the holders, Terenure. With the Leinster and future Ireland fullback Girvan Dempsey scoring two of their tries, Terenure pushed Lansdowne all the way in a closely contested affair which finished 32–30, with Lansdowne's tries coming from David O'Mahony, Glennon, and the match-clincher from McDermott. In the semi-final Dublin University were ultimately well-beaten, but not before the students had raced into a 12–Nil lead in the opening eight minutes. Thereafter however tries from Elwood, Glennon and backrow Colin McEntee steadied the ship before two Elwood dropped goals put some distance between the sides. With the wind at their backs in the second half, Lansdowne began to enjoy themselves with further tries from wing Alan Reddan, backrow Andy Doyle, McEntee, Paul O'Connor and a brace from Dillon before Elwood grabbed his second to finish off the game. Having run in ten tries in total against Dublin University, Lansdowne were widely favoured in the final against Bective Rangers. The pundits proved correct, as Lansdowne won 40–8, with a hat-trick of tries from Reddan and one a piece for McDermott and Rody Corrigan. The victory gave Lansdowne their twenty-third title, placing them one ahead of Dublin University and outright first in the all-time winners table. It was also the case that the medal-winning second-row combination of brothers Paul and Stephen O'Connor added a new layer to the Club's long tradition of multiple family members winning medals for various teams with Lansdowne. Not surprisingly, probably the proudest person at the final was their father, Rory O'Connor, for decades a larger-than-life character around the Club, whether as a player in the late 1960s and 1970s or as chairman of the social committee, team manager, fund-raiser or youth team developer. Still only in his mid-fifties, he was tragically killed only weeks later in a car crash in County Mayo.[10]

The celebrations to mark Lansdowne's 125th anniversary during the 1997–8 season included a match in October 1997 against a French Barbarians side,

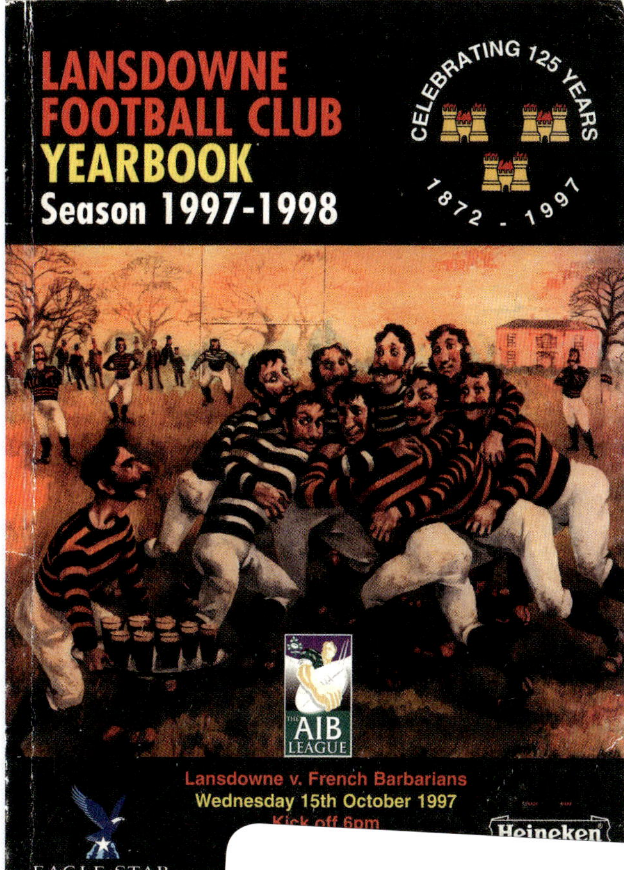

(left) The cover of the Lansdowne FC 125th Anniversary Yearbook, 1997–8.

The President and Executive Committee
of Lansdowne F.C.
cordially invite

....

to attend
Lansdowne President's XV
v.
French Barbarians

Kick-off 6.00 pm. on Wednesday, 15 October, 1997

The match will be preceded by a Drinks Reception
in the I.R.F.U. Reception Rooms (under the West Stand)
at 5.00 p.m. and followed by Dinner in
the Lansdowne Clubhouse at 8.30 p.m.

(right) The invitation card for the 125th Anniversary Lansdowne President's XV versus the French Barbarians Match and Dinner, October 1997.

managed by the great Serge Blanco and presided over by the legendary Jean Pierre Rives. In the match itself, won by the star-studded Barbarians 31–24 despite a late Elwood-inspired come-back, the O'Connor brothers lined out on opposite sides, with Paul playing in the Barbarians second-row alongside Oliver Roumat. Captained by Denis Charvet, the Barbarians scored five tries, with both Cristophe Dominici and Franck Corrihons getting two a piece with Marc Lievremont the other scorer. Lansdowne hit back with tries from the hooker Cormac Egan, Stephen O'Connor, wing Craig Whelan and scrum-half David O'Mahony.[11]

Despite a disappointing AIL campaign, the 1997–8 season still resulted in a 'double' for the First XV under the captaincy of Kurt McQuilkin, a New Zealander who had won five caps for Ireland in 1996–7. In the first half of the season the re-branded Leinster Championship (formerly the Senior League)

Leinster Senior League and Cup, 1997–8. Standing: F. Thompson (Hon. Sec.), C. Egan, E. Bohan, S. O'Connor, C. McEntee, W. Aherne, S. Rooney, G. Molloy, O. Ennis, M. Cosgrave (Coach). Seated: A. McNally (Asst. Manager), W. Clancy, D. O'Mahony, R. Kearns, K. McQuilkin (Capt.), P. Van Cauwelaert (Pres.), B. Glennon, M. McNamara, M. Dawson (Manager). Inset: S. Horgan, J. Woods, G. White (Asst. Coach).

Leinster Branch President, Caleb Powell, and Lansdowne Captain Kurt McQuilkin, 1997–8 season. Source: Des Daly Private Collection. Courtesy of UCD.

Lansdowne FC First XV trophy-winning team immediately after the final, 1997–8 season. Source: Des Daly Private Collection. Courtesy of UCD.

was won for the seventh time, with a 31–13 victory over Terenure in the final. With nine representative players unavailable for the competition, huge reliance on players from the Seconds and Thirds was rightly commended by the Club Secretary, Frank Thompson, in his annual report. After Christmas, the Leinster Senior Cup was won for the twenty-fourth time. In the first round, old rivals Wanderers were defeated 16–14, while Monkstown were beaten 26–10 in the second round, before Old Wesley were beaten 32–6 in the quarter-final with two tries a piece from McEntee and the wing Melvin McNamara. In the semi-final DLSP were beaten 30–20 in a hard-fought battle, while in the final the ultimate underdogs, Skerries RFC, were defeated 23–17 on their first occasion in the last stage of the competition. With Glennon at outhalf, the future Ireland and Lions international Shane Horgan in the centre with McQuilkin, and the carrying of the likes of Stephen Rooney, McEntee and Stephen O'Connor, Lansdowne scored two tries, the first by Glennon in the dying minutes of the first half, and the second when Glennon broke from deep to eventually give the scoring pass to the wing Willie Clancy. Fullback Rory Kearns kicked all the remaining points. Skerries kept the game in the balance right to the end, earning the plaudits of the media and the crowd. The victory also secured Lansdowne's second Cup title in a row. The demands of playing in three different competitions, and winning two of them, had ensured that a total of forty-three players had played on the First XV during the season.[12]

The 1997–8 season had also been the first in which the Leinster Branch had done away with Under-19 level competition and replaced it with an Under-20 system focused on two teams per club, with the first team playing in the J.P. Fanagan League (inaugurated in the 1995–6 season) and the re-defined McCorry Cup, and the second team playing in a separate league for a Pennant Trophy. Lansdowne's Under-20s were coached by Charlie Quinn, while the team manager was Eddie Byrne, junior, who, like his father, Eddie Byrne, senior, was a long-standing member and supporter of the Club.[13]

The season concluded in May 1998 with a First XV tour to South Africa at the invitation of the Wellington Club, which was celebrating its centenary year. Then in July, a surprise party was held at Lansdowne for Moss Keane's fiftieth birthday. Organized by Moss' wife, Anne, there were close on 300 people in

The cover of a Lansdowne FC Membership Card for the 1997–8 season.

attendance, and the celebrations went on long into the night – longer in fact than the 1.30 a.m. bar extension allowed. The arrival of the police at 2.50 a.m. finally brought matters to a close, with the resultant fine of £300 being considered a let-off. The fact that the District Court Judge who imposed the fine was understood to be a member of Blackrock RFC was deemed a fortunate occurrence in that regard.[14]

On the pitch, the increasing demands of the professional provincial franchises for access to players led to tensions with clubs. As the provinces became more successful, especially in European competition, the challenge increased for clubs with less and less access to their representative players. Fears increased about spectator attendance and playing standards in the AIL if it was to be shorn of the top players. The commencement of the 1998–9 season was overshadowed by increasing concern in the Lansdowne committee-room that the proliferation of provincial games signalled that the IRFU were 'going down the road of full professional squads'. But such issues also helped to focus attention on making sure that the structures for survival were in place regardless of such developments. To that end, plans began to be made for setting up youth teams at Under-14, Under-16 and Under-18 levels, which was something that the parents of the minis were very keen to see occurring. Likewise, in the lead in to the second iteration of the new Under-20s level of competition Lansdowne looked to put greater emphasis upon organization at that level, with the appointment of Rory MacMahon as Under-20s Controller of Rugby, and the retention of Eddie Byrne as team manager and Charlie Quinn as the coach.[15]

The increased emphasis on the Under-20s reaped immediate awards. With the long tradition of generational continuity at the Club in the guise of Karl and David Becker and Michael Quinn all following their fathers into Lansdowne colours, success was achieved in April 1999 in the J.P. Fanagan League final with a 15–7 victory against Skerries. Thereafter they went on to defeat the favourites, UCC, in the semi-final of the Under-20s All Ireland Trophy, and secured victory over Rainey Old Boys in the final.[16]

It was also of note that the Third XV won the Albert O'Connell Cup for the ninth time in the Club's history that season under the captaincy of Gavin Lee, defeating Terenure 19–7 in the final, while the Third As under Ryan McCarthy won the Junior 3 League for the seventh time. Yet such successes were over-shadowed by the most serious, life-changing event at a junior fixture in February 1999. In a freak accident, the grandson of M.J. Dunne, Mark Governey, who was playing fullback for the Lansdowne Third Bs in a match against Old Belvedere, suffered a C4 spinal cord injury following a tackle that led to an ensuing collision with another player. Unconscious and not breathing, Mark was kept alive through the administration of CPR by a nurse, Evelyn Quinn, who was also the sister-in-law of Mick and Charlie Quinn. Evelyn was at Kilgobbin that day attending to the medical concerns of a Lansdowne Under-20s game on the adjacent pitch. Mark was eventually taken to the Mater Hospital by ambulance and regained consciousness the next day, though remained on a ventilator for six months, followed by a year in the National Rehabilitation Centre. The reality of his injury was complete paralysis from the neck down and a life wholly altered overnight. The required insurance for all club players at the time only paid £500,000 for complete disability, a sum that was wholly inadequate for providing for the needs of a young man with most of his life ahead of him. As a result, Lansdowne got involved with the setting up a Trust Fund to make up the very substantial difference needed. Among the fund-raising activities, in March 2000 the Club organized a dinner on the eve of the Ireland–Wales

Albert O'Connell Cup, 1998–9. Standing: D. Flynn (Coach), D. O'Mahoney, M. Cheevers, D. Quigley, B. Geraghty, D. Fallon, B. Nestor, R. Mitchell, B. O'Connell, S. Keogh, B. Winckworth (Manager). Seated: G. Clarke, R. Mooney, I. Darcy, A. Duggan (Pres.), G. Lee (Capt.), G. Molloy, B. Kelly, K. Cleere, B. McCoy.

A match excursion ticket from the 1998–9 season.

Transland Express Train

9.15

SHANNON R.F.C.

V

LANSDOWNE F.C.

• Saturday 16th January 1999 •

£45

international at Lansdowne Road. Over the ensuing years various Lansdowne members have served as Trustees as part of the ongoing process of providing the much-needed funds to facilitate Mark living as full a life as possible. Mark went on to complete his studies at UCD with a Masters of Business Studies in 2002 and thereafter to work for Bank of Ireland in Business Services. He has also continued attending international rugby matches at Lansdowne Road and watching European Cup rugby, while also maintaining contact with Lansdowne FC, becoming an honorary life member in 2010.[17]

With regards to international rugby, the first Rugby World Cup of the professional era, hosted for the most part in Wales, dominated the opening of the 1999–2000 season. Lansdowne were represented in the Irish squad by Reggie Corrigan and Angus McKeen. On the domestic front, the season also saw another round of restructuring of the club game, when the IRFU introduced a financial support scheme. The criteria set was for Division One clubs to receive up to £33,000 per year, reducing to £22,000 for Division Two, £16,000 for Division Three, and £11,000 for Division Four.[18]

For the Lansdowne First XV, in their second year under the coaching of Michael Cosgrove, the 1999–2000 season commenced in fine style with a series of victories in the Leinster Championship against Blackrock, Dublin University, Skerries, Old Belvedere and Old Wesley, before Blackrock were beaten again at semi-final stage to set up a final against Clontarf. Pre-match uncertainty over the availability of the professional Leinster players Barry Everitt and Gordon D'Arcy, who had recently received the first of eighty-two Ireland caps, proved unfounded as Lansdowne went on to record a 33–13 victory, with Andrew O'Neill scoring two tries in a first half which also saw Enda Bohan touching down. Ray Niland added a fourth in the second half to give Lansdowne a convincing win and an eighth Leinster Championship / League title.[19]

Securing the Leinster Championship proved the best preparation for the delayed start to the AIL, as Lansdowne commenced proceedings with a 25–14 home victory over Shannon. Some patchy form thereafter meant that the last two league games had to be won in order to get into the semi-finals, a task that was duly completed against Ballymena and Young Munster. In the semi-final, Terenure were defeated 29–13 with Everitt scoring two tries, three penalties,

A Lansdowne FC Schoolboy / Schoolgirl match pass for the 1999–2000 season.

LANSDOWNE F.C.

LANSDOWNE F.C.

EAGLE STAR

SCHOOLBOY / SCHOOLGIRL
SEASON PASS 1999-2000

ADMITS BEARER TO ALL
LANSDOWNE F.C. HOME MATCHES

MICHAEL DALY
Honorary Secretary

a dropped goal and a conversion. The ensuing final was the first in the AIL's history to be contested without a Munster club in it. Instead, Lansdowne faced St Mary's in an all-Leinster affair. Considered the country's two form sides that season, both teams were packed with professional provincial and Ireland players: Victor Costello, Mark McHugh, Denis Hickie, Malcolm O'Kelly and Trevor Brennan were in the blue of St Mary's, while Lansdowne fielded the likes of Everitt, Corrigan, McKeen, Horgan, D'Arcy, McEntee, Aidan McCullen, Liam Toland and the captain, David O'Mahony. The last two had both represented Munster before later moving to Leinster. St Mary's won the closely-contested game 25–22, with a try apiece to each team and the rest of the points coming from the boots of McHugh and Everitt. Lansdowne's try came too late in the eighty-second minute when Niland finished off a move centred around Horgan and D'Arcy.[20]

The First XV's loss in the AIL final was compensated for in part by continuing success at junior levels. Captained by Bohan and with the likes of Clancy, Rooney, Stephen O'Connor and Gabriel Fulcher on the playing roster, the Second XV won the Metropolitan Cup for the tenth time in the Club's history, beating Blackrock 21–18 in the final in extra-time with a late David Quigley dropped goal. The season also saw the Third XV win the Albert O'Connell Cup for the tenth time as well, and for the second time in a row. The team had been coached by Brian Allen, a recently arrived Australian working for an asset management company in the International Financial Services Centre in Dublin's city centre.[21]

David O'Mahony in action for Lansdowne FC against Cork Constitution at the old Lansdowne Road stadium.

Having been appointed to assist Michael Cosgrave with the First XV for the 2000–1 season, Allen took over as head coach when Cosgrave had to bow out for personal reasons. The club game was still struggling with professionalism, as clubs sunk into greater financial difficulties as they tried to keep or attract players through the offer of payment or other incentives while the players themselves became more divided over the expectations of a small elite versus the realities of paying your own way for the vast majority. The junior levels of the club game were also being affected with fewer players continuing to play at lower levels as well. The decline in the number of supporters at games also negatively impacted both club finances and player motivation.[22]

Yet Lansdowne's increasing endeavours at grass-roots level continued to reap rewards despite the challenging wider rugby environment. In the 2000–1 season, the Under-20s, coached by Andy Doyle and Declan Fassbender and under their Controller of Rugby, Eddie Byrne, won the J.P. Fanagan League for the second time in three years, defeating a much-fancied UCD in the final. Having taken an early seven-point lead, Lansdowne were down 20–10 early in the second half. However, having fought their way back to a two-point deficit at 20–18 with minutes to go, the number 8 Conor Gahan pounced on a loose ball from a defensive UCD five-metre scrum to put Lansdowne ahead 25–20 in injury time, Andy Tallon having added the conversion. To rub salt in the wound, almost straight from the restart Lansdowne's captain Will Stafford scored another try, which with another Tallon conversion, left the final score-line 32–20. Three of the team – John Lyne, Niall Ronan and Tallon – went on to win Under-19 representative honours with Ireland that year also. Lyne would go on to play professionally for both Leinster and Connacht, while Ronan would do likewise with Leinster, Munster and Ireland.[23]

Metropolitan Cup, 1999–2000. Standing: D. Flynn (Coach), A. Higgins (Coach), D. Fassbender, G. Fulcher, N. Gunne, R. Geraghty, S. O'Neill, C. Egan, S. McEntee, S. Rooney, A. O'Neill, B. Winckworth (Manager), B. Corrigan (Asst. Manager). Seated: S. O'Connor, W. Clancy, K. Becker, E. Bohan (Capt.), M. Kearney (Pres.), R. Corrigan, D. Quigley, S. Cooney, S. Keogh.

Dedication to the cause was also demonstrated in other, more traditional ways. Lansdowne, like many other clubs, had a long tradition of 'Golden Oldies' teams which facilitated those who had ostensibly retired from competitive rugby to play the occasional game or tournament against others who similarly had reached a stage in life where their old rugby shorts and jerseys now seemed a bit too tight and the pitch a bit too long and wide. Alongside taking on coaching roles, participating in 'Golden Oldies' games kept players in touch with the game through meetings with old comrades and foes, and memorable trips overseas to the likes of the US, Australia, New Zealand, South Africa and Argentina. Occasionally, the Golden Oldie might forget that he had actually retired, however, as happened for Lansdowne's Frank Kenny, caught by his daughter playing for the Third Bs when they were a man short in Kilgobbin in 2000–1, thirty years after he had first joined the Club in the 1970–1 season having finished school at CUS. In that latter regard, he had also followed in the footsteps of his father and older brother before him, thereby maintaining another long-standing Lansdowne tradition.[24]

For the 2001–2 season, the former Ulster head coach, Harry Williams, took charge of the Lansdowne First XV. It was a notable occurrence in a notable season which saw the Club officially win its 100th Leinster Branch trophy when the Leinster Championship was secured for the ninth time. Under the captaincy of Rooney, and with experience of the likes of Toland, O'Connor, Bohan and McKeen up front and with O'Mahony and the former Leinster outhalf Alan McGowan at halfback, the First XV defeated Clontarf 18–16 in the league final in January 2002. A first-half try by prop Anthony Ronan was added to in the second half with a try by McGowan, who also kicked two penalties and one conversion.[25]

The Club also racked up its 101st official Leinster title that season when the Third Cs won the James O'Connor Cup for the second time. It was no ordinary success, either. In response to the shortage of players at junior levels, a group of retired senior players decided to get together for one last competition. Some were not regraded by the Leinster Branch so they took on other roles, with Glennon acting as coach, Boylan as manager, and McDermott and Conor English as the bagmen. Still not clear on the difference between Golden

Stephen Rooney receives the Leinster Senior Championship trophy from Leinster Branch President, John West, in January 2002.

Oldies and junior rugby, Frank Kenny at the age of fifty-two was the oldest member of the squad, coming on in the final as a replacement. But it was a team for the ages, or of the ages. Captained by Pat Ward, the team for the final included the likes of Paul O'Connor, Mick Kearin, Paul Clinch, John Collins and Declan Fassbender, while hamstring injuries in earlier rounds had ruled out players such as Craig Whelan, Sean Twomey and John Quinn. Playing against an Old Wesley side formed from their Under-20s, Glennon's fear was that Lansdowne's 23–3 lead at half-time would not be enough as fitness and stamina kicked in. Yet despite conceding three long-range tries in the second half, Lansdowne went on to win 33–18.[26]

With more players starting to come through from the Under-20s system at the Club, the 2002–3 season was filled with running rugby. In his second season as coach of the First XV, Harry Williams was assisted by McQuilken and Andy Doyle. On the pitch, senior players of the likes of Rooney and McKeen, who had both racked up over 100 league appearances each, were supplemented by younger players such as Karl Becker, who scored seven tries in the AIL run to a semi-final showdown with Ballymena. The semi-final place had been secured in a thrilling ten-try game against Galwegians, eventually won 34–31 by Lansdowne, with tries from Jim O'Donovan, Rooney, the Australian international Adam Magro and Stephen O'Connor. A final try by Killian Kennedy in the eightieth minute allowed the former Saracens and Wasps player Matthew Leek to level the scores with the conversion, before he won the game with a dropped goal. It was Lansdowne's ninth victory in a row that season, though unfortunately that run came to an end in the semi-final, when Ballymena dominated up front through their lineout and maul to win the game 10–3.[27]

On a brighter note for Lansdowne, the season saw the Second XV under Gareth Molloy win the Metropolitan Cup, defeating St Mary's 30–10 in the final. The competition was at that time sponsored by Leddin Finance, a company established and run by Lansdowne's Joe Leddin. The 2002–3 season also saw the launch of a new Youth Rugby Section, with a team being fielded by the Club at Under-14 level. Such activity reflected the ongoing commitment to developing all levels of rugby, a commitment which had seen the appointment in May 2001 of Fassbender as the Club's first full-time professional Rugby Development Officer. Since 1999 Fassbender had been working in the role of Youth Rugby Coordinator at the Club, so was well suited to the new role. The fruits of his labours were seen in the 2003–4 season, when Lansdowne was finally able to field two Under-20s sides, competing in a Premier and First Division respectively, with both teams finishing third in their leagues. While the Premier Division side went on to lose to Ballymena in the All-Ireland League, they thereafter reached the final of the McCorry Cup only to lose out to Blackrock. The First Division side went one better and won the inaugural Purcell Cup with victory over St Mary's. The season also saw the Lansdowne Second XV continue their winning ways with a fourteenth Junior 1 League title.[28]

The early 2000s also saw the passing of some Club stalwarts. On 20 May 2000, the same day that Lansdowne lost to St Mary's in the final of the AIL, Art Campbell passed away at the age of eighty-five. Having attended Synge Street School at a time when Gaelic football was the dominant sport, he came to rugby later on, but as soon as he joined Lansdowne in 1935 his commitment

Lansdowne FC portrait of Con Murphy. One of the most dedicated and long-serving members of the Club, Murphy was the only player to be capped for Ireland both before and after the Second World War. He was Club Captain in 1939–40 and 1944–5, as well as Club President in 1966–7.

was never in doubt. As junior match secretary in the 1940s–1950s he was synonymous for hundreds of players with life at the Kimmage Grove grounds. A manager, selector, administrator and father-figure to many, he also served as Club President in 1973–4. Two years after Campbell's death, his contemporary and similarly devoted Lansdowne clubman, Con Murphy, passed away at the age of eighty-seven in April 2002. Described by Van Esbeck as the 'most loyal and dedicated servant' that Lansdowne FC ever had, it was said of Murphy that 'not alone did he not miss a Lansdowne match for fifty years after he retired as a player, but [he] never missed a training session' either, acting as a team manager and touch judge for the First XV and also as PRO for the Club. He was a revered figure for generations of Lansdowne players and had very rightly been inducted into the Guinness Rugby Writers of Ireland Hall of Fame. As Michael Daly noted in the *LFC Yearbook* for 2002–3, 'many a "Child of Grace" passed through his shrewd rugby management' over the decades at the Club. Then in August 2002 Jack Coffey passed away at the age of eighty-two. Having come to Lansdowne in the later 1940s after playing with the Curragh Rugby Club while serving as an officer in the Irish defence forces during the Emergency, he had followed in his father's footsteps both as a Cup-winning Club Captain in 1949 and thereafter as a dedicated administrator, serving as an Irish selector as well as President of the Leinster Branch (1970–1), Lansdowne (1972–3), and the IRFU (1977–8). Another former Club President, T.C. 'Tishy' Byrne, also passed away in 2002 at the age of ninety-two, while the much younger David 'Coyler' Coyle died suddenly that year from a heart attack while out jogging. One of Lansdowne's great characters, Coyler had continued playing prop until he was almost forty, instinctively leading and teaching many other players along the way, a habit he continued thereafter as a coach. He was however possibly even better known as the keyboard player in 'Hurricane Johnny and the Jets' and later in 'Dave and the BeeBops'. His late-night turns on the piano in the pavilion after cup victories were among the more memorable Lansdowne occasions.[29]

The ongoing pressures on clubs since the introduction of professional rugby meant that club structures also had to adapt to new realities. In that regard, in 2004 Lansdowne introduced a new two-year position of Chairman of the Club, with Michael Kearney the first to take up the role. With day-to-day responsibility for running the Club, the position was in part to ease the over-burdened post of Club President, and to oversee the work of a number of other Chairmen of the various committees – Rugby, House, Finance, Sponsorship and Fund-Raising, Membership and Social – that kept the Club afloat and functioning. The primary focus of all of this re-structuring was to address the ever-increasing financial losses which had come close to threatening the Club's very survival. The need to curb expenditure, especially in relation to the costs of actually playing the game at First-team level, was the biggest challenge, but the players themselves had helped massively by agreeing to stop all payments related to the AIL matches. Unfortunately, at a time when Celtic Tiger affluence was seeing larger and larger numbers of supporters travelling to continental destinations to watch Leinster, Munster, Ulster and Connacht in European competitions, there was no trickle-down effect for the struggling clubs who remained the most natural seed-beds for future elite players.[30]

Another challenge related to the junior ground at Kilgobbin. In 1998–9 the land had been rezoned for residential building. As a result, Lansdowne and Old Wesley took the opportunity to sell to Castlethorn Construction in June 1999. As part of the sale agreement, Castlethorn undertook to provide a purpose-built alternative ground for both clubs to continue sharing. In the interim, junior rugby continued to be played at Kilgobbin for a number of years thereafter while planning permission was processed and the new ground found and laid out. Driven in particular by Frank 'Frankie' Forrest and John 'Johnnie' Lombard, this long process culminated in November 2007 with

Lansdowne FC Trustee Peter Sutherland with Club President Paddy Halpenny at the official opening of the new junior ground at Ballycorus in November 2007.

the official opening of the new ground on the Ballycorus road in Kilternan, resplendent with a clubhouse, floodlighting and three pitches. Even though once again junior rugby was squeezed further out of the city as Dublin's inexorable growth continued, the financial benefits for Lansdowne were not to be dismissed at a time of great difficulty for most Irish rugby clubs. The most important thing, as had been made clear since the 1930s with the move to the first junior grounds at Kimmage Grove, was to provide proper facilities for junior rugby to thrive in. There were several generations of hardy Lansdowne souls who looked back with fond memories upon playing careers dominated by the water-logged, windswept slopes of Kilgobbin, with reviving post-match tea and biscuits in the ground's clubhouse followed by other kinds of liquid sustenance and sociability in the Sandyford House.[31]

The challenges in the committee-room were replicated on the pitch, where in the 2004–5 season relegation from Division One was only avoided in a

Junior 3 League and Moran Cup, 2005–6. Standing: D. Flynn (Coach), C. Quinn (Coach), M. O'Laide, B. Cox, S. Mitchell, D. Becker, R. Martin, J. Quinn, P. Dunne, R. McDonnell, E. Kelly, K. Fitzduff, J. O'Regan, T. Nyhan, J. Crowley (Asst. Manager), B. Winckworth (Manager). Seated: M. Fernandez, J. Cremin, R. Horgan, D. Drummond, S. Keogh (Capt.), S. Winckworth (Mascot), O. O'Buachalla (Pres.), G. Lee, S. Collier. E. Griffen, R. Lynam.

play-off with UCC, which Lansdowne won 29–6. Coached by Andy Doyle with assistance from Pat Ward and Fassbender and initially captained by Toland before he was transferred to Croatia for eight months in his role as an officer in the Irish defence forces, the First XV was led for most of the season by Stephen O'Connor. For the play-off match, the team included one of Lansdowne's more recent, and colourful, international recruits in Felipe Contepomi at outhalf along with the likes of Rooney, Bohan, McCullen, Lyne, Ronan and the future professional Leinster and Ireland player Devin Toner on the bench. An early penalty try was added to later in the first half by wing Fiachra Baynes before McCullen put the game out of UCC's reach with a third try on forty-four minutes. A seventy-second minute try for Lansdowne's other wing, Ian Hopkins, wrapped things up with Contepomi adding the conversion to go with an earlier successful penalty and conversion. It was a fitting end to Rooney's last season on the First XV, retiring from senior rugby with a highly impressive 128 appearances for the Club in the AIL. The following season would see the retirement of two more centurions, with Enda Bohan finishing his senior career with 138 AIL appearances and Stephen O'Connor with 105.[32]

Yet not all was doom and gloom. As had happened before, junior rugby in Lansdowne shone a light in darker times. In particular, the Third As embarked upon an extraordinary run of success in the mid-2000s under the captaincy of Stephen Keogh and the coaching of David Flynn and Charlie Quinn, with team manager Brian Winckworth ably assisted by John Crowley. Having won an eighth Junior 3 League title for the Club in 2003–4, the core of the team were still there two years later in the 2005–6 season when they defeated Greystones in the Junior 3 League final 31–7 to claim a ninth such title for the Club. They then beat Clontarf 18–10 in the Moran Cup final to secure the 'double', a feat that Lansdowne had last achieved at that level in 1968–9 under Wyndam Williams, who was there in 2006 to see it done again. At the same time the Lansdowne Seconds just lost out in the final of the Metropolitan Cup, as did the Third XV in the Albert O'Connell Cup final. The season was then rounded off with a First team tour to Argentina and Uruguay and the Under-14s becoming the first Irish youth side to go on tour to Bahrain.[33]

Junior 3 League and Moran Cup, 2006–7. Standing: B. Winckworth (Manager), D. Becker, M. O'Laide, R. Martin, T. Nyhan, K. Kourilenko, D. Fallon, E. Kelly, J. O'Regan, N. O'Connor, C. Quinn (Coach), J. Crowley (Asst. Manager). Seated: S. Sexton, A. Tallon, R. Horgan, K. Fitzduff, R. McDonnell, A. Delany (Pres.), S. Keogh (Capt.), G. Lee, S. Mitchell, S. Collier. On Ground: J. Cremin, P. Dunne, S. Winckworth (Mascot), D. Drummond, S. O'Dwyer.

But the Third As were far from done. With the same management team in place, in the 2006–7 season the team went on to do a 'double' double, with back-to-back Junior 3 League and Moran Cup titles, once again with Keogh as captain and Quinn as coach. Stillorgan RFC were defeated 25–3 in the Moran Cup final on the same day that the Lansdowne Second XV took on Clontarf in the final of the Metropolitan Cup. Captained by David Upton, the Seconds won 33–32 in 'one of the most entertaining spectacles of the season', during which the future Leinster and Ireland prop Cian Healy scored two rolling maul tries for Clontarf. With tries from Vinny Goff, Stuart Meagher and two from Brendan McGeever, the decisive points came from a last-minute penalty by Andy Geraghty which put Lansdowne six points clear, which was sufficient to survive Clontarf's injury-time unconverted try.[34]

As for the Third As, not satisfied with the 'double' double', in the 2007–8 season they did the treble 'double' of titles – or 'trouble' as it was suggested at the time. Again captained by Keogh, by then the back-room team included Rory MacMahon and Gerry Maloney alongside Crowley. It was an extraordinary achievement to win three 'doubles' in three consecutive years. Throughout that extended period of success the team comprised a mix of old hands and newer blood, with the likes of Declan Drummond, Gavin Lee, Kevin Fitzduff, David Becker, James Cremin, Peter Dunne, Roy Horgan, Mark O'Laoide and Rob McDonnell appearing year after year.[35]

While such success was ongoing at the junior levels of the Club, throughout the mid-2000s the long-considered and planned IRFU redevelopment of Lansdowne Road gathered momentum. With financial assistance from the National Lottery, the formal plan was finally announced in January 2004. But it also required complex negotiations with both Lansdowne and Wanderers as co-tenants at the ground. For Lansdowne, this was to include compensation for loss of earnings during the redevelopment phase, temporary relocation to the RDS, and refurbishment of the pavilion after its use as a work-site office. An all-weather back pitch on top of a modern underground car park would also be constructed as part of the wider redevelopment. But Lansdowne also took the opportunity to utilize Club funds arising from the sale of the junior ground at Kilgobbin to construct a dramatic 5,000 square-foot extension of the pavilion that incorporated a new entrance, a horse-shoe bar and a gym that was also capable of doubling as a function room on international weekends. The new extension and upgrading of facilities would also offer the Club a means of achieving an improved income and greater financial stability in the future.[36]

Before such work came to fruition, however, concerns were raised once again about the viability of the Club remaining wholly at its Lansdowne Road location, primarily because of the potential challenges arising from only having use of a single back pitch on a shared basis and with restricted access to the main stadium. The uncertainty of the 2006–7 season in that regard had even seen a short-lived idea floated of a possible merger between Lansdowne and Monkstown FC. In the end, a simpler solution was found to facilitate sharing of the Monkstown grounds at Sydney Parade for training purposes during the time that Lansdowne were temporarily homeless. The move to the RDS took place at the beginning of the 2007–8 season. It did not prove fortuitous for the Club. Late in the day, the intended new head coach, the New Zealander Mike Brewer, was unable to take up the post, leaving no time to find a replacement. The recently appointed Club Director of Rugby, Stephen Rooney, stepped into the breach with assistance from Fassbender, since 2005 a Development Officer with Leinster Rugby. Such disruption combined with the new peripatetic lifestyle of the Club ultimately impacted results on the field. So it was that despite a final day bonus-point victory over Terenure in the AIL, Ballymena's loss to Dungannon ultimately consigned Lansdowne to Division Two for the 2008–9 season.[37]

There were some silver-linings for the Club at junior level, however. Once again, the focus on the Under-20s paid off with a first McCorry Cup title, secured with a 16–15 victory over Dublin University in the final in April 2008. Although they lost out in the final of the All-Ireland competition to UL Bohemians, the potential of the squad was there for all to see. Made up of players from St Michael's, Kilkenny, Navan, Gorey, Blackrock, Gonzaga, Castleknock, CUS, Clongowes and others drawn from the Leinster and Ireland youths levels, players such as David Kearney, Ruadhri Murphy, Eoin Sheriff, Shane Gahan, Eamonn Sheridan, Lorcan Kavanagh and Matt Healy had also all appeared for the First XV. Kearney had already shown his future potential by being the top try-scorer for the Firsts in the AIL on the back of only four appearances. Healy and Gahan had also been capped for Ireland at Under-19 level, while Kearney, Sheriff, Sheridan and Patrick Mallon had won the same honours at Under-20 level. Healy would in time switch to the wing and play for Connacht and the senior Ireland side, while Kearney would join his older brother Rob with both Leinster and Ireland. Sheriff eventually ended up playing for Saracens in London before injury cut short his career at the age of twenty-seven, while Sheridan played for Leinster before going on to spells at Rotherham Titans, London Irish and Oyonnax in France. Murphy went further afield with time spent at the Brumbies in Australia and with the Exeter Chiefs as well as playing for Ulster. William 'Willie' Earle on the other

Leinster Senior League Cup, 2008–9. Standing: P. Gore (Manager), F. Baynes, K. Ekanem, A. McCullen, E. Sheridan, D. Kearney, R. Boucher, M. Healy, J. Meagher, S. Gahan, C. Murphy, R. Lieberman, D. Marquez, C. Oosthuizen, M. Quinn (Manager). Seated: T. Conneely, D. Hewitt, R. McCarron, K. Cleere, A. Maher (Capt.), J. Kearney (Pres.), D. Toomey, A. Geraghty, P. Caldwell, S. Smyth, V. O'Dowd.

hand would go on to become the most capped Lansdowne player in the AIL by the 2019–20 season with 147 appearances. Such future career trajectories demonstrated yet again the importance of investing in the mini and youth set-ups, evidence of which was seen in activities such as the Lansdowne Under-16s going on tour to Dubai in April 2008, the Under-12s playing in Toulouse and Biarritz in May, and the Under-10s staying closer to home with a trip to Wales.[38]

The Club's primary focus in the 2008–9 season was a return to the top tier of the AIL, which from 2009–10 was to be restructured into Division One A and Division One B with eight teams in each. With Steve McIvor as head coach with assistance from Aidan McCullen and with Alan Maher as captain, the First XV returned to winning ways in the first half of the season in the Leinster Senior League Cup, the successor since 2005–6 to the Leinster Senior Cup. Having won all three of their pool matches against UCD, Greystones and Barnhall, Lansdowne defeated UCD in the quarter-finals before going on to beat Old Belvedere 15–9 in the semi-final in a match where Lansdowne's South African wing Charl Oosthuizen scored the opening try and added three penalties. The final was a tightly contested 9–5 affair against the holders, Clontarf, with Oosthuizen kicking all of Lansdowne's points. Victory was more assuredly secured, however, with a try-saving tackle by Gahan close to the end of the match. The win brought up Lansdowne's twenty-fifth Cup title. Thereafter, the First XV's endeavours to win Division Two of the AIL were well on track when they went top of the table following a 25–5 defeat of Greystones in early 2009. Despite the fact that few of the centrally contracted players managed to turn out for their clubs anymore, Gordon D'Arcy, who was returning from injury, happily mucked in with his old teammates on the day and also managed to score a try. However, a one-point loss to Dublin University in a last-day finale placed Lansdowne third in the League and out of contention for promotion. A 29–13 loss in the Division Two semi-final play-offs to Ballynahinch followed.[39]

The 2008–9 season saw continued success at junior levels, however. The Second XV under Karl Cleere won the Metropolitan Cup for the thirteenth time, while the 'trouble' Third As won the Moran Cup for a fourth time in a row by defeating Terenure 20–7 in the final. With Keogh still running the show as captain and ably assisted by the core of the team that had been playing together since the start of their phenomenal run of success back in 2005–6, the Third As had only been denied a fourth 'double' in a row because of points deducted in the league after a 38–10 defeat of Monkstown. Further success was also achieved with the Under-20s, who were coached by Willie Clancy with Fassbender back involved along with Charlie Quinn, Stephen O'Connor, Alan Twomey and David O'Mahony. With the majority of the 2007–8 McCorry Cup-winning squad retained for a second season, the J.P. Fanagan League was won for a third time in the Club's history, with the title being secured in the final round of matches by victory over the other competition contenders, UCD. Although the All-Ireland League was lost at semi-final stage in a controversial last-minute 11–10 defeat by Blackrock, a seasonal 'double' was secured by the Lansdowne Under-20s with a back-to-back McCorry Cup title. Having defeated Wanderers, Terenure and Clontarf en route to the final, UCD were overcome 24–13 in the title-deciding game.[40]

Lansdowne's last full season based in the RDS was 2009–10, when the key challenge remained securing promotion to Division One B. John Lyne was appointed Club Captain while Willie Clancy took on the role of head coach with Stephen O'Connor as his assistant. Aidan McCullen was the forwards/player coach while Gordon D'Arcy took on the role of backs coach. Mick Quinn was the team manager, with Brian Corrigan and Paddy Gore also involved in that area. The First team squad was most notable for all of the talent that had come through from the Under-20s structures in previous seasons, including the captain himself. With forty-nine players used throughout the season and with both Matt Healy and Ross McCarron breaking the Club's AIL try-scoring records with fifteen and thirteen each respectively, Lansdowne came top of the Division Two league table and thereby won promotion to Division One B for the 2010–11 season. They also won the Division Two play-offs, beating DLSP 40–8 in the semi-final before beating Bruff 17–10 in the

All Ireland League Division Two, 2009–10. Standing: D. McCarron (Chairman), W. Clancy (Coach), S. O'Connor (Asst. Coach), D. Toomey, M. Moore, J. O'Connell, C. Murphy, N. Keogh, E. Sheriff, S. Gahan, B. McKeever, W. Earle, R. Jones, S. McCarron, G. D'Arcy (Backs Coach), M. Cassidy (Video), M. Quinn (Manager). Seated: B. Corrigan (Manager), P. Gore (Asst. Manager), M. Healy, T. Connolly, A. Geraghty, R. McCarron, K. Cleere, J. Lyne (Capt.), M. Dawson (Pres.), G. Stafford, P. Flood, A. McCullen, K. Lewis, J. Meagher.

Junior 1 League and Metropolitan Cup, 2009–10. Standing: D. McCarron (Chairman), J. Maguire (Manager), M. Quinn, D. Quigley, D. Toomey, K. Kennedy, W. Earle, B. McKeever, D. Upton, R. Jones, W. Aherne (Asst. Coach), D. O'Brien (Coach). Seated: T. Conneely, A. Geraghty, F. Baynes, K. Cleere (Capt.), M. Dawson (Pres.), S. McCarron, J. Meagher, S. Smyth, S. Kelly.

final. With a total of 677 points for and 311 against in twenty-six games that season, the young side had included new faces such as Ben Horan and the former Leinster, Munster and Ireland centre Kieran Lewis. Former Connacht, Leinster and Racing Metro player David Hewitt was also in the side along with the likes of Healy, Sheriff, Gahan, Earle and the upcoming prop Marty Moore, who would go on to play for Leinster, Wasps, Ulster and Ireland. Of particular pertinence for the Club Chairman, Dermot McCarron, was the presence on the team of his sons Ross and Stuart.[41]

The last season in the RDS also saw the Second XV win the Junior 1 League and Metropolitan Cup 'double' for the fourth time in the Club's history. Coached by Daniel O'Brien and managed by Willie Aherne, the team had defeated Garda 20–Nil in the final of the Cup while the League title had been secured in early March with victory over Blackrock.[42]

Throughout the seasons 2007–8 to 2009–10 the redevelopment of Lansdowne Road had been ongoing, and ultimately cost €410 million. The last game in the old stadium had been played on 31 December 2006, between

Leinster and Ulster in front of a record attendance for the Magners League of 48,000. Demolition had commenced in May 2007, while construction was finally completed in 2010 with the first game taking place on 7 August that year. The stadium had also been re-named because Aviva Insurance had bought the naming rights for the first decade. So it was that when Lansdowne FC moved back into their new, improved clubhouse, the famous name now only applied to the Club. There was a logic to that, given that the Club had pre-dated the stadium.[43]

The welcome return for the Club to the newly refurbished and greatly extended pavilion at Lansdowne Road occurred in time for the 2010–11 season. The previous three years had required a huge commitment and body of work from a wide range of Club members to make the return happen, all of which had been overseen and driven by a committee comprising Joe Leddin, Rory Williams, Mark Dawson, Mahon Murphy, Dermot McCarron, Kieran Mulligan, Ciaran O'Reilly, David McDowell and the brothers Paddy and David Madigan. The return also coincided with the appointment of a new General Manager, Eleanor Connolly, and Finance Controller, Mary Walsh.[44]

With Lansdowne FC entering into a new phase of existence in 2010, it was of note that the preceding years had seen the passing of a number of long-serving Club members. In 2004 Sidney Minch had passed away, while the following year saw the death of Dougie Spoor and Johnny Barrett, a former treasurer and Club President in 1977–8. Canon William John Moynan, who had captained the Club in 1947–8 and served as President in 1971–2, passed away in 2009, while in April 2010 the death occurred at age seventy-seven of Michael 'Mick the kick' English, the Munster, Ireland and Lions player who had served as Club President in 1989–90 and had been inducted into the Guinness Rugby Writers of Ireland Hall of Fame in 2008. In June 2010, the 1948 Grand-Slam second-row Colum Callan passed away at the age of eighty-seven, while in July the deaths occurred of both Barry Bresnihan, who was sixty-six, and the Church of Ireland clergyman, Robin Roe, who was eighty-one. Like Mick English, both Bresnihan and Roe had played for Ireland and the Lions. Then on 5 October 2010 the legendary Moss Keane died at the age of sixty-two following a twenty-month battle with cancer. He was buried in Portarlington,

Moss Keane Commemorative Match Programme, Lansdowne versus UCC, 9 October 2010.

the home town of his wife Anne and where they had lived for many years. The grave-side eulogy was given by Donal Spring, with whom Keane had played many a match for Lansdowne, Munster and Ireland, including the legendary Munster defeat of New Zealand in 1978.[45]

It was therefore both poignant and pertinent that the inaugural AIL fixture on the brand new all-weather back pitch at Lansdowne Road in October 2010 was between Keane's two former clubs, Lansdowne and UCC. It was noted at the time that the Lansdowne squad was 'littered with current … and former professionals'. The current professionals included Leinster's Dave Kearney, Dominic Ryan and Stephen Keogh, who had also played for Munster, while those of former professional status included Lewis, Lyne and Eoghan Hickey. The emerging professional talent included Sheriff, Jordi Murphy, Tom Sexton, Jack O'Connell and John Cooney, who scored two tries in an emphatic 61–13 Lansdowne victory. O'Connell would go on to a career at Leinster, Bristol and Ealing Trailfinders. Careers with Leinster also awaited Sexton, Murphy and Cooney, with the latter two also going on to play for Ireland. Sexton eventually moved on to play professional club rugby in Australia, while Cooney transferred to Connacht and then Ulster, where he was joined in time by Murphy.[46]

The primary focus for the 2010–11 season was to win promotion to Division One A of the AIL. That task was undertaken following yet another round of IRFU restructuring with a view to having two ten-team leagues at Division One A and Division One B levels for the 2011–12 season. With Lyne as captain and the same coaching and management team in place for the second year running, other new faces in the squad included the likes of Simon Morrissey, Ciaran O'Boyle and Craig Ronaldson from the Under-21s. Ronaldson would go on to a professional career with Connacht. With an even seven wins and losses in the League, automatic promotion was secured on the last day in a winner-takes-all encounter with Buccaneers that Lansdowne won 15–Nil. The final score-line belied the real nature of the contest in a match which had remained scoreless until the fifty-sixth minute, when Ronaldson landed a penalty. He then benefitted from a scoring pass at the end of a counter-attack launched by Cooney, with the *coup de grâce* coming from a Sheridan try shortly thereafter which Ronaldson also converted.[47]

The 2010–11 season also saw Lansdowne for the first time in several years in a position to enter two teams in the recently regraded Under-21 competitions. Coached by Fassbender and Charlie Quinn and captained by David Heffernan, a future Connacht and Ireland hooker, the Premier side were unlucky to lose the League final 28–27 to UCD, but went on to victory in the McCorry Cup, defeating St Mary's 26–10 in the final. The Under-21 Pennant League team was coached and managed by Alan Flanagan, Aiden Sweeney, Phil Rice and Dave Tunney and was captained by David Sheridan. Not a single game was lost in the march to the Pennant League title, though in the Cup competition the team lost 24–21 to St Mary's in the semi-final. Further success at junior level was seen with the next generation of Third As under the captaincy of Will Stafford, the coaching of Michael Quinn junior and Nicky O'Connor, and the management of Will Sparks. Emulating the 'Trouble' team of the 2000s, and with second-generation Sparks, Quinns, Beckers, Forrests, Harveys, Whites and Gahans involved, the Junior 3 League and Moran Cup 'double' was achieved for a remarkable fourth time in six seasons. It was also the fifth Moran Cup title in that same period and the Club's twelfth in total. The season also saw some significant 'firsts' for the Under-13s, who were

Junior 3 League and Moran Cup, 2010–11. Standing: W. Sparks (Manager), R. White, B. Gahan, M. Forrest, P. Grant, G. Quinn, S. Cooney, E. Lyons, P. Harvey, C. Gahan, J. Hopkins, D. O'Neill, D. Sparks, N. O'Connor (Asst. Coach), Ml. Quinn (Coach). Seated: J. Sparks, D. Ryan, D. Becker, Mk. Quinn, C. O'Reilly (Pres.), W. Stafford (Capt.), R. Becker, M. Sheehy, S. Flynn, A. McCoy, R. Feighery.

coached by Mark MacMahon, Donal McEvoy, Andrew Curry, Vincent Ryan and Ciaran Lynch. In April 2011 they became the first Lansdowne team to win a youth-level competition when they won the Metro Under-13 League Division 1B. They then followed up in May by winning the Club's second-ever trophy at youths level, defeating DLSP, Blackrock, Belvedere and Suttonians in order to win the Under-13s Metro Cup.[48]

The 2011–12 season marked the first year with Mike Ruddock as head coach at Lansdowne. A former Welsh Grand Slam-winning coach, Ruddock brought a huge amount of experience with him, including an intimate knowledge of the Irish club game. The new assistant coach was Emmet Farrell, while Ross McCarron was commencing the first of two seasons as Club Captain. With a young team experiencing the level of competition in Division One A for the first time, it was a season for development and consolidation, with a fifth-place finish deemed a good result. More importantly, and in keeping with the Club's long tradition and ethos in that regard, the First XV were noted for playing the most attractive rugby in the AIL. Such an approach had always been a recipe for success for Lansdowne teams ever since the Club's foundation. The season also saw a notable win away to Shannon for the first time and a host of young players come through from the Under-21s, including Ian Prendiville, Scott Caldbeck, Brian Moylett, the future Ireland seven-aside internationals Foster Horan and Mark Roche, and Tadhg Beirne, who would go on to a professional career with Leinster, the Scarlets, Munster, Ireland and the Lions. There was also continued success at junior levels. The Third XV achieved the Club's first ever 'double' at that level, winning the Junior 2 League and the Albert O'Connell Cup, the former for the tenth time and the latter for the eleventh time. It was of note that the Third XV were captained by Will Stafford, coached by Michael Quinn junior and Nicky O'Connor, and managed by Will Sparks, all of whom had been part of the 'double' winning combination with the Third As the season before. With Warren Barry also

Just before the Lansdowne FC versus Old Belvedere match at Lansdowne Road, 2011–12 season.

part of the coaching team, the Third XV had gone undefeated through the season, scoring 581 points and conceding only 172. At the same time the Third As, captained by Donal Ó Cofaigh, also retained the Moran Cup, making it six such titles in seven seasons for the Club and the thirteenth overall. The financial challenges of the professional era remained, however. To that end, a new Board of Management was set up that season 'in order to tackle the major financial problems facing Lansdowne over the coming years'.[49]

Such concerns were not reflected on the pitch, where the groundwork laid in the 2011–12 season paid off in 2012–13. With Ruddock and Farrell retained as the coaching team and McCarron in his second year as captain of the First XV, the style and verve of play proved irresistible. Having won five of their first seven games in the AIL, the First XV then put together a nine-game winning streak, which included a bonus-point victory over Young Munster at the beginning of March 2013 that put Lansdowne fourteen points ahead of their nearest rivals, Clontarf, with five games to go. At that point, they were deemed 'unstoppable in their quest'. At the end of the month they wrapped things up with two games to spare in a 32–25 bonus-point victory over Clontarf. The AIL Division One A title had been won with an 'attacking brand of running, off-loading rugby' in traditional Lansdowne fashion. A young team with an average age of twenty-four, they had racked up ten attacking bonus points and an unassailable twenty-three-point lead at the top of the table by the time they defeated Clontarf and were crowned champions. Having used forty-two players to that point in the season, the winning team included the future Ulster players Clive Ross and Charlie Butterworth in the backrow along with Beirne and Earle in the second-row, and O'Connell, Sexton and Moore in the front-row, with Ronaldson guiding a backline that included Cian Aherne, Patrick O'Driscoll, Morrissey and McCarron. The star of the show against Clontarf, however, was the Under-21 centre Mark Roche, who scored two tries, including the bonus-point touchdown at the death, while he had also set up the wing Sean Carey for the first score. The number 8 Ron Boucher had gotten in for Lansdowne's other try. Throughout the AIL competition Lansdowne had conceded 292 points while scoring 524, the highest total in the history of Division One A of the competition, with

AIL Division One A, 2012–13. Standing: Backrow: K. Essex, W. Earle, A. Hoban, S. Gahan, J. Shanahan, T. Conneely, C. Toolan, S. McCarron, F. Doherty, I. Prendiville, C. O'Donnell, A. Geraghty, T. Sexton. Standing: D. Fallon, M. Cassidy (Video), P. Gore (Co-Manager), M. Quinn jnr, E. Farrell (Backs Coach), T. Daly, M. Roche, T. Combiere, T. Moran, E. Torrie, R. McCarthy, S. Kelly, M. Moore, T. Beirne, J. O'Connell, D. O'Reilly, M. Feeley, R. Boucher, C. Butterworth, D. Mannion, A. Matthews, J. Coleman, G. Stafford, C. Crowley, B. Corrigan (Manager), I. Gargan, M. Ruddock (Coach), D. Farnan, S. Rooney. Seated: J. Cooney, C. Aherne, C. Ross, C. Ronaldson, P. O'Driscoll, S. Carey, D. McCarron (Pres.), R. McCarron (Capt.), S. Collins, S. Morrissey, F. Horan, W. Walsh.

Ronaldson accounting for 249 of those. Aherne was the top try scorer on thirteen, while for the season overall Earle had appeared in twenty-three out of twenty-four games.[50]

The season also saw significant success with the Under-21s, who were coached again by Fassbender and Quinn with assistance from Freddie Mehigan and Dave Tunney and under the overall guidance of Colin Goode as Director of Under-21 Rugby. As it turned out, there were insufficient numbers to maintain two teams throughout the season, while long-term injuries to the likes of Conor Kilcoyne and Tom Farrell, the future Bedford Blues and Connacht player, further strained playing resources. Even still, the Premier side managed to go through the J.P. Fanagan League with only one defeat. As a result, a home draw was secured in the Fraser McMullen All-Ireland Cup. Garryowen were defeated 44–3 first up, while an away semi-final against Old Belvedere resulted in a fierce battle that went Lansdowne's way 8–7. In the final against Dublin University,

Frazer McMullen All-Ireland Cup, 2012–13. Backrow: M. Roche, M. Vaughan, R. Foot, J. O'Hehir, R. Lenahan, T. Farrell, P. Dooley, D. Egan, W. O'Brien, M. Mellett, T. Moran, A. McEvoy, M. Lenehan, T. Kiersey, M. Dooley, J. O'Brien. Standing: W. Barry, C. Goode, D. Fassbender (Coach), C. Murtagh, R. Keller, J. Rice, J. Flynn, A. Kelly, E. Quinn, M. O'Brien, C. Byrne, C. Kilcoyne, B. Cunningham, M. O'Neill, F. Mehigan (Asst. Backs Coach), D. Tunney (Asst. Forwards Coach). Seated: C. Quinn (Forwards coach), R. Deacon, A. Boland, B. Mylett, D. McCarron (Pres.), A. Khan (Capt.), D. McDonagh Kinkade, J. Kennedy, C. Fair-Brennan, T. Daly.

Lansdowne went 22–7 ahead, a score-line which included a sixty-metre try by future Leinster prop Peter Dooley, before the students roared back into a 26–22 lead. Team spirit and self-belief won out, however, as Richie Lenahan got the necessary try to give Lansdowne a 27–26 victory. Captained by Akhalaque Khan and with the likes of Eoghan Quinn, Tom Kiersey, Will O'Brien, Adam Boland and the future Leinster and Connacht player Tom Daly, the Under-21s had once again shown what hard work, commitment and application could achieve. As was evident with the continuing success of the Under-21s, Lansdowne's focus on developing young players was both beneficial and commendable. Further proof was seen at youth level, when the Under-17s won the Leinster Branch Metro Youth Cup for that age group that season also.[51]

Having been named Club of the year in November 2013 by the Guinness Rugby Writers of Ireland, Lansdowne looked to defend their AIL title in the

2013–14 season with Earle as Club Captain and with the same coaching team in harness once again. While the Division One A title was only decided on the final weekend of matches in April 2014, it proved to be Clontarf's year with Old Belvedere falling at the final hurdle in defeat to relegated Garryowen. Lansdowne finished fourth in the table with an even nine wins and losses, though with eleven bonus points, which, as the second highest number in the table, told a tale of close calls and running rugby. Silverware was won however by the Second XV who defeated Clontarf 36–6 in the final to secure the Junior 1 League for the fifteenth time in the Club's history, while the Under-17s went one better on their previous season by winning both the Metro Youth League and Cup for their age-grade, a 'double' success which retained the League title and secured the Cup for the first time for Lansdowne. At the other end of the playing spectrum on the international stage, it was a notable day for the Club in March 2014 when at one point in the Six Nations match between Ireland and Italy there were six Lansdowne FC players on the pitch – Gordon D'Arcy, Devin Toner, Eoin Reddan, Dave Kearney, Jordi Murphy and Marty Moore. It was further testament to the long-standing endeavours at the Club from minis upwards to develop and nurture the elite players of the future.[52]

The demands of the modern professional era saw the 2014–15 season commence with a recalibrated Club management structure, with Michael Diskin as CEO and Elayne Power as events manager supported by Fiona Nagle looking after finance and Mary Walsh as administrator. Early in the season Ruddock stepped aside as Ireland Under-20s coach in order to fully concentrate on trying to win a second AIL title with Lansdowne. The former Leinster, Connacht, Montpellier, Nice and Ireland player Mark McHugh was the new assistant coach, with further assistance provided by the former Gloucester and Wasps player Will Matthews, while Ciaran Walsh came on board to look after strength and conditioning. The Club Captain was Ron Boucher, while the former Munster player Scott Deasy in his second season with the Club took on a central role at outhalf. Once again putting faith in the youth coming through the Club systems to replace thirteen senior players who for the most part had left to take up professional contracts, the highlights of the First XV's AIL campaign included a 35–Nil victory over Clontarf at

Ron Boucher in action for Lansdowne FC against UCD, 2014–15 season.

their home ground at Castle Avenue in January in the midst of a crucial eight-game winning streak for Lansdowne. Among the try-scorers was the future Leinster and Connacht player Cian Kelleher, playing alongside fellow-Leinster Academy backs Daly, Tom Farrell – who chipped in with two tries – and Ian Fitzpatrick, a future Ireland seven's player. With the AIL reverting back to a play-off system after several years of the more traditional first-past-the-post format, Lansdowne's final tally of sixty-five points gave them a twelve-point advantage over their nearest rivals, Terenure, and assured them of a home semi-final. The ensuing nail-biting 23–19 victory after extra-time against Young Munster was only sealed at the death when hooker Tyrone Moran drove over from close range to add to an earlier try by Daly. The final was against the holders, Clontarf, and bore no reflection to the earlier encounter in January. A first-half try for Roche from a cross-field kick by Deasy and ensuing off-load by Fitzpatrick gave Lansdowne an 8–6 lead, only for them to fall behind 17–8 mid-way through the second half. A try by the backrow Joe McSwiney brought the scores back to 17–15 before Deasy kicked the winning three points with twelve minutes to go. The final score-line of

Lansdowne FC minis supporting the First XV against Young Munster in the AIL semi-final, 2014–15.

18–17 was testament to a fiercely contested game and to heroic Lansdowne defence in the closing minutes. A second AIL Division One A title in three years was thus secured.[53]

As had occurred in 2013, the Under-20s – regraded once again from Under-21 level – were not to be outdone by the First XV, demonstrating the importance of developing strength across the age ranges. While Fassbender, Quinn and Tunney continued as the coaches, Ed Lyons took over as Controller of Under-20s Rugby. With a smaller squad owing to players graduating to the senior side or no longer being age-eligible owing to the regrading process, both Conor Ganley and Ben Ridgeway captained the side. A joint-second-place finish in the J.P. Fanagan League ensured qualification for the Fraser McMullen All-Ireland Cup. A 20–13 away win against Young Munster in the quarter-final was followed by a 35–25 victory over Terenure in the semi-final. Once again, Dublin University were defeated 16–15 in another closely contested final, with Lansdowne tries from prop Ntinga Mpiko and wing Kevin O'Connor as well as a massive defensive display epitomized by the relentless tackling of backrow Jack O'Sullivan. The season also saw the Second XV captained by Dan Mannion win the Junior 1 League with a 9–6 defeat of Old Belvedere in the final, while the Third XV under Andrew Geraghty secured the second 'double' for the Club at that level, winning both the Junior 2 League and the Albert O'Connell Cup just three seasons after it had first been achieved by a Lansdowne Third XV. Like their illustrious predecessors, the 2014–15 team also went through the season undefeated. The season's silverware was rounded-off with the James Guilfoyle Cup, won by a 'hastily assembled / resurrected' self-proclaimed 'Lansdowne's Legends' team

Tom Daly in action for Lansdowne FC against Young Munster in the AIL semi-final, 2014–15.

AIL Division One A, 2014–15. Backrow: T. Beirne, W. Larkin, B. Byrne Diaper, T. Farrell, B. Moylett, J. O'Brien, J. Coleman, J. Dilger, R. Deacon, E. Quinn, G. McDonald, D. Mannion, I. Prendiville. Standing: M. McHugh (Asst. Coach), W. Matthews (Asst. Coach), J. Meagher, A. McDonagh, B. O'Connell, I. Burke, W. Wallace, C. Kelleher, R. Jones, F. Doherty, S. Gardiner, A. Conneely, P. Dooley, J. Barry, C. Aherne, D. McEvoy, C. Mylod, M. Ruddock (Head Coach), C. Goode, S. Rooney, D. Lennon, P. Gore. Seated: A. Boland, P. O'Driscoll, M. Roche, T. Moran, S. Deasy, R. Boucher (Capt.), F. Kenny (Pres.), J. McSwiney, F. Horan, T. Daly, T. Kiersey, C. Barden, I. Fitzpatrick, M. Cassidy.

at Third Ds level, in what was deemed 'the shortest Cup campaign on record' as the three competing teams played out their round-robin and final all on one Tuesday evening at Lansdowne Road.[54]

As in 2013–14, the challenge for the First XV in the 2015–16 season was scaling the heights of AIL victory once more. Unfortunately it was not to be, and a seventh-place finish in the league table reflected a season of ups and downs. Despite having the same coaching ticket in place, Deasy as Club Captain and impressive new recruits such as Eamonn Mills from Dolphin, Josh O'Rourke from Buccaneers and Matt D'Arcy returning to the club of his youth, playing

After the Match: Lansdowne FC AIL Champions, 2014–15 season.

resources were stretched through the loss to professional rugby and other opportunities of senior players such as McSwiney, Moran, Boland, Boucher, Stephen Gardiner and Aaron Conneely, and the ensuing loss mid-season of both Moylett and Farrell. With a number of the Club's Leinster Academy players also unavailable owing to graduating to full professional contracts, Lansdowne's Under-20 conveyor-belt remained as important as ever, with AIL debuts prior to Christmas for future Leinster and Ireland players Max Deegan and James Ryan, son of the 1985–6 'double' captain, Mark. Both Deegan and Ryan would go on in 2016 to play for the Ireland Under-20s, with Ryan captaining the side for both the Six Nations and Under-20 World Cup, at which Deegan won Player of the Tournament. In the interim, with Ben Armstrong joining Fassbender on the coaching ticket, the Lansdowne Under-20s under the captaincy of Jack O'Sullivan won the McCorry Cup, defeating Dublin University 36–16 in the

Frazer McMullen All-Ireland Cup, 2014–15. Backrow: M. Fitzgerald, M. Sanchez, O. Lyons, J. Barry, C. Boyle, R. Bailey Kearney. Standing: D. Tunney, D. Fassbender, E. Lyons, J. O'Sullivan, C. Joyce Ahern, M. Scalfe, K. O'Connor, J.J. Earl, R. Collins, E. Byrne, R. Barry, S. O'Heir, C. O'Donoghue, C. Goode, A. Twomey, D. Lennon. Seated: J. Delaney, J. Kelly, J. Duffy, E. Murphy, F. Kenny (Pres.), B. Ridgeway (Capt.), E. Moffitt, G. Molloy, J. Nolan, J. O'Shea.

final. The season also saw the Third XV under John Sparks retain the Albert O'Connell Cup with a 27–3 victory over Old Wesley in the final.[55]

In the 2016–17 season, with continuity in terms of coaching once again and Ian Prendiville as Club Captain, the initial focus for the First XV was the Leinster Championship. The successor to the Leinster Senior League, the Championship was the new route for qualification to the revived Bateman Cup, which itself had been reinstituted in 2010–11. Lansdowne were successful in winning their League section, but thereafter lost 16–13 in the final to Old Belvedere. Attention then turned to the AIL, in which Lansdowne came top

Lansdowne FC Under 20s Past versus Present, 2014–15 season.

of Division One A in a very tightly contested top-four ranking. They were also the top-scoring side in the regular season with 503 points for and 332 against. Having thereby secured a home semi-final in the play-offs, a hard-fought and closely contested game with Cork Constitution was lost 19–16 in the second minute of injury time. Disappointment in the AIL, however, did not detract from the relevance of the revived Leinster Senior Cup, which was played in late April. Victories over St Mary's and Terenure led to a semi-final meeting with Dublin University, who were defeated 51–7. In the final, a more closely contested match with Old Belvedere went Lansdowne's way 33–26, with two tries from Dan McEvoy along with one a piece for Barry Fitzpatrick, Prendiville and Matt D'Arcy. The Club's twenty-sixth Leinster Senior Cup title not only placed Lansdowne four titles clear above their nearest rivals, Dublin University, but also bestowed the unique distinction of being the only title-holders to have won the Cup in three different centuries.[56]

The First XV's 2016–17 campaign had seen a number of the Under-20 squad promoted to the senior side. Under the captaincy of Brian Larkin, the Under-

Donal McEvoy and Head Coach Mike Ruddock at work, 2016–17.

20s had won the J.P. Fanagan League with an unbeaten record, securing the title with a game to spare when defeating Dublin University 38–29 at College Park. For good measure, they beat UCD the following weekend in their last league game. With the two well-resourced University teams sitting in second and third place, such victories demonstrated the high standards being set by the Lansdowne Under-20s. This was seen again in the Fraser McMullen All Ireland Cup with a 24–12 victory over UCD in the semi-final. The final proved a game too far, however, as injuries and the double-edged sword of call-ups to the First XV fed into a loss to Navan. As in previous years, a number of the team went on to Leinster and Ireland Under-20 representation, with Tadhg McElroy, Greg McGrath, Paul Boyle and Oisín Dowling being capped at the latter level both for the Under-20s Six Nations and Rugby World Cup, with Boyle captaining the latter squad. McElroy went on to a professional rugby career in England, while McGrath and Dowling started out with Leinster before moving to Connacht where they linked up again with Boyle, who also won his first cap for the Ireland senior team in 2021. The 2016–17 season also saw the Lansdowne Second XV under Ed Torrie and coached by Will

Lansdowne FC Second XV Metropolitan Cup Winners, 2016–17.

Matthews win the Metropolitan Cup for the fifteenth time, defeating Barnhall 27–3 in the final.[57]

The 2016–17 season had seen several near misses for the Lansdowne First XV alongside victory in the Leinster Senior Cup. With Prendiville in his second season as captain and Ruddock in his seventh season as head coach in 2017–18, the historic culture and ethos of the Club and, as the coach himself put it, the constant focus upon 'a particular set of skills, values, behaviours and "Trademarks"', was to result in the eradication of those near misses in what turned out to be Lansdowne's most successful season ever at senior level. In November 2017 the First XV went one better on the previous season by winning the Leinster League Cup and qualifying for the Bateman Cup with a 9–Nil victory over Clontarf in the final. In January 2018 the Bateman semi-final saw Lansdowne secure a 35–15 away victory over Sligo. The final in April was against the defending champions, Cork Constitution, who had dominated the competition since its re-instatement with five titles in a row. At the end of a closely contested first half Lansdowne were only marginally ahead 8–5 through a try from scrumhalf Alan Bennie and a penalty from Deasy.

Lansdowne FC versus Young Munster, 2017–18 season.

However, three tries in the third quarter from second-row Josh O'Rourke, Ireland sevens player Adam Leavy and centre Mark O'Keefe turned the game assuredly Lansdowne's way, with a fifth and final try coming from fullback Mills to ensure a 32–12 victory. It was the Club's fifth Bateman title overall and first since 1931 and had been facilitated by the Club's tenth Leinster League title the previous November.[58]

In between winning the Leinster League and Bateman Cup, the First XV had topped the AIL Division One A table ten points ahead of their nearest rivals with sixteen victories in eighteen games. In the semi-final of the play-offs, a week after winning the Bateman Cup, Lansdowne defeated Garryowen 36–19 with tries from Bennie, hooker Tyrone Moran and two from Leavy alongside a penalty try. The final was against the defending champions, Cork Constitution, whom Lansdowne had already denied the opportunity of doing the 'double' of AIL and Bateman Cup two years in a row. The challenge for Lansdowne was to secure a first such 'double' for themselves instead. The final was a much more closely contested affair than the Bateman match two weeks earlier, with Lansdowne coming out on top 19–16. The match-clinching try was scored by

Just before the AIL semi-final, Lansdowne FC versus Garryowen, 28 April 2018.

Moran in a contest personified by the endeavours of the Lansdowne front-row, especially the player of the match, Peter Dooley. The 'double' was thus secured, while a third AIL title in six seasons also meant Lansdowne became the first team in Leinster to win the competition three times.[59]

The only unfinished business of the season was the Leinster Senior Cup, the final of which was played against Terenure three days after the AIL victory. A clearly fatigued Lansdowne were trailing 17–3 at half-time, only to rally with a devastating eight tries in the second half to run out 53–22 victors. The winning of the Club's twenty-seventh Leinster Senior Cup title also meant that all four of the 2017–18 senior club competitions – two provincial and two national – had been won by the First XV for the first time in Lansdowne's history. It was a first for any Leinster club, and was a feat only previously achieved by Cork Constitution. The season had also seen Deasy top the AIL scoring charts with 219 points, which took his Club record for the AIL to 831. Already more than 400 points clear of his nearest Lansdowne competitor, it also meant that with his previous tallies at UCC and Cork Constitution, he had scored well over 1,200 points in the AIL in total.[60]

Dan McEvoy in action for Lansdowne FC against Garryowen, April 2018.

Tyrone Moran in action for Lansdowne FC against Garryowen, April 2018.

AIL Division One A, Leinster Senior League, Leinster Senior Cup and Bateman Cup, 2017–18. Backrow: R. Kelleher, P. Dooley, W. Earle, J.J. Earle, J. Rael, M. O'Keeffe, A. Leavy, M. Mulhall, A. Conneely, C. Murphy. Standing: D. O'Sullivan, W. Matthews (Asst. Coach), M. Ruddock (Head Coach), C. Goode, W. Walsh, C. O'Brien, O. Dowling, J. Dwan, J. O'Rourke, J. O'Sullivan, N. Mpiko, G. Molloy, C. McMickan, G. McGrath, R. Collins, A. McDonagh, P. Gore, S. Rooney, M. McHugh (Asst. Coach). Seated: B. Fitzpatrick, D. McEvoy, T. Moran, A. Bennie, T. Roche, M. Cassidy (Pres.), I. Prendiville (Capt.), S. Deasy, F. Horan, E. Mills, F. Cleary, H. Brennan.

Lansdowne Second XV Trophy Winners, 2017–18.

Ian Prendiville in action for Lansdowne FC at College Park against Dublin University, 2018–19.

With Mark MacMahon taking over as Director of Under-20s Rugby, there was also continued success in the J.P. Fanagan League. Under the same coaching set-up and captained by Tim Murphy, the Lansdowne Under-20s were the only team alongside UCD to lose just two of their fourteen league games. The title was therefore decided on the last day on bonus points, with Lansdowne coming out on top. Lansdowne's fifth J.P. Fanagan League title was also the second in a row and, with the Fraser McMullan Cup in 2014–15 and McCorry Cup in 2015–16, it was also the Club's fourth Under-20s trophy in four seasons. By any standards, it was sustained and excellent success for the age-level and further testament to the coaching standards and Club investment and vision. Not surprisingly, two of the Under-20s, Peter Sullivan and Ronan Kelleher, were selected for the Ireland Under-20s that season, with Kelleher going on to a career with both Leinster and Ireland. The Lansdowne Second XV also continued their winning ways under the captaincy of Gareth Molloy, defeating Old Wesley 20–14 in the final of the Junior 1 League to secure an eighteenth such title for the Club. And back where it all begins, at minis and youth levels, the Under-14s won the Metro

Peter Sullivan in action for Lansdowne FC against Dublin University, 2018–19.

Invitational Cup while the Under-17s won both the Premier Youths League and the Leinster Youths Cup.[61]

In November 2018, in recognition of the achievements of the First XV in 2017–18, Lansdowne FC were awarded the Guinness Rugby Writers of Ireland Tom Rooney Award for a significant contribution to Irish rugby. With such plaudits comes pressure. With Mills as Club Captain for the 2018–19 season, the defence of four titles got off to an excellent start in the Leinster Senior League Cup, which was retained with a 42–5 victory over Terenure in the final in late September. After two opening losses in the AIL, an ensuing eight-game winning streak was only brought to an end in the Bateman Cup semi-final away to Garryowen, who secured a hard-fought 14–12 victory in the closing minutes. Mixed fortunes thereafter in the AIL resulted in a third-place finish in the table and an away semi-final against Clontarf, which was lost 23–15. However, there was some compensation in that in the Leinster Senior Cup the previous week Lansdowne had defeated Dublin University 49–22 in the final, with two tries a piece for Sullivan and Leavy and one a piece for Prendiville, Mills and Horan. Having done the 'double' 'double' in terms of provincial trophies, with back-to-back Leinster League and Senior Cups, Lansdowne had secured their eleventh and twenty-eighth such titles respectively, which constituted the most titles of any club in both competitions. In his final season, Deasy brought his total Lansdowne AIL points haul to 950 having played for the Club in 106 AIL matches over six years. The season also saw Earle reach 147 AIL caps, while Prendiville had amassed 112. Peter Sullivan, who had fought back from serious injury the previous season, topped the Club's AIL try-scoring statistics with fifteen. At junior level, the Second XV under the captaincy of Gareth Molloy also achieved the Junior 1 League and Metropolitan Cup 'double', with back-to-back League titles and a second Cup in three seasons. In both finals Old Wesley were defeated, 17–14 in the League and 17–13 in the Cup. The Under-17s also kept up their winning ways with the Leinster Premier Youths League title for the second year in a row.[62]

Such continuing success across all levels of club competition for Lansdowne FC was set against an ongoing discontent across the club community with the IRFU's attitude towards the club game. The close of the 2018–19 season saw renewed focus upon such issues. In an *Irish Times* interview with Gerry Thornley, Lansdowne's President, Kieran Mulligan, spoke openly about the fact that the clubs appeared to be 'the neglected child of Irish rugby'. Mulligan highlighted the problems associated with the ever-decreasing age profile of AIL players, the struggles of clubs to field teams at Third and Third A levels, the increased cost of living in Dublin for Lansdowne's traditional out-of-town players, and the perennial issue of the unavailability of those contracted to the provinces, especially when re-routed to meaningless 'A' competitions. The associated loss of players to other professional franchises outside Ireland

Ian Prendiville in action for Lansdowne FC against Terenure, 2018–19.

was also a problem – Mulligan in particular cited ex-Lansdowne players Ross Deacon, Mark O'Keeffe and Marcus Walsh who were all signed up to professional teams in the US. More needed to be done to facilitate keeping such players closer to home and playing for AIL clubs. But it was not just about the players. The clubs remained the heart and soul of Ireland's rugby communities as well as being a crucial part of local communities more generally, offering sporting outlets and social environments for so many children, youths, adults and families, while also being focal points for fund-raising activities and other socially-aware projects, offering good examples and guidance to those who joined or participated. Lansdowne under Mulligan's guidance had continued a long Club tradition in that regard, raising nearly €40,000 for local cancer support services, drugs awareness groups, employment schemes and community and resource centres.[63]

At the same time, Matt Williams raised the issue of the unsustainable business models relied upon by Irish clubs and argued for a greater connection with the provincial franchises: 'The provincial teams must support their AIL communities because it is these communities who attend the professional clubs' matches. The AIL clubs are the bums on seats for the provincial teams'. He also argued that the AIL clubs had to stop thinking short term, start planning for the long term and ultimately remember 'their reason for being'. With the *Irish Times* on something of a mission at that time, following on from an article highlighting the role of the clubs' Under-20 structures and teams in fuelling success at national level at that age-grade, John O'Sullivan also pointed out how many of the Ireland players in 2019 had come through the clubs, as demonstrated by a review of the teams playing in the last four AIL finals since Lansdowne had won in 2014–15. Both arguments implicitly advocated for greater IRFU and provincial recognition and support for the clubs in these endeavours.[64]

Such issues truly mattered, but little did the world know how they and so many other concerns would fade into the background within a few short months after the start of the 2019–20 season. For Ruddock and McHugh heading into a new coaching season with Jack Dwan as captain of the First XV, the best laid plans could never have accommodated the outbreak of the Covid-19 global pandemic in February–March 2020. With the IRFU cancelling the domestic season with immediate effect on 20 March, competitions were left incomplete and unresolved. Where finalists existed, cups were to be shared. For Lansdowne, this meant a joint Bateman Cup title. In another recalibration of the rules, Lansdowne had qualified for the Cup that season as winners of the Leinster Senior Cup in 2018–19. Having defeated City of Armagh 20–17 in the semi-final in January with a hat-trick from the Leinster Academy hooker Dan Sheehan, the trophy was thereafter shared with the other finalists, Cork Constitution. In reality, few competitions had been completed by March 2020, though the Lansdowne Under-20s had managed to secure their thirteenth win out of fourteen games in the J.P. Fanagan League in early March with a

31–28 victory over Dublin University and thereby won their third such title in four seasons.[65]

Covid-19 brought a resounding and catastrophic end to the second decade of the twenty-first century. It was a decade that had also seen the passing of a number of Lansdowne's great players, supporters and characters. In December 2012, after a twenty-five-year battle with illness, Evelyn Quinn had passed away. She had been the long-time medic and general care-giver to the Under-20s and Under-21s and rightfully the recipient of the inaugural Eoin Feighery Lansdowne Under-21s Legend Award in 2011. She had also done so much to keep Mark Governey alive pitch-side in 1999. Seamus Kelly also passed away in 2012, while in February 2013 the death had occurred of Jack Dawson, a second-generation Lansdowne stalwart and great supporter and ambassador of the Club throughout his life, who had followed in his father Michael's footsteps as a player, administrator and President, as well as having being Club Captain in 1950–1 and later serving as one of the Club Trustees from 2007 to 2012. A true believer in the Lansdowne playing tradition and ethos, Jack's four sons all followed in his footsteps, ensuring that a third generation of Dawsons were centrally involved with the Club their father and grandfather had given so much to throughout their lifetimes. The year 2013 also saw the passing of another former Club Captain and President, Paddy Berkery, as well as Ken Nuzum. In October 2016 Kevin Kelleher also passed away at the age of ninety-five.[66]

Lansdowne FC Second XV versus Old Belvedere, 2018–19.

Lansdowne FC Under 20s versus Old Belvedere, 2019–20.

The years 1995 to 2020 had proven to be both challenging and rewarding for Lansdowne. Throughout those years twenty-three Lansdowne players had played for Ireland. Ranging from one to eighty-two caps, they were: T. Beirne; J. Cooney; G. D'Arcy; M. Deegan; E. Elwood; G.M. Fulcher; M. Healy; D. Heffernan; S. Horgan; D. Kearney; R. Kelleher; K. Lewis; A. McCullen; A. McKeen; K.P. McQuilkin; M. Moore; J. Murphy; D.W. O'Mahony; C.M. O'Shea; E. Reddan; D. Ryan; J. Ryan; and D. Toner. By staying true to the traditions, ethos and legacies bestowed and valued by previous generations of Club players, administrators, supporters and families, Lansdowne had navigated the various journeys required to survive and thrive in the face of professionalism, new financial pressures, decreased spectator attendances, player-drain, a remodelled home ground and the need for a new junior ground. That success was down to being true to core values and traditions from the First XV through the Second XV, Third XV and Third As and on to the associated constant investment of time, energy and money in the ongoing development of the minis, youths and Under-19s, Under-20s and Under-21s. For all the challenges, being Lansdowne FC was what really mattered.

1872

Conclusion

2021–2022

The Lansdowne President for 2020–1, Colin Goode, was re-elected for the 2021–2 season in light of the Covid-19 global pandemic. A Club President serving more than one term had only occurred before in times of crisis: F. Denning during the First World War; F. Joynt during the Irish War of Independence; and Ernie Crawford during the first years of the Second World War. It was an exceptional measure for exceptional times. Covid-19 was only the second time in history that club rugby had been cancelled in Ireland. The first time had been following the outbreak of the First World War. But as Goode stated in the 2021–2 Yearbook, after eighteen months without any club rugby at all and as the game slowly re-emerged in the autumn of 2021, the Lansdowne colours of black, red and yellow were never more pertinent than at that time. Based on the colours of the nineteenth-century English touring cricket club, I Zingari, they symbolized the motto 'Out of darkness, through

Lansdowne FC's outdoor Covid-19 changing facilities for the Leinster Senior Cup tie with Wanderers at Merrion Road, August 2021. Source: *Irish Times*, 23 August 2021.

fire, into light'. More broadly, that motto was synonymous with the history of the Club. It had survived dark times, overcome trials and tribulations, and emerged better and stronger on each occasion. For each challenge, answers had been found, and the journey had continued. As such, the Club, like most sporting organizations, was a reflection of the society at large within which it existed. At the heart of every sporting activity is sociability – the desire and need of people to associate and interact. Sporting clubs are central to fulfilling such desire and need, and it is the people who make up the clubs – the players, administrators, supporters, members, families and visitors – that are the lifeblood of all such organizations. Fundamentally, the club is the people, and the people are the club.[1]

As long-time Club member Johnnie Lombard mused in 2014, Lansdowne grew 'from a rugby club … into a community, a family that stays with us long after we pulled our last hamstring … it is the New York City of Rugby Clubs. It is the melting pot of homeless rugby players. All are welcome with open arms'.[2] One of Lansdowne's greatest successes has been its continuing attraction for players from all parts of Ireland and beyond, a tradition sustained and built upon each generation as the names of past Lansdowne players from Munster, Connacht and Ulster encouraged later generations to do the same. Likewise,

Lansdowne versus UCD AIL Match Programme, December 2021.

the fact that the Club was never associated with any particular school or grouping encouraged a much wider spectrum of players from all walks of economic and social life to join. A greater belief in a level playing field for all who joined, both on and off the pitch, sustains those traditions and ethos.[3]

In 2020–1 Covid-19 had stopped club rugby, but in time it also offered a reminder of its pending return. With the Aviva Stadium turned into both a Covid-19 testing centre and a mass vaccination centre, those who stood in the socially distanced queues within the eastern side of the stadium could watch the return of training sessions on the all-weather back pitch, from cohorts among the 400 Lansdowne minis under the guidance of Brian Moran through to the First team squad. In a highly symbolic and appropriate fixture, the early days of the return of competitive club rugby in August 2021 saw the

Post-match celebration of the Lansdowne FC Third XV's Albert O'Connell Cup final victory, 2 October 2021.

Lansdowne First XV take on their old rivals and co-tenants Wanderers in the first round of the Leinster Senior Cup. Lansdowne won 27–3, but the result was much less important than the fact that these two old clubs, one already 150 years old and the other about to turn that age, could once again compete as they had down through the decades since 1872.[4]

By the end of September 2021, Lansdowne had brought home another trophy, winning the 2021–2 Leinster Senior League by defeating Clontarf 34–13 in the final. Then, in early October, the Third XV won the Albert O'Connell Cup for the fifteenth time in the Club's history, beating the holders Old Wesley 19–13. Further success was seen in February 2022 when the First XV defeated Young Munster 46–13 in the Bateman Cup final, thereby bringing a seventh such title to the Club exactly 100 years after the first had been secured in 1922. Finally, in March, the Under-20s retained the J.P. Fanagan League title by defeating Clontarf 38–22. Ireland's 2021 summer and autumn senior international fixtures had also seen two more former Lansdowne Under-20 players, Harry Byrne and Dan Sheehan, capped for the national team, while the 2022 Six Nations saw both Oisin Michel and Charlie Tector capped for the Ireland Under-20s. At the same time, other recent Lansdowne Under-20s, like the twin brothers Rory and Stephen Madigan, had progressed into the Club's First team squad. The Madigan brothers also represented yet another example of second-generation players, as they followed in the footsteps of their father, Paddy, at the Club. It was also the case that the Club Captain for 2021–2, Jack O'Sullivan, had himself come through the Under-20s structures at the Club as well. With Mark McHugh having taken over as head coach of the First XV, with the Under-20 structures back up and running, and with all the minis, youths and junior teams in between, so Lansdowne FC got going once again with all the volunteers, administrators, families, friends and supporters working away behind the scenes.[5]

Challenges remained, as they always do. In November 2021 the former Lansdowne, Leinster and Ireland player, Gordon D'Arcy, a forceful advocate for greater game-time for provincial players in the AIL, cited the high-scoring Lansdowne–Young Munster league clash at the Aviva on 30 October 2021 as a

Lansdowne FC versus Dublin University at College Park, February 2022

prime example of the high standard of competition available for professional players otherwise consigned to the gym at certain times of the season. His own experiences playing with Lansdowne with Shane Horgan, Barry Everitt, Liam Toland and others assured him of the veracity of the argument. Writing in the *Irish Times* in December 2021, D'Arcy also argued that

> without proper investment and vision in our club game, men's and women's, we will always be punching with one hand tied behind our back. It is important to note that the vast majority of male players in the schools rugby system start in a club. Imagine a scenario in which every player gets coached in such a way to give them the tools to play and enjoy rugby, irrespective of level. Better coaching produces better players.[6]

Lansdowne FC 150th Anniversary Logo.

The club game will always be crucial to the health and well-being of rugby in Ireland, just as it is for every sport. As a central focal point for associational culture, the clubhouse provides a place for sociability, solidarity and identification. It is at the heart of all that takes place on the pitch, but also transcends playing days into later life in public and private spheres. The administrative volunteers who keep the club machine rolling, who fund-raise to pay the debts and provide the necessary infrastructure, the coaches, team managers, drivers, medics and tea-makers from minis to First XV who keep the show on the road – this is society in microcosm, a reflection of the human condition, of the fundamentals of civil society. The lessons learnt from early years about fair play, respect for teammates, the opposition and the match officials, about teamwork, about winning and losing with equal grace, of rising to the challenge and battling adversity, are all incubated and developed within club life. If all of it is not nurtured and encouraged to grow along with the elite levels of the game, then the game itself will in time wither and die.

The history of Lansdowne FC is therefore a history of Irish associational culture in microcosm. It is a history of how positive traditions, ethos and legacies are established within civil society, and how they are developed, nurtured and sustained. And it is ultimately a history of the many, many people whose interest, commitment, compassion, drive, energy, love and passion make it all happen. Without people, there is no history. And without people, there is no Club.

Members watching in front of the Clubhouse at the Lansdowne FC versus UCD AIL match, December 2021.

Appendices

Appendix 1: Lansdowne FC Presidents and Club Captains, 1872–2022

Year	President	Captain
1872–1873		J.D. Ogilvy
1873–1874		J.D. Ogilvy
1874–1875		J.D. Ogilvy
1875–1876		D.T. Arnott
1876–1877		F.W. Kidd
1877–1878		J.W. Richards
1878–1879		G.S. Criven
1879–1880		E.H. Nunns
1880–1881		J.C. Baggot
1881–1882		J.B. Moore
1882–1883		J.B. Moore
1883–1884		J.B. Moore
1884–1885		R.G. Warren
1885–1886		R.G. Warren
1886–1887		R.G. Warren
1887–1888		R.G. Warren
1888–1889		R.G. Warren
1889–1890		R.G. Warren
1890–1891		V.C. Le Fanu
1891–1892		V.C. Le Fanu
1892–1893		F.E. Davies
1893–1894		F.E. Davies
1894–1895		S.C. Smith
1895–1896		A.A. Brunker R.P. Rowan
1896–1897		R.W. Jeffares Sr.

Lansdowne FC Presidents and Club Captains, 1872–2022		
Year	**President**	**Captain**
1897–1898		R.W. Jeffares Sr.
1898–1899		G.P. Doran
1899–1900		G.P. Doran
1900–1901		B.R. Doran
1901–1902		B.R. Doran
1902–1903		J.J. Coffey
1903–1904	H.W.D. Dunlop	J.J. Coffey
1904–1905	J. Sibthorpe	J.J. Warren
1905–1906	J.B. Moore	M.J. D'Alton
1906–1907	H. Moore	H.G. Sugars
1907–1908	W. Piggott	A.L. Leeper
1908–1909	J. Denning	M.J. D'Alton
1909–1910	R.G. Warren	G. Weldon
1910–1911	F.W. Kidd	R. Donnelly
1911–1912	R.W. Jeffares Sr.	R. Donnelly
1912–1913	A.M. Toomey	C.R. Wilson
1913–1914	J. Chambers	J. Burke-Gaffney
1914–1915	F. Denning	J. Burke-Gaffney
1915–1916	F. Denning	J. Burke-Gaffney
1916–1917	F. Denning	J. Burke-Gaffney
1917–1918	F. Denning	J. Burke-Gaffney
1918–1919	F. Denning	J. Burke-Gaffney
1919–1920	A.A. Brunker	N.M. Purcell
1920–1921	F. Joynt	N.M. Purcell
1921–1922	F. Joynt	W.E. Crawford

Lansdowne FC Presidents and Club Captains, 1872–2022		
Year	**President**	**Captain**
1922–1923	B.R. Doran	W.E. Crawford
1923–1924	J.J. Coffey	W.A. Cunningham
1924–1925	J.J. Warren	P.J. Whitty
1925–1926	R. Simons	T.V. Harris
1926–1927	J.A. Gargan	T.O. Pike
1927–1928	A.C. Sibthorpe	G.P.S. Hogan
1928–1929	M. Dawson	E. O'D. Davy
1929–1930	M.J. D'Alton	E. O'D. Davy
1930–1931	C.J. Law	J.F. McEnery
1931–1932	F.E. Davies	M.J. Dunne
1932–1933	V.C. Le Fanu	M.J. Dunne
1933–1934	F.A. Ross	T.A. O'Reilly
1934–1935	V.V. Drennan	E.J. Lightfoot
1935–1936	R.H. Lambert	J.E. Arigho
1936–1937	H. Donnelly	Rev. St.J. Pike
1937–1938	N.M. Purcell	T.P. Sinnott
1938–1939	F.W. Warren	T.J. O'Driscoll
1939–1940	W.E. Crawford	C.J. Murphy
1940–1941	W.E. Crawford	W.G. Sutherland
1941–1942	J.A. Cooke	W.G. Sutherland
1942–1943	A.H. Robinson	P. Mitchell
1943–1944	W.J. Young	N.J. Burke
1944–1945	R.H. Maunsell	C.J. Murphy
1945–1946	R.W. Jeffares Jr.	D. Hingerty
1946–1947	L.J. Heaney	C. Callan
1947–1948	A.J. Beatty	Rev. W.J. Moynan

Lansdowne FC Presidents and Club Captains, 1872–2022		
Year	**President**	**Captain**
1948–1949	R.N. Mitchell	J.F. Coffey
1949–1950	M.J. Dunne	R. Carroll
1950–1951	F.C. Conroy	J.C. Dawson
1951–1952	E.J. Lightfoot	E. Connellan
1952–1953	Lt. Col. J.J. Burke-Gaffney, MC	C.V. Crowley
1953–1954	T.A. O'Reilly	T.D. McNally
1954–1955	E. O'D. Davy	L.M. Lynch
1955–1956	J. Bell	J.P.D. Morris
1956–1957	Dr M.P. Crowe	P.J. Berkery
1957–1958	T.C. Fox	A. Twomey
1958–1959	E.W. Garland	M.A.L. Tansey
1959–1960	H.W. Jack, OBE DSc	S. Kelly
1960–1961	C.S.P. Randall	B.G.M. Wood
1961–1962	N.H. Lambert	N. Feddis
1962–1963	G.P.S. Hogan, BL	B.G.M. Wood
1963–1964	Maj. Gen. S. Collins-Powell	Dr M.D. Kiely
1964–1965	W.G. Sutherland	C. Powell
1965–1966	J.E. McEnery	A. Twomey
1966–1967	C.J. Murphy	A.T.A. Duggan
1967–1968	J.N. Garland	P.J. Casey
1968–1969	R. Mitchell	N. Dwyer
1969–1970	T.C. Byrne	Dr J. Craig
1970–1971	T.V. Davy, SC	P. Sutherland
1971–1972	Rev. W.J. Moynan	Dr E. Kiely

Lansdowne FC Presidents and Club Captains, 1872–2022		
Year	**President**	**Captain**
1972–1973	J.F. Coffey	J. Mitchell
1973–1974	A.W. Campbell	D. Power
1974–1975	H. Vard	J. Flanagan
1975–1976	J.C. Dawson	P. Inglis
1976–1977	P.J. Berkery	D. Canniffe
1977–1978	J.P. Barrett	P. Gahan
1978–1979	A. McNally	R. Spring
1979–1980	A. Twomey	P. Boylan
1980–1981	R. Carroll	M. Keane
1981–1982	L. Lynch	M. Quinn
1982–1983	S. MacHale	M. Gibson
1983–1984	P. Moorhead	V. Becker
1984–1985	K. Kelleher	D. Spring
1985–1986	N. Hayden	M. Ryan
1986–1987	Dr J. Craig	W. Burns
1987–1988	J. Maguire	J. Collins
1988–1989	P. Ward	G. Dilger
1989–1990	M. English	V. Ryan
1990–1991	P. Casey	P. Clinch
1991–1992	C. Flanagan	W. Burns
1992–1993	L. MacSherry	F. Aherne
1993–1994	C. Powell	J. Sexton
1994–1995	J. Mitchell	F. Aherne
1995–1996	B. McGann	B. Glennon
1996–1997	P. Inglis	M. McDermott

Lansdowne FC Presidents and Club Captains, 1872–2022		
Year	**President**	**Captain**
1997–1998	P. Van Cauwelaert	K. McQuilkin
1998–1999	A. Duggan	K. McQuilkin
1999–2000	M. Kearney	D. O'Mahony
2000–2001	J. Flanagan	C. McEntee
2001–2002	J. Ledden	S. Rooney
2002–2003	P. Gahan	E. Bohan
2003–2004	F. Forrest	E. Bohan
2004–2005	B. Sparks	L. Toland / S. O'Connor
2005–2006	O. Ó Buachalla	G. Quinn
2006–2007	A. Delany	D. Lavin
2007–2008	P. Halpenny	A. Maher
2008–2009	J. Kearney	A. Maher
2009–2010	M. Dawson	J. Lyne
2010–2011	C. O'Reilly	J. Lyne
2011–2012	P. Boylan	R. McCarron
2012–2013	D. McCarron	R. McCarron
2013–2014	M. Quinn	W. Earle
2014–2015	F. Kenny	R. Boucher
2015–2016	D. Lennon	S. Deasy
2016–2017	S. Coyle	I. Prendiville
2017–2018	M. Cassidy	I. Prendiville
2018–2019	K.J. Mulligan	E. Mills
2019–2020	D. Shaw	J. Dwan
2020–2021	C. Goode	J. Dwan
2021–2022	C. Goode	J. O'Sullivan

Appendix 2: Lansdowne FC Honorary Secretaries and Treasurers, 1872–2022

Honorary Secretary		Honorary Treasurer	
Duration	**Office Holder**	**Duration**	**Office Holder**
1872–1874	R.W. Morgan	1875–1876	J.R. Frazer[1]
1874–1875	J.W. Richards	1878–1879	W. Cooper
1875–1876	D.T. Arnott	1879–1880	H.F. Orr
1876–1877	J.W. Richards & G. Scriven	1883–1885	G.C. Webb
1877–1878	R.J. Baker & J.C. Bagot	1885–1887	J. Sibthorpe
1878–1879	R.J. Polden & H.W.D. Dunlop	1887–1889	D.D. Bulger
1879–1882	F.S. Searight	1889–1895	J. Sibthorpe
1882–1883	R.W. Littledale	1895–1896	G.P. Moyles
1883–1884	J.A. Denning	1896–1897	A. Bradley
1884–1890	C.F. Ruxton	1897–1901	J. Anderson
1890–1892	E.S. Jacob	1901–1904	R.S. Swan
1892–1894	E.G. Brunker	1904–1905	M.J. D'Alton
1894–1895	J. Anderson	1905–1906	W.B. Swan
1895–1900	B. Scott	1906–1909	J. Browne
1900–1903	R.W. Jeffares Sr.	1909–1914	J.A. Cooke
1903–1906	F. Studdert	1914–1929	A. Sibthorpe
1906–1913	F.C. Joynt[2]	1929–1951	L.J. Heaney
1912–1913	V. Drennan	1951–1965	T.C. Fox
1913–1923	F.C. Joynt	1965–1971	J.P. Barrett
1923–1924	N.M. Purcell	1971–1976	P.J. Moore
1924–1945	J.J. Coffey	1976–1978	D. Hannigan

1 There is no extant record of a treasurer for the years 1872–5 or 1877–8.
2 Stepped down temporarily for health reasons.

Lansdowne FC Honorary Secretaries and Treasurers, 1872–2022			
Honorary Secretary		**Honorary Treasurer**	
Duration	**Office Holder**	**Duration**	**Office Holder**
1945–1952	M.J. Dunne	1978–1983	W.G. Sutherland
1952–1957	N.J. Burke	1983–1985	H. Glynn
1957–1970	W.G. Sutherland	1985–1986	N. Feddis
1970–1976	P.J. Berkery	1986–1987	T. Gleeson
1976–1977	J. Driscoll	1987–1990	L. MacSherry
1977–1986	H.G. Governey	1990–1994	J.A. Leddin
1986	A. Browne[3]	1994–2000	P. Halpenny
1986–1989	H.G. Governey	2000–2004	A. Delany
1989–1999	F. Thompson	2004–2012	D. McDowell
1999–2007	M. Daly	2012–2015	C. Gahan
2007–2011	M. Graham	2015–2022	K. Cleere
2011–2013	D. Lennon		
2013–2015	G. Quinn		
2015–2016	M.G. Hunt		
2016–2018	D.G. Early		
2018–2022	K. Walsh		

3 Appointed in April 1986 and resigned in July 1986 owing to a new job in Boston, MA.

Appendix 3: Lansdowne FC International Players, 1872–2022[4]

Player	Years	Caps	Player	Years	Caps
Aherne, L.P.F.	1988–1992	16 (1)	Contepomi, F.	1998–2013	85 (62)
Arigho, J.E.	1928–1931	16	Cook, H.G.	1884	1
Arnott, D.T.	1876	1	Cooney, J.	2020–	
Bagot, J.C.	1879–1881	5	Corrigan, R.P.	1997–2006	32 (28)
Bailey, A.H.	1934–1938	13 (12)	Crawford, W.E.*	1920–1927	30
Barr, A.	1898–1901	4 (2)	Cronyn, A.P.	1875–1880	3
Becker, V.A.M.	1974	2	Crowe, M.P.	1929–1934	13 (3)
Beirne, T.+	2018–		Cunningham, W.A.+	1920–1923	8
Berkery, P.J.	1954–1958	11 (3)	Danaher, P.P.	1988–1995	28 (25)
Boyle, C.V.+	1935–1939	9 (8)	D'Arcy, G.+	1999–2015	82
Bresnihan, F.P.K.+	1966–1971	25 (25)	Davies, F.E.	1892–1893	5
Brunker, A.A.D.	1895	2 (2)	Davy, E.O'D.*	1925–1934	34 (5)
Bulger, L.Q.+	1896–1898	8 (3)	Deegan, M.	2020–	
Bulger, M.J.	1888	1 (1)	Doran, B.R.W.	1900–1902	8
Byrne, H.	2021–		Doran, E.F.	1890	2
Byrne, J.J.D.	1953–1955	3	Doran, G.P.+	1899–1904	8
Callan, C.P.	1947–1949	10	Duggan, A.T.A.	1964–1972	25
Canniffe, D.M.	1976	2	Dunlea, F.J.	1989–1990	3
Carroll, J.R.	1947–1950	3	Dunne, M.J.+	1929–1934	16
Casey, P.J.	1963–1965	12 (3)	Edwards, T.	1889–1893	6
Clancy, T.P.J.	1988–1989	9	Elwood, E.P.	1993–2002	35 (12)
Coffey, J.J.	1900–1910	19	English, M.A.F.+	1958–1963	16 (11)
Collins, P.C.	1987–1990	2 (1)	Feddis, N.	1956	1

4 There are 117 players listed in total. Those whose careers were ongoing at the time of publication do not have terminal dates or total number of caps. Figures in brackets are for caps won while at other clubs. * denotes Ireland Captain. + denotes players who toured with the British and Irish Lions.

Lansdowne FC International Players, 1872–2022					
Player	**Years**	**Caps**	**Player**	**Years**	**Caps**
Feighery, C.F.P.	1972	3	Lewis, K.	2005–2007	3 (3)
Fitzgerald, D.C.[+]	1984–1992	34	Lightfoot, E.J.	1931–1933	11
Freerar, A.E.	1901	3	Lynch, M.L.	1956	1
Fulcher, G.M.	1994–1999	21 (20)	McConnell, J.W.	1913	1
Gibson, M.E.	1979–1988	10 (5)	McCullen, A.	2003	1
Glennon, B.T.	1993	1	McGann, B.J.	1969–1976	25 (21)
Hamilton, A.J.	1884	1	McGowan, A.	1994	1 (1)
Healy, M.	2016–		MacHale, S.	1965–1967	12
Heffernan, D.	2017–		McKeen, A.	1999	1
Henebery, G.J.	1906–1907	6 (4)	McQuilkin, K.P.	1996–1997	5 (3)
Hingerty, D.J.	1947	4 (4)	Mannion, N.P.	1988–1993	16 (11)
Horgan, S.[+]	1999–2011	64 (10)	Moore, M.	2013–	
Jack, H.J.	1914–1921	3 (2)	Moroney, R.J.M.	1984–1985	3
Jameson, J.S.	1889–1893	7	Murphy, C.J.*	1939–1947	5
Johnson-Smyth, T.R.	1882	1	Murphy, J.	2013–	
Keane, M.I.[+]	1974–1984	51	O'Connell, W.J.	1955	1
Kearney, D.	2013–		O'Connor, P.J.	1887	1
Kelleher, R.[+]	2020–		O'Flanagan, M.	1948	1
Kelly, J.P. (Seamus)	1954–1960	5	O'Mahony, D.P.	1995	1 (1)
Kidd, F.W.	1877–1878	3	O'Mahony, D.W.	1995–1997	4 (4)
Kiely, M.D.	1962–1963	5	O'Shea, C.M.	1993–2000	35 (22)
Kiernan, M.J.[+]	1982–1991	43 (36)	Pike, T.O.	1927–1928	8
Knox, H.J.R.	1904–1908	10	Pike, V.J.	1931–1934	13
Lambert, N.H.	1934	2	Purcell, N.M.J.	1921	4
Le Fanu, V.C.*	1886–1892	11 (4)	Quinn, M.A.	1973–1981	10

Lansdowne FC International Players, 1872–2022					
Player	**Years**	**Caps**	**Player**	**Years**	**Caps**
Reddan, E.	2007–2016	71 (16)	Sheehan, D.	2021–	
Reidy, G.F.	1953–1954	5 (4)	Sherry, M.J.A.	1975	2
Roe, R.+	1952–1957	21 (17)	Smith, R.E.	1892	1
Ross, J.P.*	1885–1886	4	Spring, D.E.J.	1978–1981	7 (6)
Rutherford, J.P.*	1884–1888	5 (2)	Spring, R.M.	1979	3
Ryan, D.	2014	1	Synge, J.S.	1929	1
Ryan, J.	2017–		Toner, D.	2010–2020	70
Sayers, H.J.M.	1935–1939	10 (10)	Walsh, E.J.	1875–1876	7
Scriven, G.*	1879–1883	8	Warren, R.G.*	1884–1890	15
Sexton, J.F.	1988–1989	4 (1)	Wood, B.G.M.+	1954–1961	29 (19)
Shanahan, T.	1885–1888	5			

Lansdowne versus Dublin University, November 2021.

Appendix 4: Lansdowne FC Trophies, 1872–2022

First XV:

Leinster Senior Cup (28):
1890–1, 1900–1, 1902–3, 1903–4, 1921–2, 1926–7, 1927–8, 1928–9, 1929–30, 1930–1, 1932–3, 1948–9, 1949–50, 1952–3, 1964–5, 1971–2, 1978–9, 1979–80, 1980–1, 1985–6, 1988–9, 1990–1, 1996–7, 1997–8, 2008–9, 2016–17, 2017–18, 2018–19

Leinster Senior League / Championship (12):
1973–4, 1976–7, 1980–1, 1985–6, 1986–7, 1987–8, 1997–8, 1999–2000, 2001–2, 2017–18, 2018–19, 2021–2

Bateman Cup (7):
1921–2, 1928–9, 1929–30, 1930–1, 2017–18, 2019–20,[5] 2021–2

AIL Division One A (3):
2012–13, 2014–15, 2017–18

AIL Division Two (2):
1992–3, 2009–10

Second XV:

Junior 1 League (19):
1900–1, 1924–5, 1926–7, 1927–8, 1940–1, 1944–5, 1946–7, 1949–50, 1962–3, 1964–5, 1986–7, 1988–9, 1994–5, 2003–4, 2009–10, 2013–14, 2014–15, 2017–18, 2018–19

Metropolitan Cup (15):
1926–7, 1947–8, 1958–9, 1964–5, 1967–8, 1980–1, 1981–2, 1988–9, 1999–2000, 2002–3, 2006–7, 2008–9, 2009–10, 2016–17, 2018–19

Third XV:

Junior 2 (Minor) League (12):
1928–9, 1932–3, 1934–5, 1959–60, 1960–1, 1961–2, 1975–6, 1978–9, 1984–5, 2011–12, 2013–14, 2014–15

Albert O'Connell (Minor) Cup (15):
1957–8, 1959–60, 1968–9, 1970–1, 1980–1, 1983–4, 1987–8, 1992–3, 1993–4, 1998–9, 1999–2000, 2011–12, 2014–15, 2015–16, 2020–1

5 Owing to the cancellation of the final of the Bateman Cup because of Covid-19, the two qualifying teams, Lansdowne and Cork Constitution, were declared joint winners for the 2019–20 season.

Third As:

Junior 3 League (12):
1965–6, 1967–8, 1968–9, 1970–1, 1980–1, 1991–2, 1998–9, 2003–4, 2005–6, 2006–7, 2007–8, 2010–11

Moran Cup (13):
1957–8, 1961–2, 1964–5, 1968–9, 1976–7, 1982–3, 1989–90, 2005–6, 2006–7, 2007–8, 2008–9, 2010–11, 2011–12

Third Bs:

Junior 4 League (2):
1984–5, 1987–8

Winters Cup (2):
1965–6, 1990–1

Third Cs:

James O'Connor Cup (2):
1980–1, 2001–2

Third Ds:

Tom Fox Cup (2):
1987–8, 1995–6

James Guilfolye Cup (1):
2014–15

Third Es:

Greenlea Cup (2):
1984–5, 1987–8

Under-19s / Under-20s / Under-21s:

J.P. Fanagan League (7):
1998–9, 2000–1, 2008–9, 2016–17, 2017–18, 2019–20, 2021–2

McCorry Cup (7):
1977–8, 1986–7, 1992–3, 2007–8, 2008–9, 2010–11, 2015–16

All-Ireland Trophy / Frazer McMullen Cup (3):
1998–9, 2012–13, 2014–15

Pennant / Conall Owens Cup (1):
2010–11

Purcell Cup (1):
2003–4

Lansdowne FC Trophy Cabinet.

Lansdowne FC Bar.

LANSDOWNE FC
v
GARRYOWEN FC

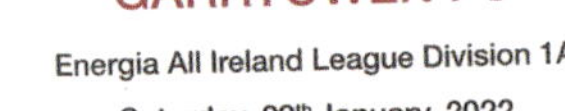

Energia All Ireland League Division 1A

Saturday, 29th January, 2022
Kick Off: 14:30

ZURICH

(left) Lansdowne versus Garryowen AIL Match Programme, January 2022.

(below) Lansdowne FC Gym.

Appendix 5: Members of Lansdowne FC killed during the First World War, 1914–1918[6]		
Members		
C.W.J. Bell	V.W. Hillyard	D.S. Smyth
G.R. Bible	T.C. Jones-Nowlan	R.S. Swan
T.S.C. Black	R.G. Kerr	T.E. Symes
W.P. Bridge	J.H.F. Leland	R.P. Tobin
J.E. Burke	C.A. LePeton	R.L. Valentine
W.S. Collen	D. LePeton	K.M. Wallace
I.M. Craig	H. Linde	E.T. Weatherill
T.J. D'Alton	L. McGrane	C. Weir
R.V. Drought	H. Moore	H.C. Weldon
J.R. Duggan	W.O. Morris	T. Whitty
L. Elvidge	A.W. Moss	C.R. Wilson
F.G. Heuston	W.J. Rice (Dublin, 1916)	L.G. Worthington-Eyre
M.A. Hill	W.A. Sadlier	E.L. Young
Former Members		
G.G. Alderdyce	H.P. Dudley	C.J. Law
J.N. Armstrong	H. Grahame	G.W. Lawder
L.M. Bayley	J.R. Hall	E.J. McCormick
A.C. Belcher	W.F. Hartley	J.T. McEntire
C.S. Burrowes	E.S. Hatte	E.J. Mahony
T.H. Clesham	F. Heffernan	D.W. Moore
G.H. Cross	J.C. Henry	W. Morton
C. Davidson Houston	H.T. Kennedy	H.L. North
J. O'G. Delmege	C.J. Kenny	J.F. Smith
G.E.B. Dobbs	A.E. Kingham	H. Stewart

6 LFC Minute Book 1902–1928, 10 Oct. 1919; Daly, 'Lansdowne and the First World War', pp 93–4.

H. Stoddart (Dublin, 1916)	J.A.H. Taylor	P. Walsh
F.M.D. Taylor	J.C. Tyndall	H.A. Warnock

Appendix 6: Members of Lansdowne FC awarded First World War Military Distinctions, 1914–1918		
	Military Cross:	
J.H. Barbor	H. Galbraith	G.W. Panter
P.C. Bell	F.G. Heuston	H.C.S. Panton
C.D. Buckley	R.G. Kerr	R.M. Patterson
J.V. Cope	G.H. McElnay	P.J. Ryan
J.F. Cox	H. Moore*	F.R. Shaw
E.W. Craig	G.L. Moss	R.P. Tobin
R.V. Drought	R.L. Murray	C.R. Wilson
H.W.G. Ferguson	S. O'Donel	G.H.B. Wilson
	Distinguished Service Order:	
P.B. Kelly	H. Moore*	T.T.H. Robinson
	Mentioned in Dispatches:	
R.N. Murray	L.G. Worthington-Eyre	
	Certificate:	
	J.E. Stokes	

* H. Moore was awarded both a DSO and Military Cross.

Lansdowne FC Second XV Honours Cap awarded to J.S. Weatherill, 1912–13 season.

Notes

Introduction – 1872

1 *Evening Herald*, 10 Oct. 1958, 4 March, 10 June 1959.

Chapter 1 – Finding a Name, Establishing the Game 1872–1899

1 M. J. O'Connor (ed.), *The History of Lansdowne Football Club* (Dublin, 1951), p. 3. For Dunlop's life see Turlough O'Riordan, 'Dunlop, Henry Wallace Doveton' in *Dictionary of Irish Biography* (online) [hereafter *DIB*]. O'Riordan states the ICAC was established in June 1872.

2 *The Sportsman*, 5 Oct. 1872; Paul Rouse, *Sport and Ireland* (Oxford, 2015), pp 84–7, 98–9, 112–16, 125–32.

3 *The Sportsman*, 5 Oct. 1872; Rouse, *Sport*, pp 137–8.

4 *Dublin Daily Express*, 11 Dec. 1872.

5 *Explanatory Circular*, ICAC Minute Book, 22 Nov. 1872.

6 ICAC Minute Book, 22 Nov. 1872, 21, 24 Jan., 22 Feb., 7 March 1873; *Freeman's Journal*, 8 March 1873.

7 *Dublin Daily Express*, 16 May 1873. Two later ICAC press releases also referenced the date of foundation as May 1872: *Dublin Daily Express*, 31 Jan. 1874; *Saunders News-Letter*, 16 March 1874.

8 *Dublin Daily Express*, 31 Jan. 1874; *Saunders News-Letter*, 16 March 1874.

9 *Dublin Daily Express*, 12 May 1873. Dunlop incorrectly dated the first event to 1872 (*History of Lansdowne*, p. 3).

10 ICAC Minute Book, 22 Oct., 29 Nov. 1873; *Dublin Daily Express*, 12 May 1783; *Freeman's Journal*, 24 Oct., 7 Nov. 1873; *Irish Times*, 7 Nov. 1873.

11 *Irish Times*, 7 Nov. 1873.

12 *History of Lansdowne*, p. 3.

13 LFC Fixture Book 1872–1951, pp 3, 15.

14 ICAC Minute Book, 9 Jan., 11 Feb., 20, 27 April 1874; *Irish Times*, 29 Jan., 25 May, 25 June, 18 Aug. 1874; *Freeman's Journal*, 30 Jan., 25 May 1874.

15 *Freeman's Journal*, 29 Oct. 1874.

16 *Irish Times*, 14 Nov. 1874; LFC Fixture Book 1872–1951, p. 171.

17 *History of Lansdowne*, pp 3, 7.

18 *Freeman's Journal*, 30 Dec. 1874; *History of Lansdowne*, pp 10–11; Rouse, *Sport*, p. 131; Edmund Van Esbeck, *One Hundred Years of Irish Rugby* (Dublin, 1974), pp 21–2.

19 *Irish Times*, 26, 28 Oct. 1875; *Freeman's Journal*, 28 Oct. 1875.

20 *Irish Times*, 25 Nov. 1875; LFC Fixture Book 1872–1951, p. 16.

21 *History of Lansdowne*, p. 7.

22 *Irish Times*, 3 Dec. 1875; ICAC Minute Book, 20 March 1874; *History of Lansdowne*, pp 7–8.

23 *History of Lansdowne*, p. 8; LFC Fixture Book 1872–1951, p. 17; *Irish Times*, 21 Feb. 1877; Gerald Siggins and Malachy Clerkin, *Lansdowne Road: The Stadium, the Matches, the Greatest Days* (Dublin, 2010), p. 33.

24 *Irish Times*, 8 Oct. 1878. See also Sean Diffley, *The Men in Green: The Story of Irish Rugby* (London, 1973), p. 25.

25 *Irish Times*, 24 Oct. 1879; *History of Lansdowne*, p. 11; 'Dunlop' in *DIB*.

26 *History of Lansdowne*, pp 11–12.

27 'Dunlop' in *DIB*; Rouse, *Sport*, p. 169; Diffley, *Men in Green*, p. 29.

28 LFC Fixture Book 1872–1951, pp 21–2; *Irish Times*, 5 March 1883. *History of Lansdowne*, p. 13 states incorrectly that the semi-final opposition in 1883 was Wanderers.

29 LFC Fixture Book 1872–1951, pp 15–22.

30 LFC Fixture Book 1872–1951, pp 25, 28, 53; Rouse, *Sport*, pp 130–1, 215–17; Van Esbeck, *Irish Rugby*, pp 16–18; information provided by Tom McCabe.

31 *Irish Times*, 15 Nov. 1880; *Sport*, 28 Jan. 1882; *The Athletic News and Cyclists' Journal*, 29 Nov. 1882; *History of Lansdowne*, pp 12–13.

32 *Sport*, 12 Nov. 1887; Rouse, *Sport*, pp 140–4. See also *Leeds Mercury*, 21 Nov. 1883; 21 Nov. 1886; *Wakefield Free Press*, 24 Nov. 1883; *Yorkshire Post*, 24 Nov. 1884; *Irish Times*, 29 Nov. 1886.

33 *Hull Daily Mail*, 17 Nov. 1887; *Irish Times*, 5–6 Dec. 1887, 23 Dec. 1890, 24 Nov., 21 Dec. 1891, 19 Dec. 1892, 26 Jan., 4 Dec. 1893, 21 Feb., 20 Nov. 1894, 29 Nov. 1898, 11 Dec. 1899; *Sporting Chronicle*, 22 Nov. 1888.

34 *Belfast Newsletter*, 11 March 1882, 27 Feb. 1897, 31 Oct. 1898; *Sport*, 8 Feb. 1890; *Irish Times*, 11 Dec. 1897, 10, 28 Feb. 1898, 7, 23 Feb. 1899; *Irish Examiner*, 24 Feb. 1894, 11 Dec. 1897, 7 March 1898; *Nationalist and Leinster Times*, 19 Nov. 1898; *Evening Echo*, 13 Dec. 1897; LFC Fixture Book 1872–1951, pp 23–48.

35 *Freeman's Journal*, 26 March, 27 Oct. 1884; *Belfast Newsletter*, 27 Oct. 1884; *Sport*, 1 Nov. 1874; *Evening Herald*, 23 July 1892, 11 April 1893, 27 March 1897; *Irish Times*, 31 March 1899.

36 Garry Redmond (ed.), *Lansdowne Football Club: Centenary 1872–1972* (Dublin, 1972), p. 17.

37 *Freeman's Journal*, 1 March 1887; *Irish Times*, 23, 29 March 1888, 25 Feb. 1889; LFC Fixture Book 1872–1951, pp 23–8; Liam O'Callaghan, 'Rugby Football and Identity Politics in Free State Ireland', *Éire-Ireland*, 48 (2013), p. 161.

38 *LFC Centenary*, p. 19.

39 *Irish Times*, 30 March 1891; LFC Fixture Book 1872–1951, pp 23–8; *History of Lansdowne*, pp 15–16.

40 *Irish Times*, 4 April 1898; LFC Fixture Book 1872–1951, pp 32–48; *LFC Centenary*, p. 25.

41 *History of Lansdowne*, pp 5, 54, 63–4; *Irish Times*, 30 March 1891; Van Esbeck, *Irish Rugby*, p. 217.

42 Van Esbeck, *Irish Rugby*, p. 70; Turlough O'Riordan, 'Bulger, Lawrence Quinlivan ('Larry')' in *DIB*.

Chapter 2 – In War and Revolution 1899–1924

1 *Irish Times*, 15 Nov. 1899; *New York Times*, 3 Dec. 1899.

2 *Irish Times*, 9 Feb. 1900.

3 *Irish Times*, 7, 9 Dec. 1901, 8 Dec. 1902, 12 Dec. 1903.

4 *Irish Times*, 23 Feb., 25 March, 6 April 1901; *LFC Centenary*, pp 29–31, 33–4.

5 *History of Lansdowne*, pp 16–17.

6 LFC Fixture Book 1872–1951, pp 49–51.

7 *Irish Independent*, 10 Oct. 1901; *History of Lansdowne*, p. 64; *Irish Times*, 24 Dec. 1901, 2 Jan. 1902.

8 *Irish Times*, 31 March, 22 Sept. 1902, 13, 17 April 1903; LFC Fixture Book 1872–1951, pp 52, 54; *LFC Centenary*, p. 33; O'Callaghan, 'Rugby Football', p. 160.

9 *Irish Times*, 4, 9 April 1904; LFC Fixture Book 1872–1951, p. 56.

10 *Irish Times*, 10 April 1905; LFC Fixture Book 1872–1951, p. 58.

11 *Irish Times*, 24, 25, 27 Nov. 1905.

12 LFC Minute Book 1902–1928, 17 April 1903; *LFC Centenary*, p. 11.

13 LFC Minute Book 1902–1928, 5 Oct. 1906, 2 Oct. 1908, 28 Oct. 1910, 3 April 1912.

14 *History of Lansdowne*, p. 5; *LFC Centenary*, pp 33, 43–4; LFC Minute Book 1902–1928, 11, 21 Oct., 27 Nov., 2 Dec. 1907, 14 Sept. 1908.

15 *Irish Times*, 10 Dec. 1906, 29 Jan., 28 Sept., 9 Oct. 1907, 11 Sept. 1911; *Evening Herald*, 21 Sept. 1907; LFC Minute Book 1902–1928, 23 Sept., 11, 21 Oct. 1907.

16 LFC Minute Book 1902–1928, 19 Oct. 1906, 4 Oct. 1907, 8 Oct. 1909; *Irish Times*, 30 Oct., 2, 5 Nov. 1906.

17 *History of Lansdowne*, pp 40–2, 55; LFC Minute Book 1902–1928, 7 Oct. 1910, 6 Oct. 1911; LFC Fixture Book 1872–1951, pp 64, 67, 70, 73, 76, 78–9.

18 LFC Minute Book 1902–1928, 19 Sept., 10 Oct., 19 Dec. 1910, 6 Oct., 8 Dec. 1913, 31 March 1914.

19 *Irish Times*, 10 Aug. 1914; Rouse, *Sport*, pp 222–30; Liam O'Callaghan, 'Irish Rugby and the First World War', *Sport in Society*, 19 (2016), pp 95–109.

20 *Irish Times*, 1, 17 Sept. 1914; *Sport*, 12 Sept. 1914; *Clifdon Society*, 24 Sept. 1914; Henry Hanna, *The Pals at Suvla Bay* (Dublin, 1916), pp 13–17.

21 *Irish Independent*, 15 Sept. 1914; *Irish Times*, 7, 17, 19 Oct. 1914; *Sport*, 17, 24 Oct. 1914.

22 LFC Minute Book 1902–1928, 5, 14 Oct. 1914; *Sport*, 14 Nov. 1914.

23 *Sport*, 5 Dec. 1914.

24 *Irish Times*, 1 Dec. 1914, 13, 18 May 1915.

25 LFC Minute Book 1902–1928, 12 April, 6 Nov. 1915.

26 *Sport*, 28 Aug. 1915; *Evening Herald*, 31 Aug. 1915; *Irish Times*, 18 Sept. 1915; *Irish Independent*, 23 July 1917; Hanna, *Pals at Suvla Bay*, pp 76, 87, 147, 164, 218, 236, 238; *LFC Yearbook 2014–2015*, pp 64–70; Siggins and Clerkin, *Lansdowne Road*, pp 103–4; information provided by Ciaran O'Mara, curator of the Lansdowne FC First World War Memorial Exhibition (see *Irish Times*, 11 Nov. 2014, 27 April 2015).

27 *Sport*, 1 Jan. 1916; *Irish Times*, 4 April 1916; *Irish Press*, 4 Jan. 1938; *LFC Centenary*, p. 40.

28 *Irish Times*, 21, 24 April 1916; *Evening Herald*, 20 April 1916; *History of Lansdowne*, pp 55, 59, 62.

29 LFC Minute Book 1902–1928, 28 Oct. 1916; Eunan O'Halpin and Daithí Ó Corráin, *The Dead of the Irish Revolution* (New Haven, 2020), pp 33, 47, 49, 72–3; Siggins and Clerkin,

Lansdowne Road, pp 104–6; J.W. Rice, Durban, to Lansdowne FC, 14 May 1987 (LFC Historical Records Folder).

30 LFC Minute Book 1902–1928, 28 Oct. 1916.

31 *Evening Herald*, 6 April 1917; *Irish Independent*, 16 April 1917; *Irish Times*, 15 Sept. 1917; *History of Lansdowne*, pp 58–9.

32 LFC Minute Book 1902–1928, 17 Nov. 1917; *History of Lansdowne*, pp 55–6, 59.

33 *Irish Press*, 4 Jan. 1938.

34 LFC Minute Book 1902–1928, 23 Nov. 1918; *History of Lansdowne*, p. 55.

35 *Irish Times*, 17 June 1918.

36 *Sport*, 28 Dec. 1918; *Irish Times*, 11 Dec. 1920; LFC Minute Book 1902–1928, 10 Oct. 1919; Michael Daly, 'Lansdowne and the First World War' in *LFC Yearbook 2016–2017*, pp 90–9.

37 Information provided by Ciaran O'Mara.

38 LFC Minute Book 1902–1928, 7, 21 Jan. 1919; John Rouse, 'Crawford, William Earnest ("Ernie")' in *DIB*.

39 R.F. Foster, *Modern Ireland, 1600–1972* (London, 1988), p. 490.

40 *Sport*, 25 Jan. 1919; *Irish Times*, 27 Jan., 24 Feb. 1919; LFC Minute Book 1902–1928, 10 Oct. 1919.

41 *Irish Times*, 5 Feb. 1962; *LFC Centenary*, pp 37–8.

42 LFC Minute Book 1902–1928, 7 May 1919; LFC Fixture Book 1872–1951, pp 86–8.

43 LFC Minute Book 1902–1928, 16 Feb., 8 Oct. 1920; *History of Lansdowne*, p. 62; *LFC Centenary*, p. 36.

44 LFC Minute Book 1902–1928, 4 Oct. 1920, 31 Jan., 30 March 1921; *History of Lansdowne*, p. 62.

45 *LFC Centenary*, pp 34, 38–9.

46 LFC Minute Book 1902–1928, 15 April 1921, 13 Feb. 1922; *Irish Times*, 14–15, 18 Feb. 1922; information provided by Ciaran O'Mara.

47 *Irish Times*, 19 Dec. 1921; LFC Minute Book 1902–1928, 19 Dec. 1921.

48 *History of Lansdowne*, pp 20, 42; LFC Fixture Book 1872–1951, p. 92; *LFC Centenary*, pp 39–41; IRFU Website, https://www.irishrugby.ie/all-ireland-leagues/men/bateman-all-ireland-cup/.

49 LFC Minute Book 1902–1928, 11 May, 4, 15 Aug., 9, 23, 30 Oct. 1922, 1 Jan. 1923; Daly, 'Lansdowne and the First World War', pp 93–4.

50 *Irish Society and Social Review*, 7 April 1923; *Irish Times*, 23, 30 April 1923; LFC Fixture Book 1872–1951, pp 95–6.

51 LFC Minute Book 1902–1928, 15 Oct. 1923; *Irish Times*, 29 Oct. 1923; *Irish Independent*, 27, 29 Oct. 1923.

52 *Freeman's Journal*, 14 Nov. 1923; LFC Minute Book 1902–1928, 10 Dec. 1923; *History of Lansdowne*, p. 59; *LFC Centenary*, pp 36–7, 43–4; Van Esbeck, *Irish Rugby*, p. 217.

Chapter 3 – Building a Tradition, Establishing a Legacy 1924–1945

1 LFC Fixture Book 1872–1951, pp 92, 95, 98, 101, 104.

2 *Irish Times*, 25 Sept. 1924, 21 March 1925; *Sport*, 20 Sept. 1924; LFC Fixture Book 1872–

1951, p. 101; LFC Minute Book 1902–1928, 9 Oct. 1925; *History of Lansdowne*, p. 33; *LFC Centenary*, p. 44.

3 *Sport*, 25 Oct. 1924.

4 *Irish Times*, 28 Feb. 1925.

5 *Sport*, 19 Sept. 1925, 21 Aug. 1926; LFC Minute Book 1902–1928, 1 Oct. 1926; *History of Lansdowne*, p. 56.

6 LFC Minute Book 1902–1928, 9 Oct. 1925, 1 Oct. 1926; LFC Fixture Book 1872–1951, pp 104–6; *LFC Centenary*, p. 45.

7 *History of Lansdowne*, pp 56, 62.

8 LFC Fixture Book 1872–1951, pp 107–8; *Irish Times*, 7, 13 Jan., 4 April 1927; *History of Lansdowne*, pp 22–3; *LFC Centenary*, pp 44–5.

9 *Irish Times*, 3 Feb. 1927.

10 *Irish Times*, 15 March, 11, 14, 16 April 1927; *History of Lansdowne*, p. 33.

11 *Sport*, 8 Oct. 1927.

12 LFC Minute Book 1902–1928, 16 Nov. 1925, 9 April 1926, 30 Sept. 1927.

13 *Irish Times*, 3 Nov. 1927; *LFC Centenary*, pp 36, 45; 'Crawford' in *DIB*.

14 *The Weekly Dispatch*, 23 Oct. 1927; *LFC Centenary*, pp 47–9; LFC Fixture Book 1872–1951, p. 110; *Irish Times*, 10 April 1928.

15 LFC Minute Book 1902–1928, 5, 12 March 1928; *Belfast Newsletter*, 5 March 1928; *Irish Times*, 6, 7 March 1927; *Irish Independent*, 3 March 2018; Siggins and Clerkin, *Lansdowne Road*, pp 128–31; *History of Lansdowne*, p. 33; *LFC Centenary*, p. 49.

16 *Irish Times*, 7 March 1928, 16 Feb. 1929; *Irish Independent*, 3 March 2018; *LFC Centenary*, p. 49.

17 LFC Fixture Book 1872–1951, p. 110; *History of Lansdowne*, pp 44, 56, 62–4; *LFC Centenary*, p. 49; *Irish Times*, 9 April 1928; Jim Shanahan, 'Arigho, John Edward ("Jack")' in *DIB*.

18 *Irish Times*, 9, 16 April 1928; *LFC Centenary*, p. 49.

19 *Irish Times*, 5, 23 April 1928; *LFC Centenary*, pp 45–6; LFC Minute Book 1902–1928, 15 April 1928; LFC Minute Book 1928–1953, 28 Sept. 1928.

20 *Irish Times*, 8, 30, 31 Oct., 1, 5 Nov. 1928.

21 *Irish Times*, 8 April 1929; *Sport*, 13 April 1929; *LFC Centenary*, p. 51.

22 *Irish Times*, 15 April 1929, 25 Jan. 1962; *Sport*, 20 April 1929; *LFC Centenary*, pp 51, 128–9; LFC Minute Book 1928–1953, 27 Sept. 1929; Terry Clavin, 'Lambert, Ham (Noel Hamilton)' in *DIB*.

23 *Irish Times*, 11 Jan., 4 Feb. 1929; LFC Minute Book 1928–1953, 27 Sept. 1929.

24 LFC Fixture Book 1872–1951, p. 117; LFC Minute Book 1928–1953, 27 Sept. 1929; *History of Lansdowne*, p. 33; *LFC Centenary*, p. 51.

25 LFC Minute Book 1928–1953, 10 Sept. 1928, 14 Oct. 1929.

26 LFC Minute Book 1902–1928, 16 April 1928; LFC Minute Book 1928–1953, 10, 24 Sept. 1928, 27 Sept. 1929, 26 Sept. 1930, 10 Sept. 1932.

27 Foster, *Modern Ireland*, p. 523.

28 Quoted in Liam O'Callaghan, *Rugby in Munster: A Social and Cultural History* (Cork, 2011), p. 174. See also pp 173–6. See also Rouse, *Sport*, p. 271; Van Esbeck, *Irish Rugby*, pp 106–7.

29 LFC Minute Book 1928–1953, 21 Oct. 1929, 3 Jan., 28 March 1930; *LFC Centenary*, pp 103–6.

30 LFC Minute Book 1928–1953, 21 Oct., 25, 26, 27 Nov. 1929; O'Callaghan, 'Rugby Football', p. 166; idem, *Munster*, p. 174.

31 *Irish Times*, 17 Feb., 25 Sept. 1930; *LFC Centenary*, pp 54, 103–4.

32 *Irish Times*, 7, 14 April 1930; *Irish Independent*, 7 April 1930; *Evening Herald*, 14 April 1930; LFC Fixture Book 1872–1951, p. 118.

33 LFC Minute Book 1928–1953, 28 March 1930; Conleth Feighery, Michael Farrell and Morgan Crowe, *The Hospital Pass: 140 Years of Dublin Hospitals Rugby* (Dublin, 2021), p. 44.

34 LFC Minute Book 1928–1953, 28 March 1930.

35 LFC Minute Book 1928–1953, 28 March, 12, 29 Sept. 1930.

36 LFC minute Book 1928–1953, 16 Dec. 1929; *Irish Times*, 9 Jan., 20 Dec. 1930.

37 *Irish Times*, 25 Sept. 1930.

38 LFC Minute Book 1928–1953, 21 April, 17, 24 Nov. 1930, 15 May 1931; *Irish Times*, 17, 21 April 1930; *Belfast Newsletter*, 18 April 1930; *LFC Centenary*, p. 11.

39 LFC Minute Book 1928–1953, 28 March, 30 June, 9 Aug., 12 Sept. 1930; Mary Law, London, to Hugh Governey, 3 Oct. 1979; Ted Pike, Guildford, to Same, 22 Nov. 1979 (LFC Historic Documents Folder).

40 *History of Lansdowne*, pp 56–7, 59, 64; *LFC Centenary*, p. 42.

41 *Irish Times*, 14 Oct. 1930.

42 LFC Minute Book 1928–1953, 23 Oct., 17, 24 Nov. 1930, 26 Nov. 1934, 25 Feb. 1935.

43 *Irish Times*, 4 April 1931; *LFC Centenary*, p. 53.

44 *Irish Times*, 6 April 1931; LFC Fixture Book 1872–1951, 121; *LFC Centenary*, p. 53.

45 LFC Minute Book 1928–1953, 9 April 1931; *Irish Times*, 11 April 1931.

46 O'Callaghan, 'Rugby Football', pp 158–67.

47 *Irish Independent*, 11 April 1931; *Waterford Standard*, 18 April 1931.

48 LFC Minute Book 1928–1953, 9 April 1931.

49 *Irish Independent*, 11 April 1931.

50 *Irish Times*, 20 May 1931; LFC Minute Book 1928–1953, 15 May 1931.

51 *Irish Press*, 23 Oct. 1931; Van Esbeck, *Irish Rugby*, pp 108–10.

52 LFC Fixture Book 1872–1951, p. 124; W.G.M. Jones, Plymouth, to Hon. Secretary, 16 June, 3, 17 Sept., 15 Oct. 1980 (LFC Historic Documents Folder). Jones's initials are incorrectly given as W.J. in the *History of Lansdowne*, p. 56; *LFC Centenary*, p. 121.

53 LFC Minute Book 1928–1953, 15 April 1932.

54 LFC Minute Book 1902–1928, 9 Oct. 1916, 12 Nov. 1917, 8 Oct. 1920; Finance Act 1925, Part II, Section 29; Rouse, *Sport*, pp 232–3.

55 O'Callaghan, 'Rugby Football', pp 153–6; LFC Minute Book 1928–1953, 26 Sept. 1930, 12 Sept. 1931, 30 Sept. 1932.

56 *Irish Times*, 4 Aug. 1932; O'Callaghan, 'Rugby Football', p. 154; LFC Minute Book 1928–1953, 17 Sept. 1932, 3 April, 9 Sept. 1933.

57 *Irish Times*, 3 Oct. 1933; LFC Minute Book 1928–1953, 10 Sept. 1934; Finance Act 1934, Part II, Section 20.

58 *Irish Times*, 2 Feb. 1932; O'Callaghan, 'Rugby Football', pp 164–6; Van Esbeck, *Irish Rugby*, pp 107–8; Rouse, *Sport*, p. 270.

59 *Irish Times*, 22, 29 Jan. 1932; *Belfast Telegraph*, 29 Jan. 1932; *Yorkshire Post*, 19 Feb. 1932.

60 *Irish Times*, 26 Oct. 1932; LFC Minute Book 1928–1953, 31 Nov. 1932.

61 *Irish Times*, 21 Jan. 1932.

62 LFC Minute Book 1928–1953, 10 Sept. 1932; *Irish Times*, 10 April 1933; *Evening Herald*, 13 April 1933; *LFC Centenary*, pp 53, 128.

63 *Irish Times*, 2 Feb. 1933; LFC Minute Book 1928–1953, 30 March, 9 April, 15 May, 12, 19 Sept., 30 Nov. 1931, 19 Jan., 15 April, 20 Oct. 1932, 3, 7 April 1933; *LFC Centenary*, p. 53.

64 LFC Minute Book 1928–1953, 9 Sept. 1933, 10 Sept. 1934, 27 Sept. 1935.

65 LFC Minute Book 1928–1953, 30 Sept., 10 Oct. 1932.

66 LFC Minute Book 1928–1953, 6, 13, 20 Nov. 1933, 6 April 1934, 22 Oct. 1934, 13 Jan. 1936; *LFC Centenary*, pp 63–7.

67 LFC Minute Book 1928–1953, 6 April 1934.

68 LFC Minute Book 1928–1953, 12 April, 27 Sept. 1935, 18 April 1941, 26 March 1945; *LFC Centenary*, pp 57, 59–61, 67.

69 LFC Minute Book 1928–1953, 10 Sept. 1934, 27 Sept. 1935, 25 Sept. 1936, 9 April, 24 Sept. 1937; *Irish Press*, 13 Sept. 1938; *LFC Yearbook 2021–2022*, p. 64.

70 *Sunday Independent*, 21 June 1936; *Irish Express*, 15 Sept. 1938.

71 *Irish Times*, 2, 8 Feb. 1940, 28 Jan. 1941, 14 Nov. 1944; *LFC Centenary*, pp 69–71, 131; Van Esbeck, *Irish Rugby*, p. 118.

72 LFC Minute Book 1928–1953, 14 April 1939, 29 March 1940; *LFC Centenary*, pp 106–7.

73 *Irish Times*, 16 Oct. 1941, 6 Oct. 1942, 23 March 1943, 17 Nov. 1945; *Irish Independent*, 27 Nov. 1941; LFC Minute Book 1928–1953, 23 Oct. 1939, 29 March, 31 Aug. 1940, 26 Sept. 1941, 25 Sept. 1942, 24 Sept. 1943, 22 Sept. 1944, 27 Sept. 1945; Van Esbeck, *Irish Rugby*, p. 117.

74 *LFC Match Programme 1996–1997*, p. 53; LFC Minute Book 1928–1953, 27 Jan. 1941; *LFC Centenary*, pp 57–9; Van Esbeck, *Irish Rugby*, p. 118.

75 *LFC Centenary*, pp 128–9; *History of Lansdowne*, pp 62–4.

76 *Irish Times*, 22 Nov. 1940, 1 April 1943, 1 Jan. 1945, 29 Sept. 1945; *Belfast Newsletter*, 2 Jan. 1945; *Irish Press*, 2 Oct. 1945.

Chapter 4 – Home-From-Home 1946–1972

1 LFC Minute Book 1928–1953, 1, 14 Jan., 18 Feb., 5 April 1946; *Irish Times*, 7 Jan. 1949.

2 *LFC Centenary*, pp 71; Barbarian FC Itinerary, Easter Tour 1946 (LFC Con Murphy Archive).

3 *Evening Herald*, 12 Dec. 1946; *Irish Examiner*, 1 Dec. 1947, 12 Oct. 1949; *Irish Press*, 10 Oct. 1949; *Irish Times*, 12 Oct. 1949; LFC Fixture Book 1872–1951, pp 193–7; *LFC Centenary*, pp 69, 79–80, 107–9.

4 LFC Minute Book 1928–1953, 11 April 1947; *LFC Centenary*, p. 69; Interview with Paul Van Cauwelaert, 13 May 2021 (LFC Transcript).

5 *Irish Times*, 17 Sept., 8 Oct. 1946; *Irish Independent*, 26 April 1947; LFC Minute Book 1928–1953, 20 Sept. 1946, 20 Sept. 1947; *LFC Centenary*, p. 67.

6 *Irish Times*, 15 March, 12 Nov. 1948, 18 Sept. 1974.

7 *Irish Times*, 30 Oct. 1948; LFC Minute Book 1928–1953, 22 April 1949.

8 *Irish Times*, 25 April 1949; LFC Fixture Book 1872–1951, p. 195; *LFC Centenary*, pp 73–9.

9 *LFC Yearbook 1997–1998*, p. 141; *LFC Centenary*, pp 47, 71, 81, 121.

10 Dublin Insurance Athletic Society 'Victory' Match Programme, 30 April 1949 (LFC Con Murphy Archive); *Irish Times*, 2 May 1949.

11 *Sunday Independent*, 27 Nov. 1949.

12 LFC Minute Book 1928–1953, 5 Dec. 1949; *Sunday Independent*, 11 Dec. 1949.

13 *Irish Times*, 24 April 1950; LFC Fixture Book 1872–1951, p. 196; LFC Minute Book 1928–1953, 19 Dec. 1949, 22 Jan., 14 April 1950; *LFC Centenary*, pp 67, 83; *LFC Yearbook 1997–1998*, p. 141.

14 *Irish Times*, 28 April, 1 May 1950.

15 *Irish Times*, 1 Jan. 1951; LFC Minute Book 1938–1953, [April] 1951.

16 *Irish Independent*, 7 Dec. 1951; *LFC Yearbook 1997–1998*, p. 141.

17 LFC Minute Book 1928–1953, 26 Sept. 1952.

18 *Irish Times*, 13, 20 April 1953; *Times Pictorial*, 25 April 1953.

19 LFC Minute Book 1928–1953, 17 April, 30 Sept. 1953; *LFC Centenary*, p. 81.

20 LFC Souvenir Match Programme, 25 April 1953; *Irish Press*, 23 Nov. 1954, 2 May 1955; *Irish Independent*, 30 April 1954, 16 Sept. 1955.

21 *Times Pictorial*, 3 Oct. 1953; *Irish Times*, 1, 8 Oct. 1955; *Evening Herald*, 10 Oct. 1958; *LFC Centenary*, pp 85, 87, 122.

22 *Irish Times*, 27 July, 22 Aug., 7, 10 Sept. 1956.

23 *LFC Centenary*, pp 87, 110–11.

24 LFC Minute Book 1959–1966, pp 3–4, 6–9, 67, 201, 211, 261; LFC Minute Book 1966–1974, p. 567.

25 *LFC Centenary*, pp 85, 87, 89, 110–11; *Irish Times*, 3 April 1959; LFC Minute Book 1959–1966, pp 13–14, 53–4, 130–1.

26 *Irish Examiner*, 29 Jan. 1954; *Irish Times*, 1 March 1958, 12 Jan. 1959; *Evening Herald*, 21 April 1958; *Irish Independent*, 12 Jan. 1959; *Longford Leader*, 18 Jan. 1959; LFC Minute Book 1959–1966, pp 13–15.

27 *Irish Times*, 25 Nov. 1954, 12 Sept. 1960, 8 June 1963; *LFC Centenary*, pp 90, 122.

28 *Irish Independent*, 25 March 1960; *LFC Yearbook 1997–8*, pp 141–5; information provided by Caleb Powell, 7 Dec. 2021.

29 Marie Coleman, 'Minch, Sydney Basil' in *DIB*; Interview with Paul Van Cauwelaert, 13 May 2021 (LFC Transcript); *LFC Centenary*, p. 90; *LFC Yearbook 2021–2022*, p. 68.

30 *LFC Centenary*, p. 122; information provided by Caleb Powell, 7 Dec. 2021.

31 *Irish Times*, 30 Oct. 1961, 30 Dec. 1963, 13 Jan. 1964; LFC Minute Book 1959–1966, pp 194–5.

32 *Irish Times*, 8 June 1963; *Irish Independent*, 13 Aug. 1963.

33 Information provided by Caleb Powell, 7 Dec. 2021; *LFC Yearbook 2004–2005*, p. 49; LFC Minute Book 1959–1966, pp 209, 319; *LFC Centenary*, p. 113.

34 *LFC Centenary*, pp 81, 125; IRFU website, https://www.irishrugby.ie/2010/07/02/caleb-powell-appointed-irfu-president/.

35 LFC Minute Book 1959–1966, pp 334–5, 348–9, 356–7, 372–3; *Evening Herald*, 24 April, 10 May 1965; *Irish Times*, 24 April, 10 May 1965; *Irish Independent*, 10 May 1965.

36 LFC Minute Book 1959–1966, pp 379–80; *Irish Times*, 22 April 1965.

37 LFC Minute Book 1966–1974, pp 455, 493, 545, 570.

38 *Irish Times*, 1 July 1967, 28 Jan. 2006; *Irish Independent*, 1 July 1967.

39 LFC Minute Book 1966–1974, pp 506, 508, 521, 535–7, 545, 568–9.

40 LFC Minute Book 1959–1966, p. 69; *Irish Times*, 2 May 1960; *Evening Herald*, 16 March 1964, 30 Nov. 1965; *Irish Examiner*, 17 March 1964; *Irish Press*, 28, 30 April, 6 May 1964; J.C. Conroy (ed.), *Rugby in Leinster, 1879–1979* (Dublin, 1980), pp 94, 96; *LFC Centenary*, p. 91.

41 Louise Asmal, Kader Asmal and Thomas Alberts, 'The Irish Anti-Apartheid Movement' in *Struggles for Freedom: Southern Africa* (2008), pp 353–5.

42 *Irish Times*, 19 Feb. 1965; *Belfast Telegraph*, 24 Feb. 1965.

43 *Irish Times*, 6, 27 Nov., 18, 22 Dec. 1969, 2–3, 5–8, 10, 12, 15 Jan. 1970; *Irish Press*, 20, 27 Nov. 1969; *Evening Herald*, 11, 13 Dec. 1969; *Irish Independent*, 1, 6 Dec. 1969; Van Esbeck, *Irish Rugby*, pp 161–2; Peter Hain and André Odendall, *Pitch Battles: Sport, Racism and Resistance* (London, 2021), pp 31–6.

44 *LFC Yearbook 1997–1998*, pp 141–3; *LFC Centenary*, p. 91.

45 Information provided by Caleb Powell, 7 Dec. 2021; *Irish Press*, 22 Feb., 24 April 1972; *Irish Times*, 20 March, 10, 24 April, 8 May 1972, 21 May 2010.

46 *Irish Times*, 6, 9, 11, 25 Sept. 1972; *Irish Examiner*, 11, 18 Sept. 1972; *Evening Herald*, 16 Sept. 1972.

47 *Irish Times*, 22 Sept., 10 Nov., 6 Dec. 1972.

48 *LFC Centenary*, pp 128–9.

49 LFC Minute Book 1966–1974, 16, 30 Aug. 1971; *LFC Centenary*, p. 1.

Chapter 5 – A Dream and a Plan 1973–1995

1 *LFC Centenary*, p. 5.

2 *Irish Times*, 6 Feb., 17 March 1973; *LFC Yearbook 1997–1998*, pp 46–7.

3 *Sunday Independent*, 18 Feb. 1973; LFC Minute Book 1966–1974, 8 Nov. 1973; *Irish Times*, 15 Jan. 1975.

4 *Irish Times*, 14 Sept. 1973; *The Guardian*, 7 Oct. 2010; Barry Coughlan, *The Irish Lions, 1896–1983* (Dublin, 1983), pp 103–4; James Quinn, 'Keane, Maurice Ignatius ("Moss")' in *DIB*.

5 *LFC Yearbook 1997–1998*, p. 141; *Irish Times*, 24 Dec. 1973; *Evening Herald*, 22 Dec. 1973; LFC Minute Book 1966–1974, 10 Jan. 1974.

6 LFC Minute Book 1966–1974, 28 June 1973; *Irish Press*, 11 June 1974; *Irish Times*, 18 June 1974.

7 LFC Minute Book 1974–1977, 6 June 1974; *Irish Times*, 25 Sept. 1974.

8 LFC Minute Book 1966–1974, 2, 29 May 1973; LFC Minute Book 1974–1977, 30 Sept. 1976, 12 April 1977; LFC Minute Book 1977–1979, 5 May, 1 Sept. 1977; LFC Minute Book 1979–1982, 23 April 1981; Conroy (ed.), *Rugby in Leinster*, pp 93–6.

9 LFC Minute Book 1966–1974, 13, 27 Feb. 1973; *Irish Press*, 28 March 1973, 11 June 1974; *Evening Herald*, 10 Jan. 1974; *Irish Times*, 2 March, 26 April 1974; Coughlan, *Irish Lions*, pp 96–101; Hain and Odendaal, *Pitch Battles*, pp 185–6.

10 LFC Minute Book 1974–1977, 18 March, 1 April 1976; *LFC Yearbook 1997–1998*, pp 181,

183; IRFU Website, https://www.irishrugby.ie/2016/09/02/michael-kearney-to-step-down-as-ireland-team-manager/; Leinster Rugby Website, https://www.leinsterrugby.ie/staff/michael-dawson/.

11 *Irish Times*, 30 June, 19 Nov. 1974, 15 April 1977; *Irish Independent*, 24 Jan. 1977; *Evening Herald*, 24 Jan. 1977; LFC Minute Book 1977–1979, 28 April 1977.

12 *Irish Times*, 26 May 1977.

13 LFC Minute Book 1966–1974, 21 Aug. 1972, 9 Jan., 2 May 1973; LFC Minute Book 1977–1979, 15 Dec. 1977, 5 Jan. 1978; Conroy (ed.), *Rugby in Leinster*, p. 97.

14 *Irish Times*, 19 Dec. 1977; *Sunday Independent*, 18 Dec. 1977.

15 LFC Minute Book 1966–1974, 16, 30 Aug., 30 Sept. 1971, 12 Sept. 1972, 13 Feb., 13 March, 29 May, 28 June, 28 Aug. 1973; LFC Minute Book 1974–1977, 6 June, 1 Aug. 1974, 25 Sept. 1975; LFC funding proposal to AIB, [*c.*1977–8] (LFC Miscellaneous, AIB Folder).

16 LFC Minute Book 1974–1977, 1, 22 April, 9 Sept., 21 Oct., 4 Nov. 1976, 20 Jan. 1977.

17 LFC Minute Book 1974–1977, 23 Sept. 1976, 12 April 1977; LFC Minute Book 1977–1979, 25 Aug., 15 Sept., 29 Nov. 1977; LFC New Pavilion Project booklet, 1978.

18 LFC New Pavilion Project booklet, 1978; Minutes of building fund committee, 30 Oct. 1979 (LFC Miscellaneous, AIB Folder).

19 LFC Minute Book 1977–1979, 11 July, 4 Aug., 15 Dec. 1977; *Irish Times*, 12 Jan. 1978; LFC Miscellaneous, Building Contract Folder; 'New Lansdowne Pavilion', *Architecture in Ireland*, 1:8 (Feb./March 1979), pp 6–11.

20 LFC Minute Book 1977–1979, 16 Oct. 1978; *Irish Times*, 19 Oct. 1978; LFC Miscellaneous, Official Opening October 1978 Folder.

21 LFC Press Release, 18 Oct. 1978; January 1977 Report and Reorganization Committee Report (LFC Miscellaneous, Official Opening October 1978 Folder and Reorganization Committee Folder).

22 LFC Press Release, 18 Oct. 1978 (LFC Miscellaneous, Official Opening October 1978 Folder).

23 *Evening Herald*, 26 March 1979; *Irish Times*, 9, 25 April 1979; *Sunday Independent*, 22 April 1979; *LFC Yearbook 1997–1998*, p. 32.

24 *Sunday Independent*, 29 April 1979; *LFC Yearbook 1997–1998*, p. 32.

25 *Irish Times*, 31 March, 19, 28 April 1980; *Sunday Independent*, 13 April 1980; *Irish Independent*, 21 April 1980.

26 LFC Minute Book 1979–1982, 26 July, 13 Dec. 1979, 24 Jan., 26 June 1980; *Irish Independent*, 8 May 1980; *Irish Times*, 24 Sept., 22 Dec. 1980; *Evening Echo*, 22 Dec. 1980.

27 *Irish Times*, 6, 13, 16, 20, 27 April 1981; *Irish Press*, 7 April 1981.

28 LFC Minute Book 1979–1982, 23 April 1981.

29 *Irish Times*, 30 Aug., 15 Sept. 1979, 20 Feb. 1980; *Evening Echo*, 22 Dec. 1979.

30 *Irish Times*, 22 Feb., 6 March 1980.

31 LFC Minute Book 1979–1982, 11 Dec. 1980; *Irish Times*, 16 May, 4 Nov. 1980, 30 Jan. 1981; Edmund Van Esbeck, *The Story of Irish Rugby* (London, 1986), pp 181–2.

32 *Irish Times*, 31 Jan., 9 April 1981; *Irish Press*, 9 April 1981; Hain and Odendaal, *Pitch Battles*, pp 192, 282.

33 *Irish Press*, 3, 21 Feb. 1981; *Irish Times*, 2, 10 March, 5 May 1981; *Evening Herald*, 7 March, 4 April 1981.

34 *Sunday Independent*, 15 Dec. 2013.
35 *Sunday Independent*, 15 Dec. 2013.
36 *Irish Times*, 2 May 1981.
37 *Irish Times*, 24 March, 2 May 1981; *Irish Press*, 9 May 1981; *Irish Independent*, 8 May 2011; LFC Minute Book 1979–1981, 23 April 1981.
38 *Irish Times*, 6 June 1981.
39 *Irish Times*, 14 April, 13 May 2020.
40 *Irish Times*, 7 Sept., 10 Dec. 1982, 20 Sept. 1983, 18 Jan. 1984, 17 Aug. 1985; *Evening Herald*, 4 March 1983.
41 LFC Minute Book 1982–1986, 5 Oct. 1982, 8 March 1983; *Irish Times*, 5, 6 Oct. 1982.
42 LFC Minute Book 1982–1986, 24 May 1984, 8 Feb., 21 May 1985; *LFC Match Programme 1985–1986*, pp 6, 15, 30.
43 LFC Minute Book 1982–1986, 6 Sept. 1982; Patrick Maume, 'Ryan, James' in *DIB*; Pádraic Conway, 'Ryan, Eoin' in *DIB*; *LFC Match Programme 1995–1996*, pp 77–9.
44 *Irish Times*, 1 Jan., 24 March, 14, 21, 28 April 1986; LFC Minute Book 1986–1989, 1 May 1986.
45 *Irish Independent*, 24 April 1986; *Irish Times*, 22 Dec. 1986, 6 Oct. 2010.
46 *LFC Yearbook 1997–1998*, p. 28; *Irish Times*, 3 Sept. 1986, 26 Jan., 13, 20, 27 April 1987.
47 LFC Minute Book 1986–1989, 24 March 1987; *Irish Times*, 20 March 1987.
48 Edmund Van Esbeck, *Irish Rugby, 1874–1999: A History* (Dublin, 1999), pp 170–5, 374.
49 *Irish Times*, 29 Feb., 16 March 1988; LFC Minute Book 1986–1989, 28 April 1988; Van Esbeck, *Irish Rugby, 1874–1999*, p. 288; *LFC Yearbook 1997–1998*, p. 28.
50 LFC Minute Book 1986–1989, 28 April 1988; *Irish Times*, 27 April 1988.
51 *LFC Match Programme 1992–1993*, pp 9–13.
52 *Irish Times*, 3, 17, 20, 24 April 1989.
53 LFC Minute Book 1986–1989, 9 May 1989; *Irish Express*, 27 April 1989; Shanahan, 'Arigho' in *DIB*.
54 LFC Minute Book 1982–1986, 3 Oct. 1983, 18 July 1985; *Irish Times*, 16 Oct. 1985, 16 Dec. 1986, 3 March, 9 June 1988, 5, 10 Jan., 12, 19, 21 Feb. 1990; LFC Newsletter, Aug. 1989; LFC Minute Book 1986–1989, 9 May 1989; LFC Minute Book 1990–1992, 10 May 1990.
55 LFC Minute Book 1986–1989, 7 Sept. 1989; *Irish Times*, 19 Oct. 1987, 29 March, 15, 16 April 1988.
56 *Evening Echo*, 2 Sep. 1989; *Irish Times*, 12, 19 Sept. 1989; *Irish Independent*, 20 Sept. 1989.
57 *LFC Yearbook 1997–1998*, pp 51–3; *Irish Times*, 22 Aug., 15 Oct. 1990, 26 March, 15, 22, 29 April 1991.
58 LFC Minute Book 1986–1989, 9 May, 21 June, 22 Aug., 5 Oct. 1989; LFC Newsletter, Aug. 1989; LFC Minute Book 1990–1992, 25 Sept. 1991.
59 *LFC Match Programme 1991–1992*, p. 3; *LFC Yearbook 1997–1998*, p. 13; LFC Minute Book 1990–1992, 2 May, 25 Sept. 1991.
60 *LFC Yearbook 1997–1998*, pp 53–5.
61 LFC Minute Book 1990–1992, 23 June 1992; *Irish Press*, 16 Oct. 1992; *LFC Yearbook 1997–1998*, pp 55–61.
62 *LFC Match Programme 1991–1992*, pp 21–6.
63 LFC Minute Book 1992–1993, 4 May 1993; LFC Minute Book 1994–1995, 12 May 1994, 11 May 1995; *Irish Times*, 18 March 1993, 25 May 1995.

64 *LFC Yearbook 2021–2022*, p. 75.

65 LFC Minute Book 1974–1977, 19 June 1975, 22 April, 21 Oct., 30 Dec. 1976; LFC Minute Book 1977–1979, 5 Jan. 1978; LFC Minute Book 1982–1986, 18 July 1985; LFC Minute Book 1986–1989, 12 Jan. 1988; *Irish Times*, 26 March 1981, 28 Nov. 1989, 12 April, 17 May 1993; *Limerick Leader*, 19 May 1982.

Chapter 6 – Rising to the Challenge: Being Lansdowne FC 1995–2020

1 *Irish Times*, 12, 26, 28, 29 Aug. 1995; Van Esbeck, *Irish Rugby, 1874–1999*, pp 214–15; O'Callaghan, *Rugby in Munster*, pp 210–12.

2 *Irish Times*, 1 Sept., 19 Dec. 1995, 5 Dec. 2000; Rouse, *Sport*, pp 313–14.

3 LFC Minute Book 1994–1995, 7 Nov., 11 Dec. 1995.

4 *Irish Times*, 26 Aug. 1995, 13 Feb., 17 Dec. 1996, 8 Jan. 1999; Van Esbeck, *Irish Rugby, 1874–1999*, pp 217–19.

5 Meeting with IRFU, 15 May 1992 (LFC Minute Book 1990–1992); LFC Minute Book 1992–1993, 8 Dec. 1992.

6 LFC Minute Book 1994–1995, 22 Sept., 5, 11 Oct., 1 Nov. 1994, 5 Oct. 1995; Interview with Paul Van Cauwelaert, 13 May 2021 (LFC Transcript).

7 *Irish Independent*, 8 Oct. 2010. On declining attendances see O'Callaghan, *Rugby in Munster*, pp 212–19.

8 *Irish Times*, 13 Nov. 1996, 1 Dec. 1999, 12 Oct. 2006; *Evening Herald*, 13 Nov. 1996; *Irish Independent*, 14 Nov. 1996; *LFC Yearbook 1997–1998*, pp 72–3, 124–5; *LFC Yearbook 2006–2007*, pp 95–6.

9 *Irish Times*, 24 Feb. 1997; *LFC Yearbook 1997–1998*, pp 63–5.

10 *Irish Times*, 21, 28 April, 5, 10, 12 May, 5 June 1997; *LFC Yearbook 1997–1998*, p. 107.

11 *Sunday Independent*, 12 Oct. 1997; *Evening Herald*, 16 Oct. 1997.

12 LFC Honorary Secretary's Report to Members, Season 1997/1998 (LFC Miscellaneous, 1998 Folder); *Irish Times*, 15, 20 April, 4, 6 May 1998; *Sunday Independent*, 17 May 1998; *Sunday Times*, 17 May 1998.

13 LFC Honorary Secretary's Report to Members, Season 1997/1998 (LFC Miscellaneous, 1998 Folder).

14 *LFC Yearbook 1998–1999*, pp 39–47, 140–1; LFC Correspondence, 23 April 1999 (LFC Miscellaneous, Frank Thompson Folder).

15 Minutes of executive committee meeting, 10 Sept. 1998 (LFC Miscellaneous, 1998 Folder); *LFC Yearbook 1998–1999*, pp 81, 103–5; *Irish Times*, 5 Dec. 2000, 17 Jan. 2001.

16 *LFC Yearbook 1999–2000*, pp 49–54; *Irish Times*, 26 April 1999.

17 *Evening Herald*, 9 Feb. 1999, 29 March 2003; *Irish Times*, 29 March 2000; *Irish Independent*, 19 March 2000; *LFC Yearbook 2005–2006*, pp 54–5.

18 *Irish Times*, 10 March 1999.

19 *Evening Herald*, 19 Nov. 1999; *Irish Independent*, 22 Nov. 1999.

20 *LFC Yearbook 2000–2001*, pp 102–3; *Irish Times*, 20, 22 May 2000.

21 *Irish Times*, 2 May, 30 Nov. 2000.

22 *Irish Times*, 30 Nov. 2000; *LFC Yearbook 2000–2001*, pp 59–64.

23 *LFC Yearbook 2001–2002*, pp 86–93.

24 *LFC Yearbook 2001–2002*, p. 54.

25 *Irish Times*, 16 May 2001; *Sunday Independent*, 27 Jan. 2002. The calculation of the number of trophies won to that point in time did not include two Third E Greenlea Cups won in 1984–5 and 1987–8 or the 1989–90 Moran Cup, which was rescinded owing to the fielding of an ineligible player (For the original calculations see *LFC Yearbook 2002–2003*, pp 113–17).

26 *LFC Yearbook 2002–2003*, pp 29–33; *Irish Times*, 7 May 2002.

27 *Sunday Independent*, 20 April 2003; *Irish Times*, 3 May 2003; *Irish Examiner*, 5 May 2003.

28 *Limerick Leader*, 29 May 2003; *LFC Yearbook 2002–2003*, p. 17; *LFC Yearbook 2004–2005*, pp 16–17.

29 *LFC Yearbook 2000–2001*, pp 57–9; *Irish Times*, 10 April, 9 Dec. 2002; *LFC Yearbook 2002–2003*, pp 41, 45, 49, 51, 93, 95.

30 *LFC Yearbook 2004–2005*, pp 36–41.

31 Minutes of executive committee meeting, 10 Sept. 1998 (LFC Miscellaneous, 1998 Folder); Land Registry, County Dublin, Folios 130644F, 184945F; *Irish Times*, 20 Sept. 2001, 18 Jan. 2007; *LFC Yearbook 2001–2002*, p. 54; *LFC Yearbook 2005–2006*, pp 120–2; *LFC Yearbook 2006–2007*, p. 19; *LFC Yearbook 2013–2014*, pp 81–6; *Evening Herald*, 30 Nov. 2007.

32 *Irish Times*, 18, 22, 25 April 2005; *LFC Yearbook 2005–2006*, p. 57.

33 *Irish Times*, 8 May 2006; *LFC Yearbook 2006–2007*, pp 46–9, 118–23, 138–41.

34 *Evening Herald*, 4 May 2007.

35 *LFC Yearbook 2008–2009*, pp 40–1; *Evening Herald*, 9 May 2008.

36 Clerkin and Siggins, *Lansdowne Road*, pp 322–4; *Irish Times*, 17 Feb. 2006; *LFC Yearbook 2009–2010*, p. 7; *LFC Yearbook 2011–2012*, pp 29–30.

37 *Irish Times*, 23, 30 April 2007; *LFC Yearbook 2006–2007*, p. 16; Interview with Stephen Rooney, 10 Aug. 2021 (LFC Transcript); *LFC Yearbook 2008–2009*, pp 51–6.

38 *LFC Yearbook 2008–2009*, pp 147–66.

39 *LFC Yearbook 2008–2009*, pp 133–9; *LFC Yearbook 2009–2010*, pp 31–5, 77–85; *Evening Herald*, 21 Nov. 2008; *Irish Independent*, 22 Nov. 2008; *Irish Times*, 9 Feb. 2009; *Belfast Newsletter*, 25 April, 5 May 2009; *Evening Herald*, 8 May 2009.

40 *LFC Yearbook 2009–2010*, pp 71–5.

41 *LFC Yearbook 2010–2011*, pp 35–7.

42 *LFC Yearbook 2010–2011*, pp 39–41.

43 Clerkin and Siggins, *Lansdowne Road*, pp 324–5; *Irish Times*, 24 Oct. 2009.

44 *LFC Yearbook 2010–2011*, pp 7, 11, 109.

45 *LFC Yearbook 2004–2005*, p. 45; *LFC Yearbook 2005–2006*, p. 125; *LFC Yearbook 2006–2007*, p. 71; *LFC Yearbook 2010–2011*, pp 31, 83, 121–3; *LFC Yearbook 2011–2012*, pp 70–1; *Irish Times*, 28 April, 2 June, 20, 31 July, 6 Oct. 2010; *Evening Herald*, 8 Oct. 2010; Quinn, 'Keane' in *DIB*.

46 *Irish Times*, 11 Oct. 2010.

47 *Irish Times*, 29 July 2010; *Westmeath Independent*, 9 April 2011; *LFC Yearbook 2011–2012*, pp 31–4.

48 *LFC Yearbook 2011–2012*, pp 35–7, 62–7.

49 *LFC Yearbook 2012–2013*, pp 30–7, 43.
50 *Irish Times*, 4 March, 1 April 2013; *LFC Yearbook 2013–2014*, pp 32–3.
51 *LFC Yearbook 2013–2014*, pp 53–7, 88; *Evening Herald*, 26 April 2013.
52 *Belfast Telegraph*, 11 Nov. 2013; *Irish Examiner*, 21 April 2014; *LFC Yearbook 2014–2015*, pp 33–8.
53 *LFC Yearbook 2014–2015*, pp 38–9; *Evening Herald*, 11 Oct. 2014, 11 May 2015; *Irish Times*, 12 Jan., 27 April, 11, 15 May 2015; *LFC Yearbook 2015–2016*, pp 34–5, 50–3.
54 *LFC Yearbook 2015–2016*, pp 38, 54–5, 64–6, 70–1, 80–5.
55 *LFC Yearbook 2016–2017*, pp 36–51, 62–3.
56 *LFC Yearbook 2017–2018*, pp 55–62.
57 *LFC Yearbook 2017–2018*, pp 62, 67, 71.
58 *LFC Yearbook 2017–2018*, p. 35; *LFC Yearbook 2018–2019*, pp 29–32; *Sunday Independent*, 22 April 2018; *Irish Times*, 23 April 2018.
59 *Irish Times*, 3, 5, 7 May 2018; *LFC Yearbook 2018–2019*, pp 58–9.
60 *LFC Yearbook 2018–2019*, pp 59, 85–7.
61 *LFC Yearbook 2018–2019*, pp 53–5, 84.
62 *Irish Examiner*, 22 Nov. 2018; *LFC Yearbook 2019–2020*, pp 24, 28, 52, 62–3.
63 *Irish Times*, 13 April 2019.
64 *Irish Times*, 25 March, 19, 25 April 2019.
65 *Sunday Life*, 5 Jan. 2020; *Irish Times*, 6 Jan. 2020; *Irish Independent*, 20 March 2020.
66 *Irish Times*, 10 Dec. 2012, 19 Nov. 2016; *LFC Yearbook 2013–2014*, pp 108, 112–15.

Conclusion – 2021–2022

1 *LFC Yearbook 2021–2022*, pp 23–4.
2 *LFC Yearbook 2014–2015*, p. 56.
3 Interview with Stephen Rooney, 10 Aug. 2021 (LFC Transcript).
4 *Irish Times*, 23 Aug. 2021.
5 *LFC Yearbook 2021–2022*, pp 31, 47.
6 *Irish Times*, 3 Nov., 22 Dec. 2021.

Index

Page numbers of illustrations are in *italic*, photos of individuals in **bold**

Set in 10.5 on 15 pt Minion
Published by Open Air
an imprint of Four Courts Press, 7 Malpas Street, Dublin 8, Ireland
www.fourcourtspress.ie
and in North America by
Four Courts Press
c/o IPG, 814 N Franklin St, Chicago, IL 60610

A catalogue record for this title
is available from the British Library.

ISBN 978-1-80151-054-7

Book design and typesetting by Anú Design, Tara
Printed in Spain by Grafo, S.A.

Stand

Pavilion

Football Ground

M.P Westland Row 1

LANE

Pavilion

19

Level Crossing

24

S.P

ROAD

B.M. 23·9

S.P

S.B.

Platforms

Lodge

Lansdowne Road Station

F.B.

Lansdowne Lodge

SHELBOURNE AVENUE

Carlton Villas

Ivanhoe